PRAISE FOR *SUICIDE SQUEEZE*

"Don Hooton helped bring the issue of teen steroid abuse into the national consciousness after the tragic death of his son Taylor. *Suicide Squeeze* reveals this moving and poignant story. The book is a must-read for all parents and for everyone interested in the integrity of sports."

—ROB MANFRED, Commissioner of Baseball

"In *Suicide Squeeze*, William Kashatus injects new life into the decade-old testimony that led to the enactment of my California legislation to crack down on steroid use by student athletes. He puts the reader inside the 'dugout' to witness the harrowing accounts of two young baseball standouts who took their lives after falling prey to steroids. We cannot forget the loss of these two young, talented men or ignore the threat that confronts anyone who seeks to get bigger fast. Laws help, but they are not enough. Continuing education on the allure of and the damage caused by steroid use is essential for parents, players, and coaches alike."

—JACKIE SPEIER, Congresswoman,
California's Fourteenth Congressional District

"With the help of Major League Baseball, the New York Yankees, and other supporters, Don Hooton and his team at the Taylor Hooton Foundation have done more than any other organization over the years to educate not only our kids but also their parents and coaches about the dangers of steroids and other performance-enhancing drugs. *Suicide Squeeze* illuminates their efforts in a powerful and engaging way. Every young person who reads this book represents a life potentially saved."

—RANDY LEVINE, President, New York Yankees, and Board Member,
Taylor Hooton Foundation

"William Kashatus has written an outstanding book that should be read by anyone who has or will have a connection with young people who play sports. *Suicide Squeeze* reads like a novel and instructs like a textbook. Kashatus has shown us the true meaning of sports and the true meaning of a coach—not a coach of a sport, but a coach of the young people who compete in sports."

—RICHARD P. BORKOWSKI,
Sport and Recreation Safety Consultant

SUICIDE SQUEEZE

WILLIAM C. KASHATUS

SUICIDE

Taylor Hooton, Rob Garibaldi, and the
Fight against Teenage Steroid Abuse

SQUEEZE

TEMPLE UNIVERSITY PRESS
Philadelphia • Rome • Tokyo

TEMPLE UNIVERSITY PRESS
Philadelphia, Pennsylvania 19122
www.temple.edu/tempress

Library of Congress Cataloging-in-Publication Data

Names: Kashatus, William C., 1959– author.
Title: Suicide squeeze : Taylor Hooton, Rob Garibaldi, and the fight against
    teenage steroid abuse / William C. Kashatus.
Description: Philadelphia : Temple University Press, 2017. | Includes
    bibliographical references and index.
Identifiers: LCCN 2016018607| ISBN 9781439914380 (hardback : alk. paper) |
    ISBN 9781439914403 (e-book)
Subjects: LCSH: Doping in sports. | Doping in sports—Prevention. | Anabolic
    steroids—Health aspects. | Athletes—Drug use—Prevention. | Baseball
    stories. | BISAC: SPORTS & RECREATION / Baseball / General. | SPORTS &
    RECREATION / Sociology of Sports.
Classification: LCC RC1230 .K37 2017 | DDC 362.29/9—dc23
LC record available at https://lccn.loc.gov/2016018607

♾ The paper used in this publication meets the requirements of the American
National Standard for Information Sciences—Permanence of Paper for Printed
Library Materials, ANSI Z39.48-1992

Printed in the United States of America

9 8 7 6 5 4 3 2 1

In memory of

Taylor Hooton and Rob Garibaldi

CONTENTS

PREFACE

One of the greatest joys of my life has been sharing a passion for baseball with my son Peter. As it has for many fathers and sons, the game has created a special bond that allows the two of us to express our love for each other in a meaningful way. But there have also been times when I seriously considered discouraging his involvement in the sport because of the dramatic changes that have occurred during the past thirty years at the professional and at the amateur levels.

Growing up in the 1970s, the only baseball I played was in the Philadelphia prep schools and later at a Division III college. My coaches were *teachers* who had a deep and passionate commitment to young people and approached the game from an educational standpoint. Intellectual, moral, and physical development were their priorities. The diamond was an open-air classroom that enabled them to impart invaluable life lessons, such as "restraint under pressure," "moral courage," and "teamwork." Just as important, I learned that there are no shortcuts to success—only hard work and perseverance. The lessons were taught in the heat of competition and within the context of inevitable failure that defines the game of baseball. Criticism was constructive—not punitive—and almost always followed by an encouraging remark. That is how I learned the game, how I tried to play it, and later how I tried to teach it.

When I began to coach my son's Little League baseball team in the late 1990s, I was appalled to discover that many coaches placed winning above everything else. Some were manipulative, behaving as if the game were about them and their children and not at all about the other kids they coached. They viewed mandatory pitch counts, playing time, and bat regulations as obstacles to be overcome instead of restrictions that preserved the integrity of the game and the safety of the children playing it. Some coaches even created year-round programs, forcing kids to choose baseball over other sports. During the summer, their teams took precedence over all other family activities. The pressure on players to perform well was ever present in games that became high-stakes affairs.

When Peter graduated to American Legion and later tournament baseball, I found that the teaching of life lessons was nearly obsolete. Personal development was often subordinate to winning. Individual success was emphasized over teamwork, and the art of deception was given equal priority to work ethic. It quickly became clear that amateur baseball had been corrupted by the egocentrism and instant gratification that plagued Major League Baseball (MLB), thanks to the boorish behavior of such star performers as Barry Bonds, Roger Clemens, and Alex Rodriguez. In fact, many tournament coaches and even some high school coaches are former minor leaguers with a "my-way-or-the-highway" attitude, or they are businessmen eager to make a buck by selling impressionable teens and their parents on the necessity of investing thousands of dollars in their tournament programs to attract Division I attention in the college recruitment process.

Oftentimes, the kids who receive preferential treatment are those whose parents pay the biggest bucks for additional services, such as conditioning programs, recruitment videos, and showcases. Some parents, encouraged by these coaches, hold their sons back in school, believing that the "extra year of maturity" will benefit them in the college recruitment process. This is especially true if the youngster is a corner infielder, outfielder, or catcher, positions that are reserved for power hitters. Even some of the most prestigious private schools become complicit by allowing exceptional student-athletes to repeat a grade or by giving those who come from modest financial circumstances "athletic scholarships" disguised as "need-based financial aid." The incentive for the school is to field winning teams and gain greater media visibility and for the student-athlete to improve his or her academic performance and allow for greater physical development. These so-called competitive advantages are laughable.

But another shortcut has emerged—a shortcut that is increasing among young ballplayers between the ages of 15 and 24—that is not at all funny. That shortcut is the growing use of appearance- and performance-enhancing drugs (APEDs)—specifically, anabolic steroids. My son and other adolescents who have chosen to rely on natural ability and work ethic alone will continue to face this temptation until the day they stop playing the game. I pray that these youngsters have the moral courage and emotional strength to reject the temptation.

This book is about two student-athletes who decided to take this shortcut and paid for it with their lives. Taylor Hooton and Rob Garibaldi were not stereotypical drug addicts or recreational users who indulged haphazardly. They were intelligent, athletically talented, handsome young men with extremely promising futures. They were not raised in communities with visible drug cultures, and they had the advantage of being surrounded by loving and supportive families with strong moral codes and healthy expectations.

Like me, their parents believed that baseball would teach their sons important life lessons. They believed that there are no shortcuts to success, only hard work. And they encouraged their sons' dreams. In Taylor's case, his aspiration was to become a starting pitcher on his high school's varsity baseball team. In Rob's case, his aspiration was to reach the major leagues. Determined to achieve their dreams, Taylor and Rob made the bad decision to begin using anabolic steroids. That's the sad irony—these kids were All-American superachievers who learned as much as they could about steroids and the cycling process because they genuinely believed that it was a healthy and productive way to improve their personal appearance, physical strength, and athletic performance. In the process, anabolic steroid use robbed them of their compassion for others, their honesty, and their personal integrity. Unable to stop their steroid use, Taylor and Rob ended up taking their own lives. Fourteen years later, their families continue to be haunted by the nightmare of their sons' tragic deaths.

It would have been easy for the Hootons and the Garibaldis to place blame for the suicides elsewhere, but they did not. They might have suspected the negligence of their sons' coaches or school and university administrators, but they never pursued litigation. Instead, for years, the two families blamed themselves for failing to recognize warning signals and changes in their sons' appearance and behavior. Only later did they come to realize that most of the current research on steroid use began in the wake of their family tragedies and as a result of their own efforts to publicize the dangers of steroids. In the end, the Hootons and the Garibaldis dealt with their grief by accepting the fact that Taylor and Rob were responsible for their own actions and, hence, their own deaths. I agree that their sons were responsible for their own fates. No one forced either of the boys to take steroids. Accepting that fact allowed the Hootons and the Garibaldis to move on with their lives, but it has not made their loss any less devastating.

To be sure, we will never know just how many young men and women are abusing APEDs. One reason is that law enforcement agencies have largely ignored the issue,[1] focusing instead on the more common issue of recreational drug abuse.[2] What we do know is that current research places the number of adolescent steroid users at 1.5 million teens and growing.[3]

It would be easy for the general public to dismiss the Hooton and the Garibaldi suicides as rare. In fact, I was among those who initially considered the boys' deaths unusual on the basis of the fact that both young men were mixing steroids with antidepressants and, in Rob's case, an additional medication used to treat attention deficit disorder. But Harrison G. Pope Jr., MD, director of the biological psychiatry laboratory at McLean Hospital–Harvard Medical School and a leading authority on steroids, has maintained that suicide attempts related to steroid withdrawal are "more common than most people suspect."[4] Pope's research convinced me that steroid use among adolescents, who are already experiencing physiological and hormonal imbalances, can often trigger suicidal tendencies, especially when the user is going through withdrawal.[5] Add to that the increasing numbers of teens in our society who are already taking antidepressants, other medications for preexisting conditions, and/or recreational drugs, and steroid use has the potential to become fatal for many, as it did for Taylor and Rob.

Suicide Squeeze: Taylor Hooton, Rob Garibaldi, and the Fight against Teenage Steroid Abuse explores the lives and deaths of these two young men, the impact of their suicides on family and friends, and their parents' ongoing fight against adolescent APED use. The title is taken from the most high-risk/high-yield play in baseball.[6] Like the base runner in a suicide squeeze, the teenage steroid user is taking a huge risk to achieve ultimate glory. Unfortunately, the odds are against him or her, because the play fails more than it succeeds. So, too, are the odds against an adolescent steroid user who hopes to escape unscathed.

This book is *not* a comprehensive study of APED use throughout amateur sports—although there is a desperate need for such a book—but focuses instead on amateur baseball, the sport that exercised the strongest influence in the lives of Taylor and Rob. It is based on their own writings; interviews with family members, friends, and coaches; contemporary newspaper accounts; national television coverage of the suicides; and the evolving research on adolescent steroid abuse by professional authorities in the fields of law, medicine, pharmacology, psychology, and public advocacy. In the process of telling the tragic stories of these two promising student-athletes, *Suicide Squeeze* examines the following issues: What messages are being delivered to teenagers and college recruits that might encourage steroid use? What are the warning signs and symptoms of anabolic steroid use? Why is there such widespread ignorance of the problem among parents and coaches? How can a steroid user be safely weaned off APEDs? How extensive is the APED problem among adolescents today? What steps must be taken to eliminate the use of anabolic steroids among teens?

Ultimately, APED abuse by our young people has little to do with the game of baseball but everything to do with our love for and commitment to our children. I wrote this book because I have dedicated a lifetime to the education of youth. I wrote it because I cannot imagine suffering the death of a child by suicide and then trying to rebuild my life. And I wrote it because the dangers of anabolic steroid use threaten not only to destroy the moral fabric of the next generation but also to compromise the physical health and mental welfare of our society's most valuable resource. I believe that our country cannot afford either risk. I hope that this book will help prevent other families from suffering the tragic loss of a son or a daughter to anabolic steroids.

William C. Kashatus
Philadelphia, Pennsylvania
October 15, 2016

LIST OF ABBREVIATIONS

AAS	anabolic-androgenic steroid
ADA	Americans with Disabilities Act of 1990
AL	American League
APED	appearance- and performance-enhancing drug
BALCO	Bay Area Laboratory Co-Operative
BMI	body mass index
CBP	Customs and Border Protection
CDC	Centers for Disease Control and Prevention
CPR	cardiopulmonary resuscitation
CSM	College of San Mateo
DEA	Drug Enforcement Agency
DHEA	dehydroepiandrosterone
DSP	Disability Services and Programs
EPO	erythropoietin
FBI	Federal Bureau of Investigation
FDA	U.S. Food and Drug Administration
FSH	follicle-stimulating hormone
HGH	human growth hormone
IFBB	International Federation of Bodybuilding and Fitness
IOC	International Olympic Committee
JV	junior varsity
LH	luteinizing hormone
MLB	Major League Baseball

m.p.h.	miles per hour
MTF	*Monitoring the Future*
MVP	Most Valuable Player
NCAA	National Collegiate Athletic Association
NFL	National Football League
NL	National League
PATS	Partnership Attitude Tracking Study
PED	performance-enhancing drug
PISD	Plano Independent School District
PLAY	Promoting a Lifetime of Activity for Youth
RBI	runs batted in
SAAS	Student-Athlete Academic Services
SI	*Sports Illustrated*
SRJC	Santa Rosa Junior College
SSU	Sonoma State University
THG	tetrahydrogestrinone
USADA	U.S. Anti-Doping Agency
USC	University of Southern California
WADA	World Anti-Doping Agency
YRBS	Youth Risk Behavior Survey

SUICIDE SQUEEZE

1

CONFRONTING BASEBALL'S
FALLEN HEROES

On Thursday, March 17, 2005, Donald Hooton of Plano, Texas, was visiting Capitol Hill to attend the congressional hearings on steroid use in Major League Baseball (MLB). Hooton was a celebrity inside Room 2154 of the Rayburn House Office Building, where the rapid fire of camera shutters echoed down the hallway. It seemed everyone wanted to have a photo taken with the unassuming gentleman from Texas, although few people outside Washington, D.C., had ever heard of him—certainly not the baseball luminaries scheduled to appear before the House Government Reform Committee that day.

Mark McGwire, formerly of the St. Louis Cardinals, was expected to be a key witness. McGwire was also the biggest star at the hearings, having broken Roger Maris's single-season home-run record of 61 when he slugged 70 homers in 1998. Three other witnesses—Baltimore Orioles outfielder Sammy Sosa, McGwire's rival in the 1998 home-run chase; one-time Oakland Athletics slugger Jose Canseco, a former A's teammate of McGwire's; and Rafael Palmeiro, another top power hitter who played for the Orioles—also commanded attention. While Canseco had already admitted to using anabolic steroids to improve his offensive performance, McGwire, Sosa, and Palmeiro were suspected of juicing, and their hitting records were now being called into question. The presence of these all-stars attracted an overflow crowd to the packed House Oversight Committee hearing. Many news reporters and curiosity seekers were turned away, left to scramble for a seat in a nearby room to watch the televised hearings.[1]

Hooton was not an all-star baseball player, a journalist, or an autograph seeker. He'd been an executive in the telecommunications industry until he had resigned to establish and serve as the president of a nonprofit organization dedicated to educating students, parents, and coaches about the signs and dangers of appearance- and performance-enhancing drugs (APEDs) among adolescents. Like McGwire and company, Hooton had come to testify before the committee on the use of steroids in baseball. Unlike the major leaguers, he had appeared before congressional committees investigating the subject on two previous occasions. Impressed by his testimony, legislators insisted that he return so that he could deliver his sobering message directly to the ballplayers. On this early spring morning, Hooton planned to tell them what it was like to suffer the loss of a 17-year-old son who followed their lead and used anabolic steroids to improve his chances of making his high school's varsity baseball team.

Taylor Hooton, a 6'3", 175-pound pitcher at Plano West High School, appeared to have everything a teenager could desire: popularity, good looks, a 3.8 grade point average, excellent SAT scores, and a well-mannered disposition that endeared him to peers and adults alike. He also had the bloodlines to become a successful pitcher. His cousin, Burt Hooton, pitched for the Chicago Cubs, Los Angeles Dodgers, and Texas Rangers in the 1970s and 1980s. His older brother, Don Jr., hurled for Division I University of Texas at Arlington. But the thing Taylor wanted most of all was to measure up to other, more physically impressive athletes. He wanted to build body mass to become a starting pitcher for Plano West's varsity baseball team. A junior varsity (JV) coach reinforced this idea by suggesting that he get bigger.

In January 2003, Taylor began injecting himself with nandrolone decanoate, often referred to as "Deca 200," and taking Anadrol orally, steroids commonly used by weightlifters. That winter, Don and his wife, Gwen, began to notice changes in their son's physique and behavior. Taylor had been spending much more time in the weight room, lifting at a feverish pace. By early spring, his 6'3" frame was carrying 205 pounds, a dramatic increase of 30 pounds. He also began to develop acne on his back and to exhibit severe mood swings. Taylor would fly into a sudden rage and then express remorse for the outburst. He would pound the floor with his fists in anger and then become tearfully apologetic. Initially, Don and Gwen did not suspect steroid use, although Taylor was exhibiting many of the tell-tale signs. Desperate for answers, they had their son screened for recreational drugs. When the tests came back clean, Taylor snapped, "Told you so," and they were momentarily relieved. Blake Boydston, the varsity baseball coach at Plano West, offered further assurance that nothing was wrong. Boydston told Don and Gwen that Taylor always came to the field "in good spirits," that he had noticed no troubling behavior, and that their son's added body mass appeared to be the natural result of weight training. Taylor had everyone fooled. Then his behavior grew more erratic.

Once, he hurled a phone through the wall, injuring a finger on his pitching hand. He pummeled his girlfriend's ex-boyfriend, sending him to the hospital with a wound that required nine stitches. He also took several hundred dollars from his parents' bank account without permission. Finally, in April 2003, Don and Gwen insisted that Taylor see a psychiatrist. Only then did the young pitcher admit that he had been doping. Although the psychiatrist convinced him to stop using steroids, the withdrawal resulted in a severe depression. On July 15, 2003, after the Hootons returned from vacation, Taylor fashioned a noose out of leather belts and hanged himself from his bedroom door. When the room was later inspected by police, vials of steroids, along with syringes and needles, were discovered. An autopsy by the Collin County medical examiner revealed the presence of metabolized steroids 19-Norandrosterone and 19-Noretiocholanolone in Taylor's system. Hooton attributed his son's death to the psychological effects of steroid use.[2]

Don Hooton was not the only parent who came to testify before Congress. Denise Garibaldi, a clinical psychologist from Petaluma, California, and her husband, Ray, were also scheduled to appear before the committee. They, too, had lost a son to steroid use. Rob Garibaldi, a polite, good-natured young man, had grown up with baseball. By age 13, the game was the most important thing in his life. At age 16, he was recruited to join a traveling all-star team sponsored by MLB's California Angels. The following year, he was named a high school All-American. Rob was a "four-tool" outfielder who could run, hit, throw, and field. But at just 5'11", 150 pounds, he lacked the muscle to achieve the vital "fifth tool"—hitting for power. To add muscle mass, the youngster began taking nutritional supplements, but to no avail. So, during the summer of 1997, he purchased steroids.

Rob would do anything to succeed in baseball, and he did not have to look far for role models. He idolized Barry Bonds, the muscle-bound San Francisco Giant outfielder who eclipsed McGwire's single-season home-run record by hitting 73 in 2001. Bonds's new record and his suspicious late-career renaissance suggested steroid use.[3] Rob also modeled himself after McGwire, who in 2010 would admit to taking steroids during his playing career as well as androstenedione, or "andro," a pill that produced testosterone for the intended purpose of building muscle mass.[4] Bonds and

McGwire, as well as a growing number of major leaguers, had benefited from the use of performance-enhancing drugs (PEDs). PEDs augmented the quickness essential to a hitter's swing or a base stealer's speed. They built muscle mass, giving players unprecedented power and increased aggression. They improved recovery speed, enabling players to heal faster from injury or muscle fatigue. Essentially, anabolic steroids allowed big league players not only to survive the grind of a 162-game season but also to pad their personal statistics and bank accounts substantially while increasing their national media exposure. At the same time, medical researchers linked megadoses of PEDs to tendon and ligament tears, kidney and liver damage, impotence, heart disease, and cancer.[5] But players like Bonds and McGwire were willing to take these risks because of the immediate gratification associated with the benefits. If major leaguers were willing to jeopardize their long-term health to achieve more immediate goals, why wouldn't an amateur player like Rob Garibaldi take that same risk to make it to the majors?

Rob matriculated to Santa Rosa Junior College and began injecting himself with Durabolin and Sustanon. By the fall of 1998, he had increased his weight to 165 pounds and hit .450 with 14 home runs and 77 runs batted in (RBI). Those numbers earned him the title of Northern California's "Junior College Player of the Year" as well as a scholarship to the University of Southern California (USC), a top Division I program and McGwire's alma mater. He had also been selected by the New York Yankees in the forty-first round of the 1999 amateur draft. But Rob chose to attend USC, where he continued his steroid use. His prodigious hitting helped the Trojans earn an appearance in the 2000 College World Series. The future looked bright. Rob had become the "five-tool" player scouts had predicted. *Baseball America* identified him as one of the country's top 100 college prospects.[6] But steroids also altered his personality and behavior. Over time, he became violent, delusional, and depressed. Cut from the team for being a "behavior problem" by the coaches at USC in 2001, within a year, Rob was placed on an involuntary hold at Psychiatric Emergency Services in Santa Rosa, California. He had assaulted his father and threatened suicide. When he finally confessed his steroid use, Rob explained to his parents that he had simply been following the actions of his role models, Bonds and McGwire. When seized by 'roid rage, he would scream, "I'm a ballplayer, and this is what ballplayers do!" Undrafted at age 24, Rob became despondent. Unable to see the connection between his steroid use, delusional behavior, and depression, he suffered from withdrawal and addiction for two years. Finally, on October 1, 2002, Rob fatally shot himself, putting a tragic end to a once-promising life cut short by APEDs.[7]

Mark McGwire and Jose Canseco, who formed Oakland's "Bash Brothers," led the A's to a world championship in 1989. Their prodigious offensive production was fueled by steroids. *(By Tom Dipace / Polaris Images.)*

The suicides of Taylor Hooton and Rob Garibaldi captured the attention of Congress, which launched an investigation on steroid use in MLB. The timing could not have been better, since the hearings coincided with the publication of Canseco's scandalous book, *Juiced*, which revealed the rampant use of steroids in the big leagues.

Canseco flattered himself as a pioneer, boasting that he had "single-handedly changed baseball by introducing anabolic steroids into the game."[8] During his playing days, the Cuban American slugger attributed his prodigious power hitting to excessive weight training. But that was only part of his story. In fact, he began using anabolic steroids in 1985 when he was in the minor leagues. Juicing was rare among ballplayers at the time, so Canseco was a guinea pig for the PEDs that were just beginning to infiltrate the black market. In the process, he developed a chiseled physique and the phenomenal strength and speed required to set power-hitting and base-stealing records.[9]

In 1986, Canseco, who began his career with the Oakland A's, was voted the American League's Rookie of the Year for his 33 homers and 117 RBI. Two years later, he was the league's Most Valuable Player (MVP), hitting 42 homers and stealing 40 bases, a very rare combination of speed and power among major league players at the time. Together with Mc-Gwire, Canseco formed Oakland's "Bash Brothers" and led the A's to a World Series title in 1989. By that time, he had experimented with anabolic steroids and human growth hormone (HGH) so extensively that he was known as "the Chemist" among ballplayers and trainers throughout the league. Canseco also shared his knowledge with fellow players, including McGwire and, after being traded to the Texas Rangers in 1992, Palmeiro, Juan Gonzalez, and Ivan Rodriguez.[10]

By the mid-1990s, the "steroid era" was in full swing, and doping spread throughout the major leagues. Motivated by the lure of big money, a place in the record books, or the simple desire to remain in the game, players began using anabolic steroids in increasing numbers, despite the fact that Commissioner Fay Vincent had issued a 1991 memo specifically prohibiting the drug's use.[11] Doping was an "open secret" in the major leagues, which still operates on the unspoken rule that "what's said and done in the clubhouse, stays in the clubhouse."[12] The evidence could be found in the unprecedented numbers of home runs being hit each season. Between 1995 and 2003, there was a total of eighteen 50-homer seasons.[13] To put things in perspective, there were only three 50-home-run seasons between 1961 (the year after Maris and Mickey Mantle both topped the mark) and 1994.[14] That's just three 50-homer seasons in thirty-two years, compared to the eighteen 50-homer seasons recorded in nine years during the steroid era.

At the height of the steroid era was the 1998 home-run race to break Maris's single season record of 61, which generated exceptionally positive publicity. McGwire and Sosa became national heroes that summer, revitalizing baseball after the 1994–1995 work stoppage. Fans flocked to the ballpark whenever the St. Louis Cardinals came to town just to watch McGwire take batting practice. The Associated Press and most television outlets paid close attention to the rivalry throughout the summer. It was a close race until August, when McGwire broke away. Finally, on September 8, the Cardinal first baseman hit his record-breaking 62nd home run of the season before a sellout crowd at Busch Stadium in St. Louis. Interestingly, the historic event came against Sosa's Chicago Cubs. The two rivals hugged each other before McGwire went into the stands to embrace Maris's children.[15] It was a made-for-national-TV moment.

McGwire would finish the season with 70 homers. Later, he would be hailed as one of the top 100 players of the twentieth century by *Sporting News* and one of the top 30 by MLB.[16] Ironically, the steroid scandal began to unravel that same season when AP writer Steve Wilstein reported seeing a bottle of androstenedione, an over-the-counter muscle-enhancement product that boosts testosterone levels, in McGwire's locker.[17] Although "andro" was legal in the United States at the time and not banned by MLB, McGwire, embarrassed by the discovery, initially denied using the substance.[18] Nevertheless, the incident piqued the curiosity of sportswriters, who began to make the connection between PEDs and tape-measure home runs.

Public suspicion of steroid use in the majors was heightened in 2001, when Bonds eclipsed McGwire's single-season home-run record with 73. Suspected of doping since the late 1990s, Bonds had been long and lean and no more than 190 pounds when he played for the Pittsburgh Pirates earlier in his career. But by 2001, he weighed 225 pounds, most of it rock-hard muscle. His broad shoulders and huge biceps gave him the appearance of an NFL linebacker rather than a baseball player. In addition, Bonds's late-career explosion in offensive production was unparalleled in baseball history. Even as the San Francisco outfielder took aim at Hank Aaron's career home-run record of 755 in 2007, a grand jury was investigating him for possible perjury and tax-evasion charges stemming from his involvement with an alleged steroids ring.[19] Other events also suggested that MLB had a serious steroid problem.

In a *Sports Illustrated* (*SI*) cover story that ran in June 2002, Ken Caminiti, a former San Diego Padre, admitted that he had used steroids during his National League (NL) MVP-winning 1996 season, when he hit a career-high .326 with 40 home runs and 130 RBI, and for several seasons afterward. He expressed no regret about his use. "It's no secret what's going on in baseball," said the retired Caminiti. "At least half the guys are using steroids. They talk about it. They joke about it with each other." He also revealed that steroid use was a widely accepted—even necessary— choice for ballplayers looking for a competitive edge and financial security. "If a young player were to ask me what to do," Caminiti added, "I'm not going to tell him it's bad. Look at all the money in the game: You have a chance to set your family up, to get your daughter into a better school. . . . So I can't say, 'Don't do it,' not when the guy next to you is as big as a house and he's going to take your job and make the money."[20]

Caminiti's confession marked a major turning point in the steroid era. A week later, Senator John McCain (R-AZ) called for a Senate subcommittee hearing. Senator Byron Dorgan (D-ND) opened the June 18, 2002, hearing by citing the *SI* cover story as a "call to action" to determine whether "legislative action was necessary." Before the hearing ended,

McCain and Dorgan told Commissioner Bud Selig and Players Association Executive Director Don Fehr that a strict drug-testing program at the Major League level must be negotiated during collective bargaining. Two weeks later, the players' union reversed its position and agreed to random drug testing for the first time in its history.[21]

Now, three years later, in March 2005, Congress was threatening to play hardball with baseball's antitrust exemption again.[22] This time, however, the issue hit closer to home. According to Representative Henry A. Waxman (D-CA), the ranking Democrat on the House Government Reform Committee, the growing use of steroids among adolescent youth was the primary reason for the hearings: "Kids are dying from the use of steroids. They're looking up to these major league leaders in terms of the enhancements that they're using. And we have to stop it."[23] Waxman's concern was echoed in the testimonies of Don Hooton and Denise Garibaldi.

Hooton, usually a soft-spoken, bespectacled individual, took a hard-line approach. After telling his son's story, he informed the legislators that experts identified the "usage of steroids among our high school kids at about 5 to 6 percent of the overall population." Some of the experts said that "more like a million kids are doing steroids." "In some parts of the country," he continued, "studies show that the usage among high school junior and senior males is as high as 11 to 12 percent." Of course, Hooton was speaking of the entire adolescent athletic landscape—not just baseball—as well as a growing number of female teenagers who used steroids to enhance their appearance. In the most damning portion of his testimony, Hooton rebuked "the poor example being set by professional athletes as a major catalyst fueling the high usage of steroids amongst our kids." "Our kids look up to these guys," he said. "They want to do the things the pros do to be successful." He went on to deliver three sobering messages aimed directly at the players who were called to testify that day:

> First, I am sick and tired of having you tell us that you don't want to be considered role models. If you haven't figured it out yet, let me break the news to you that whether you like it or not—you are role models. And parents across America should hold you accountable for behavior that inspires our kids to do things that put their health at risk and teaches them that the ethics we try to teach them around our kitchen table somehow don't apply to them.
>
> Second, our kids know that the use of anabolic steroids is high among professional athletes. They don't need to read Mr. Canseco's new book to know that something other than natural physi-

cal ability is providing many of you with the ability to break so many performance records, that provide you with the opportunity to make those millions of dollars. Our youngsters hear the message loud and clear—and it's wrong. [That message is] "If you want to achieve your goal, it's okay to use steroids to get you there because the pros are doing it." It's a real challenge for parents to overpower the strong message that's being sent to our children by your behavior.

Third, players who are guilty of taking steroids are not only cheaters—you are cowards! You're afraid to step on the field to compete for your positions and play the game without substances that are a felony to possess without a legitimate prescription, substances that have been banned from competition at all levels of athletics. Not only that: you are cowards when it comes to facing your fans and our children. Why don't you show our kids that you're man enough to face authority, tell the truth, and face the consequences. Instead, you hide behind the skirts of your union. And with the help of management and your lawyers, you've made every effort to resist facing the public today.

What message are you sending to our sons and daughters? That you're above the law? That you can continue to deny your behavior and get away with it? That somehow you're not a cheater unless you get caught?

It was a powerful indictment of the egotistical stars assembled that day and the fast-paced, synthetically altered, narcissistic culture they had created in the major leagues. Hooton challenged not only their manhood but also their failure to uphold the integrity of the national pastime and the heroes who shaped it. And he did not forget to address the players' union, which permitted the boorish behavior through its collective-bargaining agreement, or management, for its extremely lenient drug policy. Essentially, Hooton took on the entire baseball establishment, calling for all parties to get their proverbial house in order.[24]

Denise Garibaldi followed with an impassioned plea to parents, coaches, and athletes at all levels of sport. She asked that they view her son's death as a "wake-up call" on steroid usage. "Let's not fool ourselves," she said:

Kids use steroids because they work—and work well. Physical results are fast. High school and college students have the desire to look good. Pressure is enormous to do whatever it takes to achieve the goals of being bigger, stronger, and faster. Both males and females bulk up to get that euphoric feeling of having athletic superiority or that perfect body. Once teammates start using, others may feel the need to use so as to be competitive. Steroid usage gives a competitive edge, but it's cheating by all ethical standards.

Garibaldi also criticized the "win-at-all-costs" attitude that prevails at all levels of sport, which has resulted in a "growing demand for steroids" among youngsters, who "absorb the influence and example of their role models" in professional sports. It has also resulted in "coaches who look the other way" and "parents who push their kids to obtain scholarships" in the sports they are playing. Instead, parents, coaches, and pro athletes must "accept the responsibility of encouraging the health and well-being" of young athletes. Garibaldi closed her remarks with a five-point reality check:

- Performance-enhancing dietary supplements promote a mindset that prompts steroid use later.
- The psychiatric symptoms associated with steroid withdrawal persist for a year or more after the abuser stops.
- An undetermined percentage of steroid users become addicted, continuing to take steroids in spite of physical or psychological problems, irritability, rage, depression, and negative effects on social relations.
- Drinking alcohol or taking any other drug, including prescription medication, compounds the adverse effects of steroids.
- The most dangerous effect of steroids is suicide.[25]

The connection between steroids, the role modeling of major league stars, and adolescent doping was not new. In 2004, U.S. Surgeon General Richard Carmona declared that teen steroid abuse was "less a moral and ethical issue than a public health issue." "If youngsters are seeing their role models practicing this kind of behavior, and it seems to be acceptable," he explained, "then we need to do something about it, because it is a serious health risk."[26] But Don Hooton and Denise Garibaldi gave an immediacy and powerful force to the problem by giving it a human face in the eyes of the public. They hoped their sobering testimonies would have a strong impact on the star performers who had come to testify, one that would give meaning to the tragic deaths of their sons. It was not much to ask of a sport and its players who had captured the imagi-

At the congressional hearings on steroids in baseball in March 2005, Don Hooton delivered powerful testimony on the fatal impact of steroids on his son and the responsibility of major league ballplayers as role models for young people. He was joined by Denise Garibaldi, a clinical psychologist who lost her son Rob to steroid addiction. Denise offered an impassioned plea to parents and coaches to develop a greater awareness of the symptoms and dangers of teen steroid use. *(By Jay L. Clendenin / Polaris Images.)*

nations of youngsters for generations. Baseball was, after all, a child's game played not only for the entertainment of youngsters but also for the lessons it teaches, such as "respect for one's health," "development of personal character" and "fair play." They are lessons that parents hope their children will learn and embrace to prepare themselves for the inevitable challenges that life brings their way, lessons often modeled by the heroes a youngster adopts in childhood and remembers for the rest of his or her life. That hope may sound naïve for a game that has become a multi-billion-dollar industry, but people like the Hootons and Garibaldis still entertain a deep-seated belief in heroes and their ability to deliver when needed most. For them, the hearings were not about baseball and the rampant use of steroids in the majors; they were about the health and psychological welfare of our country's children and the pressing need to prevent other youngsters from using anabolic steroids. They understood what was at stake. Sadly, the ballplayers did not. If Don Hooton and Denise Garibaldi believed that McGwire and the others would come clean, they were sorely disappointed.

Mark McGwire (*above left*) sat throughout the hearings, deflecting most of the questions directed to him with the refrain "I'm not here to talk about the past." *(By Andy Mills, Newark Star-Ledger / Polaris Images.)* Former teammate Jose Canseco (*above right*) was viewed by other players as a traitor when he published *Juiced,* a tell-all book about steroid use in Major League Baseball. *(By Chris Maddaloni, Roll Call / Polaris Images.)*

The players entered the hearing room trailed by an army of lawyers—insurance that they would not incriminate themselves. Once seated at the witness table, McGwire read an emotional opening statement that suggested he would make amends. "My heart goes out to every parent whose son or daughter was a victim of steroid use," said the former Cardinal slugger, expressing his sympathy for the Hooton and Garibaldi families. But any hope that McGwire would admit wrongdoing was quickly dashed when he declared, "My lawyers have advised me that I cannot answer these questions without jeopardizing my friends, my family, or myself." Afterward, Big Mac sat calmly, deflecting most of questions with the pathetic refrain, "I'm not here to talk about the past." For a man who had conducted himself with class and dignity during his quest to break Maris's single-season home-run mark in 1998, McGwire's refusal to cooperate was disgraceful—and he knew it.

Canseco, considered a traitor by the other players after publishing his tell-all book, was not much more forthcoming. Stating that he could not answer some questions unless he was "given immunity from prosecution," the former A's slugger insisted that an "overzealous prosecutor" in Florida might try to revoke his probation on an unrelated offense. The remark diminished whatever admiration he may have enjoyed by coming forward in the first place. It aroused suspicions that Canseco's book was simply a scheme to generate the money to pay off the substantial legal bills he had run up. Sosa proved to be just as cowardly. Although he flatly denied using steroids, his words held little weight for anyone who had followed his career. Within one year of being traded from the White Sox to the Cubs in 1992, Sosa transformed himself from a scrawny shortstop into a muscle-bound slugger. Not wanting to explain the remarkable change in physique or the offensive numbers it had enabled him to achieve, the Dominican outfielder pretended that his English was not good enough to allow him to understand the questions asked by the congressional panel. It was a shameful performance.

Palmeiro was the most arrogant witness. Looking up from a prepared statement, he pointed his finger at the committee chairman, Representative Tom Davis (R-VA), and declared, "Let me start by telling you this: I have never used steroids. Period."[27] It is likely that few of those attending the hearing believed him. Prior to the 1995 season, Palmeiro had hit more than 30 home runs only once in slightly more than eight major league seasons. Setting aside 1993, when he hit 37 home runs, the native Cuban averaged 15 homers per season. But starting in 1995, Palmeiro began a streak of 38-plus home-run seasons that continued through 2003. If the Oriole first baseman believed he could dupe Congress, he was mistaken. Later that summer, Palmeiro became the first major baseball star to be suspended from the game after testing positive for the potent anabolic steroid Stanozolol, more commonly known as Winstrol.[28]

The behavior and scripted testimonies of these baseball stars were shameful. Steroid use in MLB was an open secret. Everyone associated with the game knew about the doping—the trainers who were treating injuries they had never seen before, the players who were injecting themselves and the teammates who were watching them do it, the sportswriters who were joking among themselves about the juicers, the general managers who were knowingly acquiring players on steroids, and the owners who were openly encouraging the home-run boom for the increasing profits it generated. None of them had the moral courage to speak out against it. Instead, they simply turned and looked the other way.[29] Just as pathetic was players' ignorance of the influential example they set as role models to our nation's youth. They simply failed to understand the implications of their doping on the adolescents who idolized them.

Unlike professional athletes, teenagers are much more susceptible to the physiological and psychological effects of steroid use because of the natural hormonal imbalance associated with adolescence. While elite athletes know the side effects of steroids and can afford to pay for the genuine article, kids are clueless and purchase less expensive substances that may be contaminated and hence even more dangerous. Adolescents also tend to believe that they are invincible, able to take dangerous risks without suffering the potential consequences. As a result, many teenagers desperate to enhance their athletic performance, improve their self-confidence, and/or attract the opposite sex are quick to resort to muscle-building steroids. Taylor Hooton and Rob Garibaldi had proven that the consequences of taking APEDs can be fatal.

McGwire, Canseco, Sosa, and Palmeiro just did not get it. If they did, they certainly did not have the moral courage to admit to their failures as role models. They embodied Don Hooton's earlier charge that ballplayers who juice are "not only cheaters [but] cowards."

Still, the biggest of the cheaters and cowards was not even present. Bonds was the one player who should have been forced to testify, the player whom Rob Garibaldi most idolized. But Bonds, already embroiled in an investigation of the Bay Area Laboratory Co-Operative (BALCO), a San Francisco–area sport supplement company that supplied anabolic steroids to professional athletes, was not subpoenaed by Congress at the request of prosecutors in that case.[30] His public humiliation began a year later with the publication of *Game of Shadows: Barry Bonds, BALCO, and the Steroids Scandal that Rocked Professional Sports* by Mark Fainaru-Wada and Lance Williams, investigative reporters for the *San Francisco Chronicle*. The book alleges that Bonds used Stanozolol and a host of other steroids to propel himself into the history books as the game's greatest home-run hitter, and it quickly turned public opinion against the embattled Giants' slugger.[31] In 2011, his problems worsened when he was indicted on an obstruction of justice charge in the government's investigation of BALCO.[32] Bonds continued to be punished by baseball writers in 2013, when they denied him entry into the Hall of Fame in his first year of eligibility.[33]

Together with the weak defense of baseball's shallow drug policy by Commissioner Selig and Fehr, the executive director of the players' union, the spectacle of the ballplayers' pathetic performances left the Hooton and Garibaldi families infuriated and largely discouraged about the possibility for change. Still, they had at least one reason for optimism.

Deeply moved by the testimonies of Don Hooton and Denise Garibaldi, Commissioner Bud Selig made Major League Baseball a founding partner of the Taylor Hooton Foundation. *(Courtesy of the National Baseball Hall of Fame Library, Cooperstown, NY.)*

According to Don Hooton, after the hearings ended, Sandy Alderson, the executive vice president of baseball operations for the commissioner's office, assured him that his testimony would change MLB for the better.[34] He made a similar remark to Ray and Denise Garibaldi.[35] And then MLB immediately made good on its promise.

The next year, Selig enlisted former U.S. Senator George J. Mitchell (D-ME) to lead an investigation into the use of PEDs in MLB. On December 13, 2007, Mitchell released the results of his investigation in a 409-page report that identified the names of eighty-nine major league players suspected of having used steroids or drugs, evaluated the effectiveness of the MLB Joint Drug Prevention and Treatment Program, and made recommendations on the handling of illegal drug use in the past as well as in the future.[36] In response to the Mitchell Report, MLB adopted the strongest drug policy in all of professional sports, one that strictly forbids the use of anabolic steroids without a prescription and includes stiff penalties as well as a testing policy conducted on a random basis throughout the year.[37]

But Selig, deeply moved by the deaths of the two young ballplayers, was determined not only to clean up the game but also to prevent other youngsters and their families from falling victim to steroid abuse. To that end, MLB became a founding partner in the Taylor Hooton Foundation by donating $1 million in 2005 and pledging additional funding as well as other forms of support in the future.[38] In doing so, Selig enabled the foundation to launch the most aggressive grassroots antisteroid educational program in the nation.

In the end, Taylor Hooton and Rob Garibaldi had forced MLB to restore competitive balance and a sense of integrity to the national pastime as well as to honor the game's past history of providing worthy role models for American youth. What follows are the tragic stories that led to this change.

2

FOR LOVE OF THE GAME
AND SONS

For those who have grown up with baseball, the game remains a love that is not easily forgotten. The memories are so vivid that they seem to have occurred yesterday: stepping into a major league ballpark for the first time, seeing the plush green playing field, and eating hot dogs and peanuts while cheering the hometown team on to victory. Other recollections are more personal, such as gripping the seams of a baseball, trading baseball cards with neighborhood friends, pretending to throw or hit like a big league hero, and getting that first hit in Little League. Such treasured childhood memories evoke powerful emotions for those who hold them. But the memories that tug at the heartstrings, the ones that are most intimate, involve our fathers.

Baseball, at its most basic level, is a game that endears fathers and sons to each other. It is about fathers passing down the stories of their own baseball experiences, playing catch in the backyard in the twilight hours after supper, pitching batting practice, and, in many cases, coaching their sons in Little League. Those years are the "Wonder Years" for fathers and sons, a period when they form a strong bond around a shared love before the inevitable distancing of adolescence occurs.

Some fathers try to extend the Wonder Years. Often, they are men who played the game at a higher level, either in college or in the minor leagues. Baseball allows those fathers to live vicariously through their sons' achievements, regardless of whether the sons appreciate the ongoing involvement. If asked, many of those dads would say that they would be pleased with and proud of their sons no matter what they did for a living—but secretly, they entertain big league dreams for their boys. Some even try to help make those dreams come true, for the love of the game and the love of their sons. Over time, the two loves can become inseparable.

D on Hooton was tired of moving his family around the country. It was the spring of 1999, and his job as a telecommunications software executive had already forced them to relocate three times in the last ten years. Gwen, his wife, and their older children, Mackenzie, age 19, and Donald Jr., age 18, had grown accustomed to change, adjusting to each new home with little difficulty because they all had each other. But now that Mackenzie and Donald were away at college, Taylor, the youngest child, at age 13, had no sibling at home.

Gwen had actually planned it that way. "Don just wanted to have two children, but I really wanted three," she recalled. "I pleaded with him to have just one more child, because Mackenzie and Donald would be going off to college, and at least we'd have someone else in the house a little while longer." Don relented, and Taylor was born on June 10, 1986, while the Hootons were living in Birmingham, Alabama. At 10 pounds, 3 ounces, he was a big baby, one who "stole his mother's heart the instant he was placed in her arms." When Gwen brought him home from the hospital, the family was complete.[1]

Both Mackenzie and Donald doted on their little brother, who immediately won them over with his cute smile and mischievous bluish-green eyes. Like most little brothers, Taylor gravitated toward Donald Jr., bonding around a mutual love of baseball. "We were a baseball family," said Don, who instilled a love for the game in his sons at an early age. "Taylor began playing T-ball when we lived in Sarasota, Florida, around the same time that Donald was playing for a team that made it to the Babe Ruth World Series in Concord, New Hampshire. Gwen and I were always driving the boys to practice or to a game, and when we weren't doing that, they'd be out in the backyard playing catch."[2]

Don was not as passionate about baseball as his sons were. His playing days had ended after Little League, when he had to find part-time jobs after school because his family came from modest financial circumstances. Initially, Don mowed lawns and did other odd jobs around the neighborhood. When he was in his teens, he was hired to sweep floors at a Morgan Lindsey store, and later he worked as a delivery boy at a pizza shop. During his college years, Don paid his tuition at the University of Louisiana by working as

Taylor Hooton was a standout Little League player for Lower Gwynedd, in southeastern Pennsylvania. *(Courtesy of Taylor Hooton Foundation.)*

a roughneck in the oil fields off the shores of the Bayou state. There was simply no time to indulge in baseball, something his parents considered a "child's game." Thus, Don's childhood ended with Little League. For him, baseball was an "enjoyable pastime," especially after he and Gwen had sons of their own. He also viewed the game as "an effective way for his sons to learn life lessons" and such values as "fair play," "sportsmanship," "perseverance," and "teamwork." Therefore, he encouraged their participation in the sport and supported their involvement in it.[3]

Taylor's love for baseball deepened when the Hootons moved to Ambler, a suburb of Philadelphia. One of the reasons was his older brother's example. Donald was a standout pitcher for Wissahickon High School who attracted considerable Division I interest. Selected by the *Philadelphia Inquirer* as the "Suburban One Conference Player of the Year" as a senior, he went on to play college ball at the University of Louisiana at Lafayette and later at the University of Texas at Arlington.

Taylor, who was playing for the Lower Gwynedd Little League at the time, was inspired to pitch by his brother's success. He was further encouraged by his cousin, Burt Hooton of the Los Angeles Dodgers. "Dad took us down to spring training at Vero Beach when Burt was pitching for the Dodgers," recalled Donald. "Burt invited us onto the field to have a catch with him and tried to teach us the knuckle-curve. It was a big deal for both of us, but especially for Taylor, because he was so young."[4]

Taylor experienced immediate success on the mound. One of the best young players in Lower Gwynedd, there was not a season when he did not make the All-Star team. He had much more natural ability than his older brother and was able to throw harder and faster at an earlier age. Coaches who saw Taylor pitch agreed that he had a pretty high ceiling. The challenge, however, was to keep him motivated to work hard to realize his tremendous potential, especially after Donald left for college. Don and Gwen had other concerns, too.

Each time the Hootons relocated, Taylor had to start all over again. Not only did he have to adjust to a new environment and a new school; he also had to make new friends. On the surface, Taylor was a gregarious kid who entertained others with his creativity, quick wit, and slapstick humor. Once, when he was 9 years old, Don and Gwen were having a dinner party. Taylor decided that he could make some money by acting as a waiter. Dressed in black pants and a white dress shirt with a bow tie, he placed a small jar for tips on a tray, folded a white towel across his arm, and circulated the room, taking drink orders. After Don mixed the drinks, Taylor, tray with tip jar in hand, served each guest, making sure he or she deposited a dollar or two in the jar. On other occasions, he entertained friends by pretending that he was going down an escalator. Hiding the lower half of his body behind a set of kitchen cabinets, Taylor walked forward, slowly bending his knees until he completely disappeared from view. It broke everyone up but also endeared him to others.[5] What concerned his parents, though, was that Taylor did not want to disappoint his peers, even if it meant conforming to their preferences. In the past, Taylor had relied on Donald to validate his choice of friends and to make sure that he mixed with good kids. But now that Donald was away at college, there was no assurance that he would maintain those kinds of friendships.

With Taylor approaching his high school years, Don was convinced that he had to plant roots. As devout Christians, Don and Gwen believed that Taylor, like his older siblings, would find refuge in his faith during the turmoil that would inevitably come with adolescence. But peer pressure could be overwhelming for a teen, no matter how strong a foundation had been laid at home. It was important to find a healthy environment in which Taylor could grow, one that complemented the strong Christian values the Hootons embraced as a family. So Don resigned as the vice president of marketing for a high-tech telecommunications software company and took a job with Tandem Computers, headquartered in Plano, Collin County, Texas.

Plano appeared to be an ideal home for a family. Situated between Fort Worth to the west and Dallas to the east, Plano, with a population of some 270,000 residents, is one of the most exclusive suburban communities in the nation.[6] CNN's *Money Magazine* routinely designated it as one of the best places to live in the United States, and *Forbes* called it one of the safest.[7] With a median household income of $82,000—almost 60 percent above the national average—Plano's residents enjoyed many of the advantages that come with significant wealth.[8] Lucrative employment opportunities could be found among the city's many corporate headquarters, including Alliance Data, Cinemark Theatres, Dell Services, Hewlett Packard Enterprises, J.C. Penney, and Siemens PLM Software. Plano's schools consistently scored among the highest in the nation. The secondary system was also unique: ninth and ten graders attended one of six high schools, while eleventh and twelfth graders attended one of three senior highs—Plano, Plano East, and Plano West. In 2012, *Newsweek* identified the city's three senior high schools among the very best in the country.[9] They not only produced an impressive number of National Merit Semifinalists each year but also cultivated many successful athletes.

High school football is a religion in Plano. Bleacher lights shine brightly over the city every Friday night in the autumn as residents flock to the high school gridiron, much like their parents and grandparents did in the glory days. Between 1965 and 1994, Plano Senior High, the oldest of the three senior high schools (dating to 1891), went to the state championship game on ten occasions, winning seven titles. Although Plano East (est. 1981) and Plano West (est. 1999) have yet to capture a state title, the two schools boast twelve district titles between them.[10] In addition, the three senior high schools have produced more than a dozen NFL players, including Charlie Peprah and Kyle Bosworth of the Dallas Cowboys and Justin Blalock and John Leake of the Atlanta Falcons.[11] And the school district spares no expense in its effort to maintain its storied football tradition.

In 2004, the Plano Independent School District (PISD) built a $15 million stadium and indoor practice facilities for the three football teams.[12] Cost was not an issue, since Plano is one of the most affluent school districts in the state. The same year, for example, PISD gave $130 million, or 32 percent of its budget, in property tax revenue to other school districts outside Collin County. The "gift" was mandated by Texas's "Robin Hood" law, which requires affluent districts to give a percentage of their property tax revenue to property-poor districts outside the county.[13]

While baseball takes a back seat to football in the city, Plano West finished first in the nation after winning the Texas state baseball championship in 2008, ending the season with a 40–2 record. Plano East has been more successful in producing major league talent, including Jake Arrieta, currently a Cy Young award–winning pitcher for the Chicago Cubs; Wes Bankston, formerly a first baseman for the Tampa Bay Devil Rays and the Oakland A's; and Matt Young, formerly an outfielder for the Atlanta Braves and the Detroit Tigers.[14]

With a reputation for impressive homes, low crime, quality schools, and competitive sports, Plano seemed to be a good fit for the Hootons, who had become comfortable living in an affluent suburban environment. Some of Don's new associates at Tandem were not as enthusiastic, though. They tried to discourage him from moving to Plano, insisting that its residents were "snobbish" and "hypercompetitive." They viewed the city as a place where parents and kids tried to "one-up each other" with their considerable incomes, expensive houses, fashionable cars, and designer clothes. They also warned Don about the city's rash of teen suicides in the 1980s and a series of heroin overdoses in the mid-1990s—a reflection of the so-called poverty of affluence that plagues wealthy suburbs, where parents substitute material rewards for the more essential emotional support that every child craves. But Don dismissed their advice as "plain and simple jealousy."[15]

On July 4, 1999, the Hootons moved into a $400,000 house at 5633 Lindsey Drive, a few blocks away from the brand new Plano West Senior High School. The house was located in the exclusive Castlemere neighborhood made up of four- and five-bedroom, single-family homes, most of which were built in the mid- to late 1990s.[16] Shortly thereafter, the family joined Prestonwood Baptist Church, one of the largest and fastest-growing megachurches in the nation, with more than eleven thousand members. Prestonwood had recently built a seven-thousand-seat worship center and was planning a Sports and Fitness Center to accommodate an already thriving sports ministry for more than one thousand youngsters. Together with a well-attended Bible fellowship class, vacation camps, and outreach programs, Prestonwood's various youth sports leagues offered the kind of faith community the Hootons desired for their young son.[17]

In August, Taylor entered the eighth grade at Renner Middle School. A handsome youngster with an infectious smile and a mischievous spark, he was also a very sensitive person who could make others feel comfortable and get a laugh at the same time. Realizing the awkwardness of being the "new kid in school," Taylor immediately put his skills to work to make some friends. Near the end of the first week, another new student, Mark Gomez, joined his English class.

"Hey, new kid, did you do the summer reading?" he blurted out, holding up a thick text.

Gomez, a shy youngster, froze like a deer caught in headlights.

Sensing the discomfort, Taylor tried to put him at ease: "Well, you've gotta complete this book by tomorrow!"

The class broke up. Taylor was just hitting his stride as a "class clown."

Gomez, who had just relocated to Plano from Seattle, would become one of his closest friends. It did not take long, since the two boys lived just a few blocks away from each other and shared a passion for baseball.

"Taylor had a real presence," Gomez said. "Growing up, I wasn't very social. I had a hard time making friends. But Taylor made me feel welcome. Our friendship just took off once I found out that he loved baseball."

Taylor, a lanky pitcher–first baseman, and Gomez, a speedy outfielder, became inseparable. They played in the same city baseball league, made the same All-Star teams, and hung out together at school and on the weekends.

"By summer, Taylor was already six feet tall," recalled Gomez, "and he could bring the heat. He also had poise—nothing seemed to shake him. When you consider all that, he was very intimidating on the mound."[18]

By the autumn of 2000, when Taylor entered the ninth grade at Shepton High School, he appeared to be a well-adjusted, ebullient adolescent with friends from a variety of social backgrounds. He had also dedicated his life to Jesus Christ, as had his parents and siblings, who were rebaptized on that occasion. A popular member of Prestonwood Baptist's Bible school, Taylor expanded his circle of friends through his involvement in church activities.[19] Reverend Neil Jeffrey, who taught Sunday Bible classes at Prestonwood, remembered Taylor as an "engaging youngster" who was "very popular" at the church. "I got to know Taylor pretty well during his first two years of high school," said Jeffrey. "Since he was an athlete and I used to be a high school athlete, our conversations often revolved around sports. Unfortunately, our sports ministry program was not nearly as developed as it would become in later years, so Taylor played baseball for Shepton High School and, later, Plano West."[20]

Jill Griffin, a math teacher at Shepton, remembered Taylor as a "sweet kid" who "always seemed to have a smile on his face." He quickly endeared himself to Griffin with his politeness and his interest in geometry. "That particular geometry class was really smart, and Taylor was right up there," she recalled. Griffin was in only her third year of teaching, so she admitted that she "wasn't as concerned about the content of the material" as much as "knowing her students and how to interest them in her course." "Geometry is like a sieve for the entire math curriculum," she explained. "It can make or break you. So I really tried hard to connect with each kid by learning their interests and then by making as many connections as possible between those interests and the subject matter." Naturally, Taylor loved baseball, and Griffin "rode that interest for all it was worth" by attending baseball games and then making relevant connections to

At Shepton Junior High School, Taylor endeared himself to students and teachers with his charming personality and infectious sense of humor. *(Courtesy of Taylor Hooton Foundation.)*

geometry. In the process, she became Taylor's favorite teacher, and he developed a strong interest in math.[21]

Although Taylor played other sports when he was growing up, baseball had become his favorite by high school. It was easy to fall in love with the game if you were a kid growing up in the Dallas–Fort Worth area in the mid-to late 1990s. The Texas Rangers, who played in nearby Arlington, were regulars in the postseason. They won American League Western Division championships in 1996, 1998, and 1999, increasing their fan base each year. The future looked especially promising in 2001, when owner Tom Hicks signed shortstop Alex Rodriguez of the Seattle Mariners to the most lucrative deal in baseball history: a ten-year, $252 million contract. While some fans and sportswriters maligned the signing, believing that Hicks tied up valuable payroll space that could have gone to improving other areas, such as pitching, Rodriguez was one of the top performers in the game and had the potential to become the greatest player of all time.

A-Rod's rise to stardom was meteoric. An outstanding scholastic athlete at Westminster Christian School in Palmetto Bay, Florida, Rodriguez, a shortstop, batted .419 and stole 90 bases to lead Westminster to the national championship in his junior year. In his senior year, he was even better, hitting .505 with 9 home runs, 36 RBI, and 35 steals in 35 attempts. Named first team prep All-American, Rodriguez was selected as the USA Baseball Junior Player and was widely regarded as the top prospect in the country.[22] The 17-year-old prodigy turned down a full baseball scholarship at the University of Miami, opting to sign with the Seattle Mariners after being selected in the first round of the 1993 amateur draft. He made his major league debut a year later.

In 1996, A-Rod became the Mariners' regular shortstop. It was his breakout season. He hit 36 home runs, drove in 123 runs, and led the American League (AL) with a .358 batting average, the highest for an AL right-handed batter since Joe DiMaggio hit .381 in 1939. He also led the AL in runs (141), total bases (379), and doubles (54). Selected by both *Sporting News* and the Associated Press as the Major League Player of the Year, Rodriguez came close to becoming the youngest MVP in baseball history, finishing second to Juan Gonzalez of the Texas Rangers. Between 1997 and 2000, A-Rod set the AL record for homers by a shortstop, becoming just the third member of the so-called 40-40 club, with 42 home runs and 46 stolen bases. He made three All-Star appearances, won two Silver Slugger awards, finished among the top 10 candidates for AL MVP each year, and established himself as the Mariners' franchise player after Seattle traded superstars Randy Johnson and Ken Griffey Jr.

After the 2000 season, A-Rod became a free agent and signed with Texas, where his power hitting improved dramatically. In 2001, Rodriguez produced one of the top offensive seasons ever for a shortstop, leading the AL with 52 home runs, 133 runs scored, and 393 total bases. He also tied for the league lead in extra base hits (87), ranked third in RBI (135) and slugging (.622), and established Rangers' club records for homers, runs, and total bases. In 2002, A-Rod hit a MLB-best 57 home runs, 142 RBI, and 389 total bases, and he won his first Gold Glove Award for outstanding defense. His 109 home runs in 2001–2002 are the most ever by an AL right-handed batter in consecutive seasons.[23]

Rodriguez's offensive prowess, chiseled physique, and all-American lifestyle made him the baseball hero of every kid who followed the Texas Rangers, including Taylor Hooton. "Taylor idolized A-Rod because he was big and strong and could crush the ball," recalled his mother, Gwen. "He'd talk about him all the time, saying that he wanted to be just like him."[24] By outward appearances, A-Rod seemed to be the ideal hero, at least during the early years of his career. He gave back to the community by establishing the Alex Rodriguez Family Foundation, which sponsored charities dedicated to orphans, AIDS and HIV research, disaster relief, family support, and childhood poverty. Rodriguez was also a loyal husband and a good citizen on and off the field.[25] Kids need sports heroes like that. They yearn to feel connected to a celebrity athlete and bask in the glow of their athletic triumphs. It is normal for youngsters to identify themselves with such heroes, especially preteens and teens who are seeking an identity independent of their parents, their very first heroes. During this process of self-definition, a sports hero often communicates the romantic yet realistic idea that a youngster can transform his or her life into something great. In so doing, the sports hero has the potential to play an extremely influential role in shaping a youngster's outlook, behavior, and self-image.[26] A-Rod was just the kind of sports hero the Hootons desired for their son, one who appeared to fit the Christian values they embraced as a family.

Don and Gwen were strict parents in the sense that they wanted their children to be responsible for themselves and their behavior. Predictably, Taylor had to meet certain expectations: lying, cheating, and stealing were completely unacceptable; his bed had to be made every morning, and his bedroom had to be kept clean; outdoor play was emphasized to prevent vegetating in front of the TV; the grass had to be cut by the time Don returned from work on Friday; if Taylor broke something, he had to fix it himself instead of paying someone to do it; and he had to earn good grades. To be sure, there were occasional exceptions. If Taylor was having difficulty with his studies, for example, his parents were always willing to help him. Don usually assisted with math and science; Gwen assisted with history, English, and writing. Similarly, when the demands of school prevented Taylor from cutting the grass or cleaning his room, his parents would cut him some slack. But in general, failure to abide by the rules—especially those involving lying, cheating, and stealing—was punishable by "grounding."[27] These were not unreasonable expectations for a Christian family like the Hootons, although few of Plano's other families were as rigid in holding their children accountable. Taylor was aware of that fact, and while he may not have appreciated "toeing the line" at home, he never wanted to disappoint his parents, especially his mother.

Taylor and Gwen had a special bond that grew even stronger after the family moved to Plano. With Don on the road most of the time and Mackenzie and Donald away at college, Gwen and Taylor became good friends. Naturally, they loved and trusted each other, but they also genuinely liked each other's company, which is not always the case with a parent and child. It was not unusual for them to enjoy a mid-week dinner and movie

Taylor had a special affection for his mother, Gwen, a schoolteacher. With his older siblings away at college and his father often away on business, Taylor spent countless hours with his mom after school and on weekends. *(Courtesy of Taylor Hooton Foundation.)*

together, "just to break up the routine." Taylor could also joke with his mother without seeming disrespectful. Once, en route to a baseball game, Gwen felt the sudden need to relieve herself.

"Oh, Taylor," she despaired, "we've got to hurry up and get to the field. I have to go to the bathroom!"

Never one to pass up the opportunity for a wisecrack, Taylor set her up with the question, "Momma, can you do something for me?"

"What's that!" she cried, growing more desperate by the moment.

"Just think, 'N-I-A-G-A-R-A F-A-L-L-S'!"

They also enjoyed the special intimacy between a mother and her youngest child. Neither would ever want to disappoint the other, and if by chance one did, the guilt was overwhelming. "There were times I had to work late and couldn't pick him up after school," recalled Gwen, an elementary school teacher. "He'd have to walk home by himself, and that really bothered me, especially if it was raining. I'd ask myself, 'What kind of a mother are you, letting your son do that?' But he never complained." Similarly, Taylor went to great lengths to please his mother. He wanted her to be proud of him, to reinforce all the love and trust she had for him. On those rare occasions that he did disappoint her, Taylor became unglued. Once, Gwen confronted him about leaving the house when his father had grounded him. Taylor snapped, either embarrassed by being caught or angry for being falsely accused. Regardless, the next day at school, he was so remorseful that he e-mailed Gwen and apologized for "flipping out." Admitting that he had "been crying all day," Taylor "swore on his life" that he "never left the house." "I love you with all my heart, Mom," he added. "I wish you could find some way in your heart to forgive me."[28] Naturally, Gwen complied. "Taylor never wanted to disappoint me, *especially* me," she said. "If he screwed up, I'd always tell him, 'Hey, dude, things like that happen. It's a learning experience. Shake it off. Let's learn from it and move on.'"[29]

By 2002, the year Taylor entered Plano West Senior High School, the Hootons were confident that they had chosen the right place to raise their youngest child. Together with the strong values and the sense of personal responsibility they cultivated at home, Plano, its public schools, and the Prestonwood Baptist Church offered the perfect environment for an all-American kid to grow.

Ray Garibaldi was a self-employed building maintenance contractor in Northern California, but his true passion was baseball. He grew up playing the game and was good enough to earn a spot as catcher at San Francisco State. In the 1960s, Garibaldi caught on with a few independent minor league teams in Latin America, fulfilling a boyhood dream to play pro ball. Ray would probably have continued to lead that lonely existence if he had not met Denise Della Santa, a petite, blonde-haired beauty with a contagious smile. She allowed him to see life's other possibilities and the joys of having a family of their own. The couple married in 1974 and purchased a small, one-story house on Bramble Court in Foster City, a middle-class suburb of San Francisco. Over the next four years, Denise gave birth to two sons: Raymond, on January 26, 1976; and Rob, on September 15, 1978.

Ray embraced fatherhood with the same enthusiasm that he had once reserved for playing baseball and looked into coaching the sport. When Raymond turned six, Ray began to scrutinize the local Little League and did not like what he saw. Foster City, with a population of just ten thousand, attracted younger, highly educated couples who worked in the Silicon Valley's emerging high-tech industry. Like Ray and Denise, they were ambitious people who wanted the very best education and community programs for their children.

But the older residents were entrenched in the ways of the past. Most of the men who coached the local youth teams had been doing so for decades, long after their own children had stopped playing. These "semi-professionals" believed in negative motivation, not encouragement. They emphasized winning rather than developing the youngsters' skills and manipulated playing time, giving the advantage to the most naturally talented kids. There were no background checks, no training program for aspiring parent-coaches, and no desire to improve the shabby quality of the sandlots. "It was a very unhealthy situation," recalled Ray, who quickly got himself appointed to the local Little League board. "It took some time to get rid of those older coaches, but we did and replaced them with new parents who placed teaching above winning."

Soon, Ray was a board member of the Foster City Little League, which sponsored ten teams for a total of one hundred twenty youngsters. Operating on a philosophy of positive reinforcement, Ray created an exemplary Little League program in which all the kids enjoyed equal playing time, regardless of ability, and life lessons were emphasized. Ray also spearheaded a training program for aspiring parent-coaches, creating detailed guidelines on everything from how to conduct a practice to game management. "The system worked so well that in a few years, we actually had competition among the parents for coaching positions," he said.

At the same time, Ray cultivated his sons' interest in baseball by taking them to major league games. Since Foster City was fairly close to both San Francisco and Oakland, the Garibaldis followed the Giants and the A's. "When Robbie was four and Raymond was seven, Denise and I took them to 'Little League Day' at Candlestick Park, where the San Francisco Giants played," said Ray. "While we're sitting in the stands, I could see Robbie's eyes were as big as saucers. 'Do these guys get paid to do this?' he asked. When we told him that they did, he blurted out, 'That's what I want to be when I grow up—a baseball player!'"[30]

Rob's passion for baseball actually began the year before, when Ray gave him a small brown leather glove and taught him how to play catch. "Throw it right here," said Ray, pointing to his chest. "No matter how big or small the person is, just hit him in the chest, and you'll be fine." Robbie did as he was told, and his father, pleased as punch, just started chuckling. "I've got a ballplayer here," he thought. "No doubt about it." Many years later, Rob would identify that cherished memory as the "moment I fell in love with baseball."[31]

Denise was even more smitten by Raymond and Robbie, both of whom she regards as "warm and caring people" who loved "being around our family." When she discovered in their early years that both of her sons were dyslexic and that Robbie also struggled with attention deficit hyper-

Growing up in Foster City, California, in the 1980s, Rob Garibaldi had a childhood that revolved around baseball and family. *Clockwise from lower left:* Ray Sr., Rob, Raymond, and Denise. *(Courtesy of the Garibaldi Family.)*

activity disorder, she learned as much as possible about child and educational development to meet their needs. In fact, Denise eventually earned a doctorate in clinical psychology and opened a private practice. Yet somehow, she also managed to make baseball a priority. "It was a 'family thing' for us when the boys were young," she recalled. "Raymond was the first to play, and Robbie, like any younger brother, wanted to be just like him. Their father coached both of them in Little League, and I was 'Team Mom,' often keeping the scorebook at games."[32] Both Raymond and Rob viewed their mother as a "best friend." She was the one who gave them "huge hugs and kisses" when they were sad, the one who "listened" when they were discouraged, and the one who "protected" them whenever the real world dealt a serious setback.[33]

Robbie, being the youngest, also had a big brother to look out for him, although Raymond did not always appreciate the task. Robbie could be very demanding. He insisted on playing with the older kids on their Bramble Court cul-de-sac, regardless of the game or level of competition. Once, during a pick-up basketball contest, the neighborhood bully, a 13-year-old, started harassing Robbie, who was only 6. Twice, Raymond, age 8, stopped the game and warned him of the consequences if he continued the harassment. But the bully just stood there laughing at him. "After the third time, I kicked him in the nuts as hard as I could," recalled Raymond. "He wasn't laughing after that. He was on the ground, holding his balls and puking his brain out. Robbie loved it. He was the one laughing now." Rob would remember the incident for the rest of his life.[34]

Raymond also learned early on that he would have to tolerate his younger brother's obsession with baseball. When Raymond, at age 7, started to play Little League, Robbie became inconsolable. It was bad enough that he had to sit and watch from the bleachers as his older brother played and his father coached a game that was his passion; the fact that Raymond was wearing a "baseball uniform" (i.e., Robbie's perception of a baseball uniform: a colored T-shirt and a pair of generic white baseball pants) only increased his jealousy. It was as if they were rubbing salt into an open wound. When the Garibaldis returned home, Robbie protested. "Dad, I can play with those kids," he insisted, tears streaming down his face.

"You're still too young, Robbie," said his father, which only made matters worse.

"You always say that, and it's not fair!" he screamed, before stomping off to his bedroom and slamming the door behind him for effect.

Ray, a bear of a man with a huge heart, understood his son's disappointment. No one devotes that much of his life to baseball without possessing a deep and abiding love for the game, a love that is often passed down to a son. After a few minutes, Ray walked into Robbie's room to console him.

"Listen, Robbie," he began. But his young son, who had his head buried in a pillow, cut him off: "No, just leave me alone, Dad!"

"Robbie, if you stop crying, I'll make you a deal."

His curiosity piqued, the youngster removed the pillow.

"What is it, Dad?"

"I spoke with the other coach, and we both agreed that you can be the team's bat boy," said Ray.

"Bat boy? What's that?"

Ray explained the duties and that Robbie could be in the dugout with the other players and have his very own "uniform."

"But I want to play!" the youngster insisted.

Ray had expected this response and was prepared for it. "I'll make you another deal," he added. "After the game, if you are the best bat boy you can be, I'll throw you the ball until my arm falls off or until it gets dark."[35]

Robbie agreed, and Ray was true to his word. "Dad coached all my Little League teams from the time I was seven, and Robbie was always right there, like a shadow," said Raymond. "He couldn't get enough base-ball. If he didn't get his fair share of my dad's time after practice was over, he'd have a fit. So the three of us would stay out on the field for hours afterward, just so Robbie could get all the fielding or hitting he wanted."[36] But it was not *all* baseball when the boys were young.

Family was also important to the Garibaldis. Both Denise and Ray came from close-knit, Italian Catholic families who cherished not only the nuclear unit but the extended unit as well. Thus, it was important for Raymond and Rob to spend time with their grandparents, aunts, uncles, and cousins and to learn about their interests. Denise's parents, Al and Elva Della Santa, owned a condo at Lake Tahoe, so the boys learned at an early age to ski on water and on the slopes. They also learned carpentry from Al, who owned several apartments in downtown San Francisco. Ray's parents, Ben and Eva Garibaldi, lived in South San Francisco and often babysat for all their grandchildren. Ben, an avid fisherman, indulged his grandsons by organizing family vacations around the sport. Of course, invitations were limited to males only. Occasionally, vacation plans would be altered, and moms would be included for camping in various states. Among the most favored cousins was Joe Garibaldi, who lived in nearby Pacifica. The three boys spent extended weekends "tearing apart Grand-ma's house" by playing some kind of sport, both indoors and outdoors. However, since Joe, a year younger than Raymond, also loved baseball, it became the sport of choice.[37]

Although Rob also participated in the local soccer and basketball leagues, he just could not get enough baseball, especially after he began playing Little League. Rob, a left-hander, played many different posi-tions, but he excelled at pitching and hitting. He also had a competitive instinct that shone whenever he stepped onto the mound.[38] For example, in July 1990, during a Little League All-Star tournament, Robbie faced Tom Brady, who would go on to quarterback the NFL New England Patri-ots. Brady, who played Little League in San Mateo, California, was a very good hitter. He was also much taller and stronger than most of the kids, especially Robbie, who was small for his age. The two youngsters faced each other, which was quite a spectacle because Brady, who was close to 6' tall, towered over Rob, who was just 4'9." Determined to strike Brady out, Rob had to settle for a fly out to center field instead. After the game, the *Foster City Progress* ran a "David-and-Goliath" feature story about the event, predicting "good things to come" for both boys.[39]

Rob, age 12, who counted the A's among his favorite Major League Baseball teams, played for the Little League Majors' team by the same name. *(Courtesy of the Garibaldi Family.)*

Rob's cousin, Joe Garibaldi, also recognized Rob's competitive drive. Joe was an exceptional ballplayer. Drafted by the Texas Rangers after high school, he placed a higher priority on his education and chose to attend San Diego State. A left-handed pitcher and power hitter, Joe recognized many similarities between himself and his younger cousin and encouraged him. "Rob, Raymond, and I were very close growing up," he said. "We always seemed to be at each other's houses. We'd go out to the local Little League field and play home-run derby. One of our dads would pitch. Raymond and I hit from home plate, but since Robbie was much younger, we let him hit from just behind second base. After the first few times, he said that he didn't want to have the advantage and insisted on hitting from home plate, too. I was impressed. He might not have hit many home runs from there, but he could drive the ball pretty far for his age."[40]

Despite his competitive drive, Rob was a compassionate person who tried to help out less talented teammates. By the time he was in his second year of Little League, he had an exceptional knowledge of the game and how to play all nine positions. "Rob was more of a surrogate coach than a player," recalled his father. "If another kid had difficulty understanding a particular position, Rob would take the time to explain it and even show him how to play the position. He was always trying to help out the weaker players. I was very proud of that, because it was something he did naturally. I never asked him to do those things."[41] Perhaps his compassion for others was a result of Rob's own educational struggles, or he had learned from the examples of his parents. Regardless, it was a quality that Rob demonstrated throughout his life.

In 1993, the Garibaldis decided to leave Foster City for Petaluma, California, a slightly larger city that was home to an emerging telecom industry. Since Denise was finishing her doctorate, she was looking for a place to establish a private practice for children with learning disabilities. Petaluma offered that opportunity as well as a public school district that had a strong program for special needs students. The plan was to have a house built there while Rob completed his eighth-grade year in Foster City.[42] Raymond, a high school junior, accepted the decision, but Rob was devastated by it. In a school essay titled "Speculating on My Future," he wrote:

> I am building my own house in Foster City. It's going to have two storys, five bedrooms, and a three-car garage for my three cars. One will be an antique show car, another one will be a BMW to drive around the city, and the third one will be a Ferrari to drive on weekends only.
>
> I will be able to afford all this, because I will be playing pro baseball with the Oakland A's and autographing baseballs for money. In my spare time, I will be teaching little kids baseball.

Interestingly, the description of the house matched that of the one Denise and Ray were building in Petaluma. The only difference was that they would not be living in Rob's house. Instead, Rob would be "living with [his] girlfriends and making [his] own decisions."[43]

According to Christina Reed, Rob's first girlfriend, "he didn't want any part of the move." "He called Petaluma 'Cow Country' because of all the cattle farming, and he was really very bitter," she recalled. "We were friends, first and foremost, so we could talk to each other about anything. I knew exactly how he felt." Reed had to deal with the sad knowledge that her closest confidant would be leaving her within the year. "I guess Rob's parents tried to make it easier by allowing him to finish out his eighth-grade year in Foster City while they went ahead to Petaluma," she said. "But in some ways that made it worse for both of us, because we knew our 'breakup' was inevitable." It was also around this time that their peer group began to experiment with drugs and alcohol. Considering his bitterness about the move to Petaluma as well as the absence of his parents, it would have been easy for Rob to indulge in either of those "experiments," but he refused. "Rob was obsessed with baseball," said Reed. "He wouldn't do drugs or alcohol, because he believed it would hurt his health and his ability to play the game."[44] Instead, Rob remained "mad at [his] parents for a year" after the family relocated to Petaluma, not only because he was leaving "great friends and his first girlfriend" but also because he "had no say in the decision."[45]

Petaluma, in Sonoma County (1993 population: forty thousand), was named by the Coast Miwok Indians. "Petaluma" means "hill backside" and refers to the town's proximity to Sonoma Mountain.[46] After gold was discovered in 1849, pioneers flocked to the frontier town, whose location along the Petaluma River made for productive farming in the nineteenth century. Steamships navigated the river between Petaluma and San Francisco, carrying agricultural produce to the burgeoning population of the Bay Area. Petaluma was soon known for its grain mills and chicken-processing industry, which eventually made it the "Egg Capital of the World." In the twentieth century, residents turned to cattle farming and wine making, but by the late 1990s, Petaluma was home to a growing telecom industry. Two of the better-known success stories are Advanced Fibre Communications (now Tellabs) and Cerent (now Cisco).[47]

Petaluma is also an attractive combination of the past and the present. Victorian homes that survived the 1906 San Francisco earthquake can be seen throughout the downtown Historic District, as can several other architectural styles. Quaint shops and a variety of restaurants can be found along the riverfront along with a yacht club and a snug harbor for power and sailboat enthusiasts. The rustic setting regularly attracts Hollywood producers, who have shot more than twenty feature films on location, including such blockbusters as *American Graffiti* (1973), *Basic Instinct* (1992), and *Cheaper by the Dozen* (2003).[48]

Drawn by the telecom industry, young upwardly mobile professionals like the Garibaldis settled in Petaluma, steadily increasing the population. By 2000, 54,548 individuals, 19,932 households, and 14,012 families were residing in the city, with a median family income of $71,158.[49] These families placed a high priority on education, and most became actively involved in their children's schooling. While St. Vincent de Paul High School and Harvest Christian School (grades K–8) offered residents a private education, the Petaluma City School District provided a quality public education through its several elementary schools, two junior high schools (Kenilworth and Petaluma), and two four-year high schools (Petaluma and Casa Grande). Casa Grande High School, in particular, was one of the best public high schools in Northern California, known for an exceptional Academic Decathlon team that represents Sonoma County on a regular basis at state-level competitions.[50] Petaluma also catered to young families, sponsoring a variety of colorful family-oriented events throughout the year, ranging from the "Butter and Egg Days Parade" to an "Art and Garden Festival," and from "Victorian Holiday Events" to the "Annual Antique Fair."[51]

Finally, Petaluma is just under forty miles from the Bay Area where the San Francisco Giants and Oakland A's play, making Candlestick Park and the Oakland Coliseum very accessible to the Garibaldis. Rob was a fan of both teams, especially Oakland, because his Little League Majors' team was named the A's and he idolized Mark McGwire. Oakland's first-round draft choice in the 1984 free-agent draft, McGwire shattered MLB's rookie home-run record with 49 in 1987 and was unanimously voted the AL Rookie of the Year. The 6'5" first baseman with a boyish-looking face and bright red hair immediately became Rob's hero. "Rob's very first baseball card was Mark McGwire's 1984 Olympic baseball card," recalled his mother, Denise. "He knew *everything* about Mark—his hitting statistics, how he wore his uniform, the way he ran around the bases after hitting a home run. He truly was Rob's first baseball hero."[52] Like Rob, McGwire was a hard-working athlete with a shy personality, who actively avoided the media during his years in Oakland. Undoubtedly, the youngster identified with those traits, which endeared the A's first baseman to him even more.

McGwire did not disappoint his young fan, either. During a ten-and-a-half-year career with Oakland, he was selected for or voted to nine AL All-Star teams and won two Silver Slugger Awards (1992, 1996) and a Gold Glove (1990). Most impressive, McGwire hit a total of 363 home runs for the Athletics, setting a new franchise record.[53] His most famous homer with the A's was a game-winning solo shot in the bottom of the ninth inning in Game 3 of the 1988 World Series against the Los Angeles Dodgers. The home run gave the A's their only victory in that Fall Classic, which they lost in five games. But the following season, Big Mac teamed up with Jose Canseco to propel the A's to the 1989 World Series. For Rob, it was a dream series, pitting the A's against the San Francisco Giants, his two favorite teams. Ray managed to get tickets to one game and took both Rob and Raymond, who were in awe of their very first World Series game. Oakland swept San Francisco in four games in the famous "Earth-quake Series."[54] In 1996, his last full season in Oakland, McGwire belted a MLB-leading 52 homers, set a career-high .312 average, and led the AL in both slugging percentage (.730) and on-base percentage (.467).[55] McGwire signed with the St. Louis Cardinals after that season, but Rob continued to follow his career closely. "Loyalty" was one of Rob's defining traits.

Rob also idolized Barry Bonds, who grew up in neighboring San Mateo. Although Bonds did not play for the Giants until 1993, Rob paid careful attention to his career as a Pittsburgh Pirate and took special pride in his ownership of the slugger's 1986 Topps rookie card.[56] Signed by the Pirates in the first round of the 1985 draft, Bonds was a *Sporting News* All-American from Arizona State University. He made his MLB debut on May 30, 1986. Although he went on to lead all NL rookies with 16 home runs, 48 RBI, 36 stolen bases, and 65 walks, Bonds finished sixth in Rookie of the

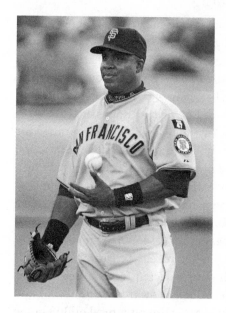

When Barry Bonds signed with the San Francisco Giants as a free agent in 1993, he became another of Rob's heroes. *(By Armando Arorizo, Prensa Internacional / Polaris Images.)*

Year voting. He was an exciting and dynamic player who immediately captured the imaginations of the fans. With Bonds as their lead-off hitter and left fielder, the Pirates experienced a dramatic increase in attendance. Between 1987 and 1993, when he became a free agent, Bonds hit .283 and averaged 27 home runs, 85 RBI, and 36 stolen bases each season. He won two NL MVP awards (1990, 1992), three Gold Gloves (1990, 1991, 1992), and three Silver Slugger Awards (1990, 1991, 1992), and he made two All-Star Game appearances (1990, 1992).[57] He was the complete package, a five-tool player who could field, run, throw, hit, and hit for power, and the cornerstone of an impressive lineup that also featured first baseman Bobby Bonilla, center fielder Andy Van Slyke, and shortstop Jay Bell. Despite their talent, the Pittsburgh Pirates, winners of three straight NL East titles (1990, 1991, 1992), failed to advance to the World Series.[58]

In 1993, Bonds signed a free-agent contract with the San Francisco Giants worth a then-record $43.7 million over six years. To honor his father, Bobby, who spent the first seven years of his MLB career with the Giants, Barry wore his jersey number, 25.[59] Rejuvenated by the homecoming, he hit .336 and led the NL with 46 home runs and 123 RBI en route to his third MVP award.[60]

With Bonds's return to the Bay Area, Rob could see his two baseball heroes on a regular basis, at least until 1996, when McGwire left for St. Louis. Despite that fact and the many advantages Petaluma offered, the youngster was still miserable after his family's move from Foster City. For the first few months, he "cried himself to sleep at night." Initially, he found it difficult to make friends at Casa Grande High School, and he felt "lonely and forgotten" until he met Josh Fuchs. Fuchs "made him laugh" with his off-color jokes and zany sense of humor. Although he was not very interested in baseball, Fuchs loved to skateboard and rollerblade, and he coaxed Rob out of his shell by getting him involved in those activities. They became fast friends as well as each other's confidants. Fuchs taught Rob that he really did not need "a hundred friends, just one or two true ones."[61]

P.J. Poiani was another close friend whom Rob met on the JV baseball team as a freshman. Although Poiani was a year older, the two boys shared a "quiet and shy" disposition and a strong passion for the game. "We clicked right away," Rob later recalled in a college essay. "We have such a strong friendship because of our honesty with and trust in each other. P.J. is the only person I trust with my life."[62] If Fuchs and Poiani were like surrogate brothers, Bob Leslie was Rob's surrogate father.

Leslie was the varsity baseball coach at Casa Grande. He had been a stellar high school pitcher with a decent fastball. But when he matriculated to Division II Sonoma State, he developed a devastating slider that attracted the attention of several pro scouts. Drafted by the Houston Astros, Leslie blew out his shoulder before he could realize his big league dream.[63] Instead, he channeled his love of the game into coaching high school kids. Everything about him screamed "baseball": the athletic gait of a former pitcher, the smokeless tobacco he had chewed since age 13, a competitive instinct that surfaced whenever he stepped onto the diamond, and the passion with which he spoke of the game.[64] At Casa Grande, Leslie did not have the same talent or number of players to choose from as the larger high schools in Northern California, but he got the most from his players, who tended to be scrappy, overachieving kids. He was a taskmaster who believed in tough love, but he also had a wonderful rapport with his players. He listened to their concerns, earning their trust and confidence. It was his way of using baseball to teach life lessons, and the approach endeared him to the kids.[65]

When Rob was promoted to the varsity team as a sophomore in 1995, Leslie took him under his wing. "Bob was very, very good for Rob," said Ray Garibaldi. "If Rob had a problem, he wouldn't hesitate to go to Bob with it. Although Rob loved basketball and soccer—and was good at both—Bob saw the potential he had for baseball and steered him in that direction. He also allowed Rob to both pitch and play center field, which was becoming rare at that time. Most all of the pitchers didn't play a field position—rather, they concentrated on pitching. No, Bob was extremely careful with Rob, because he knew that he could play Division I baseball."[66]

At the same time, Ray was heavily involved with the Casa Grande baseball program. He joined the Booster's Club and volunteered to upgrade the baseball field by raising funds in the community, building the mound, infield, and drainage system.[67] He attended every game, and, if Leslie or his assistant coach, Paul Maytorena, was thrown out for arguing with the umpire, he stepped in to coach. Ray's friendship with Leslie became so close that it impeded Rob's ability to become independent of his father, a natural desire for any adolescent. "Bob would talk to me about everything that was going on with Rob," he admitted, "especially if there was a personal problem."[68] While Ray undoubtedly viewed himself as looking out for his son's best interests, Rob would probably have resented his interference if he had known about it.

Nevertheless, Rob's baseball career flourished under Leslie's tutelage. In Rob's sophomore year, the Casa Grande Gauchos won the North Bay League title and made a run at the North Coast Sectional Championship, played at the Oakland Coliseum. Although the Gauchos failed in their bid for a return to the sectionals, the team clinched the North Bay title for the next three years. In 1996, Rob, a junior, pitched and played center field. He also led the team to a 19–6 record with a .460 batting average, which earned him All-League, All-Section, and All-State honors. The following season, the Gauchos lacked the dominant pitching and hitting they had enjoyed the previous two seasons. It was a young team with only four seniors, including Rob. In addition, the roster had to be cut from eighteen to just twelve players due to disciplinary problems.[69] "We have to manufacture runs," Leslie admitted in a March 1997 newspaper interview. "We realize that we aren't going to hit three home runs each game. Every game, win or lose, will be up to us. Nothing is going to come easy this season."[70] Despite their "underdog" status—or maybe because of it—the players formed a close-knit bond. Regardless of each one's role, the kids worked hard and genuinely enjoyed playing with each other.

Rob and Adam Westcott, a sophomore first baseman, became especially close, as they were thrust into the role of team leaders. "For every hour the other kids put in on the field or in the classroom, Rob puts in three," said Leslie. "On and off the field he's such a hard worker."[71] All the hard work paid off that season, as the Gauchos clinched their third-straight league title, and Rob once again earned All-League, All-Section, and All-State honors. But he also learned about the hard and painful realities of life while in high school.

During his last few years at Casa Grande, Rob lost two of his closest friends Josh Fuchs and Westcott. Fuchs was killed in an automobile accident in Rob's junior year, and Westcott met the same fate in his senior year. Struggling with feelings of grief, Rob suffered prolonged periods of depression. "Until then, I had never lost anyone close to me," he later wrote in a reflective essay:

I was confused. Sometimes I felt isolated and I tried to avoid the pain, so I resisted the necessity of letting go of Josh and Adam. Instead, I kept them with me. But Coach Leslie was there for me. He helped me understand that I could not go around grief, that I had to go through it. Going through grief meant that I didn't love them any less. I would always love them. But I also had to respect myself, and I could only do that by appreciating my own life and the people in it. Once I could do that, I would be happy again.[72]

Rob also arrived at the painful realization that he would have to go to a junior college to improve his grades if he hoped to be academically eligible for a Division I program. He struggled with his studies. Since elementary school, he had attended special education classes, had a tutor, and listened to books on tape. "I'm still not a great reader," he admitted in his senior year, "but I'm getting better. I just have to work harder than others."[73] Again, Rob followed the counsel of his baseball coach, who emphasized the importance of a positive attitude despite occasional discouragements. "Whenever I get real frustrated, I take a break from my homework and get back to it later," he explained. "Nothing's ever that bad. Getting mad doesn't help."[74]

Leslie might have used baseball as the vehicle for his teaching, but the lessons he imparted were invaluable. "Coach Leslie saw my potential and believed I could succeed," wrote Rob in his college admissions essay. "He also taught me what is truly important about life: a positive attitude, discipline, camaraderie, loyalty, and hard work. He gave me the confidence to succeed, whether it's on a baseball field, in a classroom, or in everyday life."[75]

Leslie cared. He was a special teacher-coach who made a meaningful difference in Rob's life. That's why the cruelest thing that happened to Rob in his senior year was learning that Leslie was fighting a losing battle with cancer.

3

"YOU NEED TO GET BIGGER"

In spring 2002, Taylor Hooton and his best friend, Mark Gomez, were starters on Shepton High School's baseball team, a feeder for Plano West. Taylor, a lean 6'3", 175-pound pitcher, played first base on days when he did not start. Gomez, the center fielder, was 20 pounds lighter and only 5'8" tall. Compared to other kids their own age, both youngsters lacked the size and weight to compete at the varsity level in the fall—and they knew it.[1]

High school and college coaches, as a general rule, expect corner infielders to hit with power or, if they pitch, to throw hard and fast. Taylor could not hit consistently with power. He was more of a gap hitter who occasionally drove a ball deep to the warning track. His tall, lean build was ideal for a pitcher, but at age 15, he had yet to grow into it. As a result, his fastball topped out at 80 miles per hour (m.p.h.). Gomez also struggled to hit with power, although he was a prototypical center fielder with the speed necessary to steal plenty of bases and cover a lot of ground in the outfield.[2] It came as no surprise then that the Shepton coach told both boys that they "needed to get bigger" if they hoped to make Plano West's varsity squad the following year. "Those were his exact words," recalled Gomez in an interview. "He said, 'You need to get bigger.' He didn't say, 'Here's a workout routine' or 'Here's a diet plan.' He just said, 'You need to get bigger.'"[3]

To be sure, the coach also did not say, "You need to get bigger by doing steroids." He may have been suggesting that the two boys go on a diet high in protein and carbohydrates or that they work out with free weights. But many of the student-athletes in the PISD interpreted such advice as a license to "get bigger" quickly and in any way possible—in other words, it was an open invitation to do steroids.

"Coaches don't come out and say, 'Take steroids,'" explained Billy Ajello, another close friend who played catcher for Plano West's varsity squad and who spoke with Jere Longman of the *New York Times* in a November 2003 interview. "Freshman, sophomore, junior year, they tell you you're too small. A kid thinks high school sports are everything: 'I have to take [steroids] to get to the next level, to get bigger and stronger to play.' I think if the coaches knew for sure, certain ones would pull a kid aside and say, 'What are you doing?' I think others would turn their heads and wouldn't say anything to the kid."[4] Don Hooton did not see it that way, at least not in the case of the Shepton baseball coach.

"I honestly believe that the coach was *not* suggesting that Taylor take anabolic steroids," he said after his son's death. "I've always said that Taylor was ultimately responsible for what happened to him. He didn't need to take steroids to get bigger. He chose to do that. But I also believe that there needs to come a time when a coach cannot make that kind of statement unless he's been trained to show a kid what kind of diet and exercise to do."[5]

Interestingly, one of the assistant principals, a former steroid user, had recently spoken with the baseball team about the dangers of the drug. Perhaps he believed that there was a problem at the senior high school and hoped to limit it by giving these impressionable freshmen and sophomores a reality check. "He told us that he had used steroids in the past and mentioned the things that could happen to you—the acne, how you could lose your hair at an early age," said Gomez. "Basically his message was 'Don't do it.'"[6]

Taylor and Gomez took this advice, at least in the short term. But when they entered Plano West as juniors in the fall of 2002, the temptation to "get bigger" by using steroids became overwhelming. The combination of wealth; parental pressure to achieve, both in the classroom and on the athletic field; and peer pressure to win games and to look good for girls made the school an especially fertile ground for PEDs. In an August 12, 2004 article, students told Paul Kix of the *Dallas Observer News* that Plano West had a "problem with steroid use," although estimates differed on the severity. According to Kix, one student indicated that 80 percent of the males—athletes *and* nonathletes—were doping, while another claimed that one-third of the football team juiced. Still another student contended that steroid use was a problem limited to a few athletes and body builders at the school. But none of the students denied that it was a problem at the school or that most students were aware of the problem.[7] The following year, Gregg Jones and Gary Jacobson of the *Dallas Morning News* interviewed more than one hundred current and former high school students, coaches, and parents, who revealed that steroids were readily available and commonly used by students in North Texas high schools, including Plano West. The findings of the four-month investigation included the following:

- High school students easily obtained steroids, often from dealers who were friends, classmates, and sometimes varsity athletes.
- Coaches rarely confronted players or alerted their parents, even when they suspected steroid use. Some cited the fear of a lawsuit from angry parents as a reason for remaining silent.
- Federal and local law enforcement agencies devoted little time to curbing steroid use because of tight resources and more urgent drug-related priorities.
- The Internet served as a virtual hangout where teenagers and adults exchanged information about buying and using steroids and picked up tips on managing side effects. Although dozens of websites sold steroids, the *News* found that area high school students preferred to buy the banned drugs from friends or acquaintances.
- Many teenage steroid users were nonathletes. Inspired by the sculpted bodies of teen models and ubiquitous images equating muscularity with sex appeal, these "vanity" users took steroids to impress classmates and potential girlfriends.
- Steroids led teens to abuse other drugs as they attempted to manage steroids' side effects, such as sexual impotency, suppression of natural testosterone production, and mood swings by taking Viagra, the fertility drug Clomid, and sedatives.[8]

Although it is difficult to determine the severity of adolescent steroid use in the Dallas area at the time, it is clear that a serious problem existed and was not limited to northern Texas.

National surveys indicated the growing use of steroids among American teens. The University of Michigan began studying national trends in legal and illicit drug use by teens in 1975. Questions about steroid use were added to the survey in 1989. Titled *Monitoring the Future*, the Michigan survey revealed a sharp increase in adolescent steroid use between

1998 and 2002. Prior to 1998, the overall annual prevalence rate was fairly stable among eighth and tenth graders, ranging between 0.9 percent and 1.2 percent. But in 1999, adolescent steroid use jumped from 1.2 percent to 1.7 percent in both eighth and tenth graders. Use was much higher among boys, increasing from 1.6 percent in 1998 to 2.5 percent in 1999 in eighth graders and from 1.9 percent to 2.8 percent in tenth graders. In other words, adolescent boys increased their use by nearly 50 percent in a single year. Among tenth graders, steroid use continued to increase, reaching 2.2 percent in 2002. In twelfth grade, there was a different trend: steroid use fell from 1.9 percent overall in 1989 to 1.1 percent in 1992—the low point. Between 1992 and 1999, however, use increased more gradually, reaching 1.7 percent in 2000. In 2001, use rose significantly among twelfth graders to 2.4 percent, possibly reflecting a cohort effect with the younger, heavier-using cohorts as they became older.[9]

Another national survey, the "Youth Risk Behavioral Surveillance," conducted by the Centers for Disease Control and Prevention (CDC), revealed even higher rates of teenage doping. Between 2001 and 2003, steroid use among ninth graders rose dramatically from 5.8 percent to 7.1 percent. A significant increase was also found among tenth graders (4.9 percent to 6.1 percent) and eleventh graders (4.3 percent to 5.6 percent). Like the Michigan study, however, the CDC survey revealed a modest increase in use among twelfth graders, from 4.3 percent in 2001 to 4.9 percent in 2003. The survey also detailed the prevalence of steroid use by gender and race, revealing that 6.1 percent of students nationwide had taken steroid pills or shots without a doctor's prescription one or more times during their lifetimes. In addition, the prevalence of lifetime illegal steroid use was higher among black males (5.4 percent) than black females (1.9 percent) and higher among twelfth-grade males (6.4 percent) than twelfth-grade females (3.3 percent) students. Overall, the prevalence of lifetime illegal steroid use was higher among whites (6.2 percent) and Hispanics (7.2 percent) than blacks (3.6 percent) and higher among white females (5.6 percent) and Hispanic females (6.6 percent) than black females (1.9 percent). The prevalence of lifetime illegal steroid use was higher among ninth-grade females (7.3 percent) than twelfth-grade females (3.3 percent).[10]

While the statistical totals are different, both surveys show that adolescent steroid use was increasing nation-wide between 1998 and 2002; that boys were juicing in greater numbers than girls; and that eighth, ninth, and tenth graders were abusing steroids in greater numbers than older high school students, possibly due to the need to "get bigger" to play competitive sports at the varsity level. These trends, together with the high-achieving, sports-dominated culture of Plano West, suggest that Taylor Hooton was a prime candidate to experiment with steroids.

To be sure, steroid use at Plano West Senior High School could be found in many sports, although the football players with their huge biceps and gorgeous girlfriends set the tone for other male students at a school where "looking good" was of primary importance. It was just another part of the teen culture that emphasized fashionable clothing, expensive cars, and machismo behavior.[11]

Amid such extreme affluence, Don and Gwen Hooton struggled to keep their son grounded in their own middle-class values. After Taylor passed his driver's test, for example, he inherited his older brother's black Dodge Ram pickup truck but had to pay $100 each month for the insurance. To maintain the vehicle, his parents insisted that he find part-time employment. He found two jobs: one working a concession stand at a local AMC movie theater and a second scooping ice cream at a Maggie Moo's shop. Realizing that his peers did not have to work to pay for their more expensive cars and spending money, Taylor was embarrassed by the jobs and complained to his parents. "It was a battle when Taylor entered senior high," admitted Don. "Once, a schoolmate totaled a $50,000 Cadillac Escalante he'd been given for his sixteenth birthday. The father didn't blink an eye. The very next day, he went out and purchased a brand-new one for him. That's an awful fast environment to grow up in. We had different expectations for our children. We just didn't hand things to Mackenzie and Donald, and we weren't going to do that for Taylor, either. We raised our kids to work for what they wanted."[12]

Initially, Taylor compromised. While he continued to pay for his car by working part-time jobs, he remained active in youth programs at Prestonwood Baptist Church and earned good grades, carrying a 3.8 grade point average. Taylor also tried to keep pace with his wealthier peers. He spent hours on his hair, changing the color and spiking it. He started to wear more expensive clothing, an earring, and pricey Oakley sunglasses, which he wore on the back of his neck, lenses facing out. He outfitted his pickup with an ear-splitting stereo system and thundering exhaust pipes.[13] Although being popular was the major priority in his life, Taylor tried hard not to disappoint his parents. Gwen's approval, in particular, was still extremely important to him. Shortly after he had his ear pierced, for example, he wrote his parents a letter trying to justify his decision:

I know y'all don't like my earring. But I REALLY want to keep it in. I don't see it doing any harm or even looking that bad. It's not like

I'm doing drugs, drinking, or getting a tattoo. I've never ever been in any trouble with the law, and my grades are pretty decent. I see myself as a good kid. I can use the earring as a motivation to make good grades and keep them up. . . . Besides, Mackenzie got earrings when she was three months old, and Donald has one, plus they both have tattoos. I know it's a LITTLE different but still. Please consider this, 'cause it is what makes me happy.[14]

Taylor was appealing to Gwen's maternal sympathy. He knew that his father, who acted as the family disciplinarian, was angry about the earring and less forgiving. Don viewed earrings and tattoos as "juvenile," confirmation that an adolescent still had not grown up. In the business world, such childish symbols gave a prospective employer a poor impression, and he just did not understand why they were necessary. But for Taylor, the earring was an important means of gaining acceptance among his peers, many of whom also had them. It was also his way to define himself as a "playa" (player) in a teen culture that viewed earrings and tattoos as "cool" or, in the parlance of that culture, "tight" and "keen."

"Taylor was da man!" wrote one friend in a September 2003 reflective essay after Taylor's death. "He always had my back. He was my bro, my pal, and my party sidekick. Whenever we met up, he'd have that twinkle in his eye and say, 'What up playa?'"[15] There were at least a dozen similar testimonials written about him. Nearly every one of his friends admired Taylor for his apparent self-assurance and uncanny ability to make others feel better when they were having a bad day. "Taylor knew when something was on your mind and knew how to cheer you up with his quick-witted mirthful remarks," wrote Matt Koenig:

He could turn the most somber moment into one of the most remarkable few minutes of your life. He was the kind of kid everyone dreams of becoming. Taylor had a certain aura that followed him wherever he went. He was always happy and humorous, which allowed him to make however many friends he desired. He taught me how to deal with difficult situations, what phrases to say to bring laughter to a dull party, and how to take action when opportunity arises.[16]

To be sure, all the student testimonials tend to portray Taylor as a popular, self-assured young man who had all the answers to life. What they do not say is that he was struggling with serious self-esteem issues.[17] Teens

In 2003, while Taylor adapted to the affluent teen culture at Plano Senior High School by spiking his hair and wearing an earring, he remained a high-achieving student and an active member of the Prestonwood Baptist Church. *(Courtesy of Taylor Hooton Foundation.)*

typically deal with the problem in many ways, but one of the most common approaches is to gain respect on the athletic field. Another common approach is to improve one's physical appearance to be attractive to the opposite sex. By most accounts, Taylor was trying to do both. He had his heart set on not only making Plano West's varsity baseball team but also becoming the no. 1 pitcher in the starting rotation. He came to believe that steroids would help him achieve that goal—and he did not have to look very far for proof of his theory.

The hometown Texas Rangers were widely suspected of abusing anabolic steroids. Between 2000 and 2004, when MLB began testing for PEDs, the Rangers' roster was loaded with juicers, including Rafael Palmeiro, Juan Gonzalez, Ken Caminiti, John Rocker, Randy Velarde, and Alex Rodriguez, Taylor's favorite player.[18] "Taylor just loved A-Rod," said Gwen Hooton. "He was his hero. In fact, we had his 17th birthday at the ballpark in Arlington, just because he wanted to see Alex play. He talked about it all the time."[19] No doubt, Taylor had also heard the rumors of steroid abuse among the Rangers. Although it is impossible to determine whether he decided to follow A-Rod's example, it is hardly a coincidence that the same kind of peer pressure led Taylor's baseball hero to begin doping.

A-Rod had been a four-time All-Star and a consistent .300 hitter who had already captured an AL batting title when he arrived in Texas. The sky was the limit for him. He was on his way to becoming one of the greatest baseball players of all time, which seemed to justify the outrageous ten-year, $252 million salary that Rangers owner Tom Hicks paid him. But Rodriguez was also very impressionable and struggled to gain the acceptance of a veteran clubhouse that would become notorious for its steroids culture.

Alex Rodriguez of the Texas Rangers was Taylor's baseball idol. *(Courtesy of the National Baseball Hall of Fame Library, Cooperstown, NY.)*

"When I arrived in Texas I was young and naïve," he admitted in a February 16, 2009, *SI* article. "I felt an enormous amount of pressure. I felt like I had the weight of the world on top of me and I needed to perform at a high level every day. I wanted to prove that I was worthy of being one of the greatest players of all time."[20] When he tested positive for anabolic steroids in 2003, Rodriguez was traded to the New York Yankees. Six years later, on February 17, 2009, he finally admitted to using illegal PEDs between 2001 and 2003, when he played for Texas.[21] Taylor might have suspected as much; if so, it may have provided more incentive to begin doping. After all, A-Rod was his role model, and if using steroids was what it took to make him the premier player in MLB, juicing would certainly help Taylor secure a spot as a starting pitcher on his high school varsity baseball team.

If his pitching ambition was Taylor's primary reason to begin doping, improving his physical appearance was a close second. According to Emily Parker, the girl he began dating during the summer of 2002, Taylor was very disappointed with his physique and went on steroids "for his looks," because at school, "every guy was big."[22] Parker, who was a year younger than Taylor, was a cute girl with high cheekbones and a gorgeous smile. She was attracted to Taylor in part by his good looks, but mostly because of his gregarious personality and the manner in which he had quickly won over her family. Unlike most teens, who shy away from adults, Taylor always greeted Parker's father with a firm handshake and, looking him directly in the eye, asked how he was doing. According to a letter provided by the Hooton family, Parker's father, Tom, considered Taylor to be "a fine young man."[23] In fact, Tom Parker told his daughter that Taylor was the "only boy who [he] felt always had her best interests at heart" and that he "always put her ahead of himself."[24]

In another letter to the Hootons, Emily's mother, Christie, wrote, "If I could have hand-picked a boy to hang out at my house every day with my daughter, Taylor was the one. He was so incredible to us and our children."[25] According to Christie Parker, her young son, Luke, "worshipped" Taylor, who was like a "big brother" to him. "They'd spend hours together playing basketball or Nintendo or cruising around Plano in Taylor's pickup truck," she wrote.[26] But all this admiration did not improve Taylor's self-esteem, which was inextricably tied to his physical appearance.

At 6'3", Taylor was taller than everyone in his family, but he did not have the muscular physique of his brother or the stocky build of his father. According to Parker, from the very beginning of their relationship, Taylor "wanted to get on steroids" so he could "get bigger," and he was constantly "thinking [about] how he could get the money" to purchase them.[27] Billy Ajello knew it, too.

In a March 3, 2004, interview on *60 Minutes*, Ajello told CBS reporter Jimmy Stewart that he had tried to discourage Taylor when he learned that his friend was considering doping. But Taylor had insisted. "I'm not just doing it for baseball," he had said. "I'm doing it for myself."

"No high school baseball career is worth taking steroids," Ajello had told his friend. He had even described the health risks involved, but Taylor "blew [him] off."[28]

In Taylor's mind, juicing was acceptable, even desirable. It was not as though he were snorting cocaine or injecting himself with heroin. Those were addictive hallucinogenic drugs that sapped your strength and made you look emaciated. Anabolic steroids, on the other hand, improved strength and appearance and increased athletic performance. Even the name—*appearance- and performance-enhancing* steroids—suggested that juicing was a healthy practice. In addition, Taylor saw other student-athletes getting bigger and stronger. Due to the lack of secrecy about the issue at Plano West, he knew how they were getting those results. "Doing steroids was like a cult activity," said Patrick Burke, another one of Taylor's close friends. "It was elitist and treated with a wink and a smile in the hallways. Any *real* discussion about steroids, in terms of procuring the drugs or injecting them, was done behind closed doors and away from the student population, or as much as possible."[29] Taylor craved that kind of attention from his schoolmates. If doing steroids was the way to get it, so be it. "It was almost like people looked up to you for using steroids," explained Parker. "It was cool. It wasn't something you were ashamed of, or kept to yourself, or were secret about. It was what people wanted to do. Steroids were almost a way of life. I was used to hearing about so many guys who did it." So when Taylor told Parker he wanted to begin juicing, it "didn't even faze" her.[30]

One weekend in January 2003, Taylor told Mark Gomez that he had a friend at nearby Frisco High School whose older brother could sell them steroids.

"Oh, really?" said Gomez, who was also eager to crack Plano West's varsity.

"Yeah, man, I need to bulk up," replied Taylor. "Season's coming up. Why don't you come with me when I buy the stuff?"

Gomez hesitated.

"C'mon, I promise it'll be tight," Taylor assured him, using the local slang for "good."

Gomez agreed. "I actually thought it was a cool idea," he remembered.

The next day, Taylor stole $450 from his mother's bank account using her ATM card. He had never stolen anything before; it was a violation of not only his family's moral code but also his own. But his desire to do steroids had become a compulsion.

Taylor drove with Gomez to the Borders Bookstore on Preston Road to meet the dealer. The two teens walked inside and sat down at a table in the small café. Shortly after, a muscular young man in a sleeveless T-shirt and gym shorts sat down at their table. The 19-year-old dealer, a former wrestler at Frisco Senior High School, flattered himself a major player in North Dallas's seedy drug culture.

After a brief conversation, the dealer slid a brown package across the table. Inside were some syringes; a vial of Deca 300, an injectable steroid that promotes lean muscle gain; and a bottle of Anadrol, another injectable steroid (that can also be taken orally) to supplement the Deca. The package amounted to an eight-week supply of two of the most popular PEDs. Gomez, impressed by the dealer's calm, professional manner, sat there in awe: "I was like, 'Wow! I can't believe this is happening right here in front of me.'" Taylor placed the package in his coat pocket and reached across the table to shake hands, pressing $450 into the palm of the dealer.[31]

He had made his decision.

Rob Garibaldi had also been told that he needed to get bigger ever since 1995, when he was a 5'9", 130-pound sophomore at Casa Grande High School. He was not blessed with his father's stocky frame or his older brother's 6'2", 200-pound build. Rob had to work hard to gain weight and keep it on. Although he ate like a horse and lifted weights four to five days a week, Rob could not increase his muscle mass.[32] It just did not seem fair.

The speedy center fielder hit .460 to lead the Gauchos to a 19–6 record and the North Bay League title in 1996. He had all the tools for a Division I prospect except the ability to hit with power.[33] When the Gauchos played in the North Coast Sectional Championship at Oakland Coliseum that spring, among the dozens of pro scouts and college recruiters in the stands, only one approached Rob. His name was Butch Baccala, a senior cross-checker scout for the Cincinnati Reds. According to Denise Garibaldi, Baccala told her son, "You're good, but you're also not big enough yet." She also said that every time the scout saw Rob play after that, he would say the same thing: "Gotta get bigger."[34]

Rob Bruno also told Garibaldi he needed to get bigger. Bruno was the manager of the NorCal Angels, a traveling All-Star team sponsored by MLB's California Angels. He was also a salesman for a nutritional-supplements company and a former power lifter. Impressed by Rob's natural athletic ability as well as by his performance at the Sectional Championship, Bruno offered the scrawny youngster a spot on his roster. The Garibaldis jumped at the opportunity. The NorCal Angels were an elite amateur team that competed in showcase tournaments across the county. Showcase tournaments were becoming a huge business in the late 1990s, offering talented young baseball players the opportunity to perform before hundreds of pro scouts and college recruiters. Because of his learning disability, Rob could use whatever advantage he could find to gain college admission. In addition, Bruno claimed that he could help Rob "get bigger." To that end, he started the young ballplayer on weight-gaining supplements to complement an already rigorous weight-training program. Bruno assured the Garibaldis that the supplements were safe and would allow their son to eventually bulk up to the 185 pounds necessary to attract the attention of professional scouts and Division I recruiters.[35]

"Obviously, we're going to tell a kid what they need to do to get bigger and stronger," he explained to Mark Fainaru-Wada of the *San Francisco Chronicle* when asked about his training program for youngsters. Bruno told Rob, "Use [nutritional] supplements to complement a solid weight-

In high school, Rob played for the NorCal Angels, a traveling All-Star team sponsored by the California Angels. It was during this time that Rob realized he would have to add muscle if he was going to become a Division I baseball player. *(Courtesy of the Garibaldi Family.)*

training program, because if you're going to be a great athlete, you need to be stronger."[36] The Garibaldis trusted Bruno. "At the time, we thought it was a good idea," recalled Denise. "We trusted him. He'd already worked with our nephew, Joe Garibaldi, as well as other young men who ended up playing pro ball. We also knew Rob couldn't gain the weight on his own, and if nutritional supplements could do that for him, and if it could improve his game, we didn't see any danger in it."[37]

Paul Maytorena, the assistant varsity baseball coach at Casa Grande, confirmed that there were no health risks involved in taking nutritional supplements. Maytorena, who holds a degree in exercise science from Sonoma State University, was a professional trainer at a local health club. He agreed to monitor Rob's use of supplements and to provide Denise and Ray with information about the substances he was taking.[38] "When I first started with Rob, he was only 130 pounds," said Maytorena in an interview. "What I remember saying to Rob when he began was that he needed to get bigger and that a careful weight-training program together with supplements would help him do that." The youngster followed the advice and gained 10 to 15 pounds pretty quickly, increasing his weight to about 145 pounds. "That's where he should have been for his size, which was 5'9" or 5'10", and his physical stature," said Maytorena. "But after that, Rob's body plateaued, and he couldn't gain any more weight, even with the supplements."[39] As careful as Maytorena had been in monitoring Rob, there were no guarantees that the supplements he was taking were not tainted.

Since the early 1990s, nearly 25 percent of the nutritional supplements that are sold over the counter have contained steroid precursors (i.e., creatine, protein, glutamine, and nitric oxide) or steroids themselves, a practice known as "cocktailing."[40] Prior to 1990, when Congress passed the Anabolic Steroid Control Act (Title XIX of Pub. L. 101-647), body builders had only a few categories of supplements to choose from. The most popular were protein products and vitamin and mineral derivatives. None of these supplements were nearly as effective as anabolic steroids in building muscle size, strength, and recovery ability. But after 1990, when steroids were classified as a "controlled substance," the supplement industry witnessed a huge spike in sales. Manufacturers began to attract body builders and weight lifters by marketing their products with such catch terms as "anabolic," "steroid replacer," "hormonal," "testosterone," and "metabolic." They also discovered that if they combined some of the best supplements, the result was a "synergistic effect," similar to that of small doses of steroids. According to Fainaru-Wada and Lance Williams, authors of *Game of Shadows: Barry Bonds, BALCO, and the Steroids Scandal that Rocked Professional Sports*, the discovery provided the incentive for some manufacturers to add creatine and other steroid precursors to their products to attract an even bigger market.[41] Still others, like Victor Conte of BALCO, used their supplements businesses as fronts to distribute anabolic steroids.[42]

Conte used his steroid connections to build a nutritional-supplement business into a $47 million industry by 1999.[43] He began by experimenting with HGH, also known as "somatotropin" or "somatropin," which stimulates growth, cell reproduction, and cell regeneration in humans.[44] HGH is prescribed medically to treat children's growth disorders and adult growth hormone deficiency, but it has been abused by athletes wanting to increase muscle mass at least since 1982.[45] Conte also experimented with erythropoietin (EPO), an essential hormone for red-cell production used in treating anemia, Crohn's disease, and ulcer colitis.[46] EPO has also been used as a blood-doping agent in endurance sports, such as boxing, cycling, distance running, and the triathlon.[47] The primary reason athletes use EPO is to improve oxygen delivery to muscles, which directly improves their endurance capacity. It also increases the likelihood of stroke by increasing red-cell mass beyond the natural levels, which, in turn, reduces blood flow in the body. Both HGH and EPO were banned in the 1990s by the International Olympic Committee (IOC) and the National Collegiate Athletic Association (NCAA).[48] But athletes continued to use them, because traditional urine testing cannot identify them. Conte was responsible for that, too. According to Fainaru-Wada and Williams, he devised a testosterone-based balm called "The Cream"—a mixture of synthetic testosterone and epitestosterone—to mask steroids in the urine.[49]

Federal investigators targeted Conte and BALCO in 2001. The investigation was made public two years later, when a federal grand jury subpoenaed some thirty professional athletes who were regular BALCO customers, including San Francisco Giants' slugger Barry Bonds.[50] A year later, in 2004, Congress amended the Anabolic Steroid Control Act (Pub. L. 108-358) to ban over-the-counter supplements containing steroid precursors; increase penalties for making, selling, or possessing illegal steroid precursors; and allot funding for preventative education for children.[51] Not until 2009, however, did the federal government address the selling and distribution of nutritional supplements tainted with steroids.[52]

When the BALCO story broke, steroids were already a growing problem among teens. Surveys revealed that between 3 percent and 11 percent of American teens had used them. In California alone, more than twenty thousand adolescents were believed to be doping, not just to improve their athletic performances but also to improve their physical appearances by losing weight or gaining muscle. Many of these teens, including Rob Garibaldi, began by using nutritional supplements and later advanced to steroids.[53]

When Rob graduated from high school in June 1997, he was 5'11" and weighed 150 pounds after three years of weight training, tossing down protein shakes, and ingesting nutritional supplements that were most likely laced with anabolic steroids.[54] In his mind, doping was the next logical step. Rob disdained recreational drugs and had no respect for those who indulged in them. He knew that they presented serious health risks and that those whose use went unchecked could overdose. But Rob did not place steroids in the same category. For him, steroids were simply an "extension of supplements," a healthy means to achieve his ultimate goal of playing in the major leagues.[55] "Rob wasn't a kid who was just looking for beach muscle," P.J. Poiani, a close friend and teammate, told Fainaru-Wada of the San Francisco Chronicle. "He was a kid whose every hope and dream centered around baseball. And you do whatever it takes."[56] Garibaldi even said as much. In fact, as a senior at Casa Grande High School, Rob told Andrew Jowers of the Santa Rosa Press Democrat that "pro ball is my dream and has always been my dream" and that he would "give it my very best shot to make it to that level."[57]

According to Fainaru-Wada, Brian Seibel, another close friend, said that Rob told him that he "wanted to get bigger and stronger" and that "steroids were the way to do it."[58] After graduation, Seibel, a nonathlete who had no interest in doping, agreed to accompany his friend to Mexico, where it was easy to purchase steroids. The two teens told their parents they were going on a three-day camping trip and headed south to Tijuana. When they arrived, Rob walked into the first pharmacy he saw and was directed to a nearby physician's office. After Rob handed over some cash, the physician gave him a prescription for Sustanon, a popular steroid composed of four testosterones. Rob then returned to the pharmacy, where he purchased syringes, needles, and an eight-week supply of the drug. Rob hid the package behind a stereo speaker, and the two friends drove back across the border. The entire transaction took fewer than twenty minutes and cost between $250 and $300, about two-thirds of the money Rob had received as graduation gifts.[59]

When Rob returned to Petaluma, Poiani taught him how to cycle. "Rob was scared of needles," Poiani told Fainaru-Wada, "so it was kind of comical watching him inject the needle into his butt. It got easier the more he did it." Poiani remembers that his friend completed the eight-week cycle before he entered the College of San Mateo (CSM) in August, when he was 8 to 10 pounds bigger.[60] Poiani, a user himself, had become not only Rob's "best friend" but also a role model. Rob admired his "work ethic" in transforming a once 5'9", 135-pound body into a chiseled 180-pound physique. He insisted, "P.J. is buffed only because of his dedication and hard work." "I have never met a person who works as hard as he does in the gym or on the baseball field," he added. "I hope half of his work ethic rubs off on me."[61] Poiani would continue to monitor Rob's cycling for the next year.

Denise Garibaldi was less impressed by her son's "best friend." "Rob did not have the street smarts to teach himself how to dope," she said. "P.J. was instrumental in getting him started. He worked at a GNC store and introduced Rob to Ephedra, a supplement for performance enhancement. It was banned by the FDA in 2006, because it was associated with heart attacks and high blood pressure leading to stroke. P.J. was very intelligent when it came to supplements and steroids. He was also cycling himself. In fact, he later admitted that some of the steroids Rob purchased in Tijuana were for him." P.J. was "very capable of manipulating Rob," Denise added.[62] Rob's brother, Raymond, also believes that Poiani not only encouraged but also taught his younger brother to dope. "Looking back," he said, "I remember that P.J. went from being a normal-sized kid to Hulk Hogan within a year of graduating high school." Once Rob saw the increase in body mass, he decided to follow P.J.'s lead. "Robbie might've been more cautious about using than P.J., but there's no doubt that he was juicing," added Raymond. "The summer after his high school graduation, he was lifting like a maniac, and there's no way a normal person could have the strength or stamina to do that. The funny thing is that Rob had long, lean muscles, so you really couldn't tell just how much weight he was adding to his body."[63]

In August 1997, Rob enrolled at CSM, a baseball powerhouse and a "family school." Ray Garibaldi had attended and played for the college, and Rob's cousin Joe Garibaldi had pitched there and attracted the attention of Division I San Diego State University, where he matriculated on a baseball scholarship. At first glance, the school appeared to be a good fit, but Rob's enrollment turned out to be a mistake.[64] "Rob was extremely disappointed with the coaching at San Mateo," said Denise. "There was also a lot of drug use on the team and on campus, and Rob was very outspoken about not using any kind of recreational drug because of the negative effect it could have on his health."[65] Rob told his parents that he was not going to play baseball at the school. They were astounded by his decision but respected it. When Bob Leslie learned of Rob's situation, he urged him to redshirt that season and transfer to Santa Rosa Junior College for the following school year.[66]

Rob missed home desperately for the one semester he spent at CSM. He constantly phoned Poiani, telling him that he had "made the wrong decision."[67] College, in general, proved to be especially challenging for Rob. He quickly became frustrated, because the classes "covered much more material and in a shorter time than those in high school." Having to listen to lectures for long periods of time was difficult because of his "attention span problems." Test taking was even more difficult. Rob complained that he would "blank out and forget everything" during an exam. The day of an exam was a "nightmare" that "just ate [him] up inside." Academically, Rob admitted that he "felt like an absolute loser." But he tried to "take it a step at a time" and do the "best" he could. "If I can get through this," he wrote, "I can realize my dream of being a pro baseball player."[68] Sadly, Rob did not realize that he possessed the talent to pursue other things, including teaching, coaching, and writing.

Among the many essays he wrote during that semester, one is especially impressive—and hilarious. Titled "How to Clean a Messy Room," it reveals his wonderful sense of humor as well as his potential for writing:

> If you were to walk into my messy bedroom, you would see clothes everywhere, dirty dishes, soda cans, and ants. The ants are attracted to the sugar from the food left under my bed. Your first approach would be to find the food and the dirty dishes . . . under my bed, behind the stereo, on top of the television, and in my closet. Take the dishes downstairs and place them in the kitchen sink. Mom

will take care of them. Throw the unfinished food in the garbage. Dad will take care of that.

Speaking of garbage, there's a lot of that in my room, too. But you would have to pick up all the dirty, smelly clothes, jock straps, etc. (need I say more?), off the floor to find it. After placing those dirty clothes in the hall hamper for Mom to wash, use some bug spray to kill all the living insects still crawling around the floor. After that, vacuum up all the dead insects. You can put on a pair of gloves to pick up the larger bugs that would choke the vacuum.

Now that you can see the carpet, it's time to clean the closet. The first challenge is to get inside. Be careful of the avalanche that awaits. Once inside, start throwing all the clothes on the bed. Don't try to figure out what's dirty and what's clean—just wash everything. While Mom washes the clothes, vacuum the closet floor and place the shoes in order. When Mom finishes drying the clothes, hang them back up in the closet by order of color. The stripes go next to the stripes, the whites next to the whites, and the baseball shirts have their own section. . . .

Finally, get the Windex and clean the television, the windows, and the sliding mirrors. Organize the CDs and tapes. Change the bed sheets because you never know what happened between them. . . .

The whole process may take a few hours. Please leave plenty of time![69]

The essay is classic for a male teen, revealing the natural chaos in which he lives as well as his ongoing dependency on his parents. Rob realized that he was in transition. Although he was not yet an independent adult, he was no longer a child, and he had the satirical ability to laugh at the contradiction. He certainly had the potential to become a good writer had he chosen that path.

During the 1998 spring semester, Rob returned to Petaluma to coach his high school baseball team. Being reunited with Leslie, however briefly, made him feel good about himself again. Leslie had a way of doing that for his players. Although Leslie was suffering from mouth cancer and the unyielding pain caused by several facial skin grafts, he always made time for Rob when he was well enough to attend practices or games. Maytorena, who had been Leslie's assistant, was in effect the head coach, and Rob was his assistant. The arrangement was difficult for both of them. "As an assistant coach, the kids felt comfortable talking to me," said Maytorena. "But now I'm a twenty-eight-year-old head coach, and that means I have

Casa Grande High School baseball coach Bob Leslie was a mentor to Garibaldi. Despite a valiant struggle against lip cancer from years of chewing tobacco, Leslie remained a guiding light for the baseball prodigy after his graduation in 1997. *(By Chad Surmick, Santa Rosa Press Democrat. Courtesy of Amy Leslie Frydenlund.)*

to be the disciplinarian. There's a certain distance that must to be maintained between a head coach and his players."[70] Rob, on the other hand, was caught in "no man's land." Although he was an extremely talented high school player and commanded the respect of the team in that capacity, he did not enjoy their respect as a coach. He would have to earn it, which proved to be difficult. "Rob was just a year out of high school," explained Maytorena. "There wasn't much of an age difference between him and the kids on the team. I loved him, and I understood he was having problems making the transition from high school to college, so I welcomed him back with open arms. But we also had a very talented team that year. Jonny Gomes, a future major leaguer, was a sophomore on that team. His older brother, Joey, was a senior. He would go on to become an All-American at Santa Clara before turning pro. So there were many meetings between the captains, Rob, and myself to straighten out the chain of command."[71]

By June, Leslie's cancer—called desmoplastic malignant melanoma— had spread from his lip to his brain stem. Although this type of cancer was extremely painful, the Gauchos' coach still managed to spend his time wisely. For the past three years, Leslie had joined with former major leaguer Joe Garagiola and MLB to educate youth on the harmful effects of spit tobacco.[72] Shortly before playoffs, he gathered the team in the dugout for one final "life lesson." "Unfortunately, the cancer has spread to a difficult place in my head, and surgery is out of the question," he began. "Death is near. No one knows if it will be next week, or next month. The last three weeks have been tortuous because of the pain, but I plan to be with you as long as possible."

The dugout was quiet; the players were stunned by the news. After composing himself, Leslie posed the question: "If there was no tomorrow, how hard would you work today?"

It was a rhetorical question, one designed to motivate ballplayers. There was a pregnant pause while the question hung in the air for each teen to ponder.

The Gauchos' beloved coach went on to discourage his players from using tobacco. He explained that the cancer began in his mouth, the result of chewing tobacco since the age of 13. "Why?" he asked. "Because it was the 'cool' thing to do. It was part of baseball's culture, chewing, spitting, and having that chew bulging from my mouth. And I'd still probably be chewing had they not cut my mouth."

Tears began to flow openly among the players; the only sound to be heard was sniffling, weak attempts to stifle the sadness.

Leslie now turned to the real meaning of his bout with cancer—what he had learned about himself during the ordeal.

"Before I had the cancer, I was angry, frustrated all the time," he admitted. I was always in a hurry. Since I've known about the cancer, though, I'm a better person, a better husband and friend. I take time now. I slow down and just see things for what they are."

"I'm also a better coach. Some of the seniors will remember that I didn't have much patience. It was my way or the highway, and I'd lose a lot of kids because of that approach."

The seniors remembered and nodded their heads in agreement.

"But now I understand that it's more important to listen, to try to understand a player's difficulties with the game and then work with him to improve his performance. Now I have a better idea of how to instill a love of the game in my players."[73]

When Leslie finished, there was not a dry eye in the dugout. His players stood up, gathered around him, and draped their arms across each other's shoulders. It was their way of embracing a coach they had grown to love.

After the players went onto the practice field, Leslie pulled Rob aside. "The Lord is going to take me soon, Rob," he said. "But whenever you need me, just look up to the heavens and ask for my help, strength, and friendship. I'll be there for you."[74] Then the coach embraced his former player.

On June 6, 1998, Leslie stepped into the third-base coaching box for one last time. The Gauchos were playing archrival Petaluma High for the North Coast Section 2A title. A crowd of 1,500 spectators packed the bleachers. Sensing it would be the coach's final game, they gave him a standing ovation. Casa Grande won, giving a final victory to an exceptional coach who was posthumously voted California's 1998 Coach of the Year. He died nine days later, on June 15, leaving a wife and a 14-month-old baby daughter. Leslie was just 32 years old.[75]

Rob was devastated. He not only spiraled into a prolonged depression but also became consumed by the memory of his beloved coach. He wore Leslie's uniform no. 22 when he played for Santa Rosa Junior College that fall and would write constantly about him in his journal and in college essays for the next few years. "I miss him tremendously," he wrote a year later. "I still don't understand why God takes the best people away."[76] Rob slowly came to realize that Leslie would "want him to be happy" and that he had to "move on with [his] life." "I am sustained daily by what he taught me about baseball and about life," Rob wrote in a 1999 speech to his teammates at Santa Rosa Junior College. "Coach Leslie taught me to make the best out of what God gave you. Attack your weaknesses, instead of complaining about them. Set your goals high and try to make them your strengths."[77]

"Bob's death was especially hard on Rob," said Maytorena. "If he had any other interests at that point in his life, he gave them up to focus completely on baseball. It's like a switch went off in his life. He was obsessed with the game after that. I just chalked it up to his way of dealing with Bob's death."[78] Poiani also noticed Rob's obsession with his dream to become a professional baseball player. "He took another cycle of Sustanon and started lifting like crazy," recalled Poiani. "It was a long cycle, because I remember at the time thinking, 'What the hell are you doing?' I mean you're supposed to take six- to ten-week cycles, and Rob was into something like fourteen weeks. It was crazy. He blew up at that point, I mean, for his standards, which were pretty cautious to that point."[79]

Like Taylor Hooton, Rob Garibaldi had come to believe that the only way he could achieve his dream was by doping. He, too, made a fatal decision.

As a junior at Plano West High School in 2004, Taylor was a swing player, starting on the junior varsity and pitching in relief for the varsity. *(Courtesy of Taylor Hooton Foundation.)*

4

"MOM, COME LOOK AT MY GUNS!"

Taylor Hooton was obsessed with getting bigger, and not just to make Plano West's varsity baseball team—he was also doping to improve his physical appearance. Beginning in January 2003, when he started using, Taylor lifted weights at the local YMCA every day, sometimes twice a day. When he would get home, he would look at himself in the mirror, flex his biceps, and boast, "Mom, come look at my guns!"

"Looking good, Taylor," Gwen Hooton would say, unaware of her son's secret. It became a daily routine between them.

Don Hooton, who was proud of his son's work ethic, also complimented him on his increasingly chiseled appearance. Neither parent suspected steroid use. Even if they did, they would not have recognized the signs.[1]

In fewer than two months, Taylor added 30 pounds of mostly muscle to his once lean frame, increasing his weight from 175 to 205 pounds. He was blowing through his weight-lifting routine. One week, he was bench pressing 120 pounds, doing four sets of ten repetitions each. Within a month's time, he had almost doubled the weight, increased the number of sets, and hardly broke a sweat. At one time, his clothes hung off his body as if they were a size too large, but now they accentuated his musculature. He even bought smaller sizes to show off his new body. Once he walked the halls at school, intimidated by the impressively built football players. Now he was the one doing the intimidating, strutting the halls with his chest jutting out as if daring one of those same players to challenge him.[2] The steroids were working.

"All the girls loved Taylor, and he knew it, too," said Lindsay Forester, a friend since middle school. "He was good-looking and athletic. What girl wouldn't be attracted to a guy like that?" Forester could be objective. She prided herself on being a "guy's girl" who liked to play sports and had a lot of "guy friends." She also spoke her mind, even if it was not always appreciated. "Taylor's girlfriend, Emily, and I didn't get along too well," said Forester. "I guess we tolerated each other for Taylor's sake. That's what I liked about him, though. He was loyal to his friends. Not a whole lot bothered him. He was easy-going, just an all-around good guy. If he got into an argument with you, he immediately wanted to fix it. He didn't want people to be mad at him." But things changed when Taylor began doping.

If the two friends got into an argument, Taylor would hold a grudge. They would go for days without speaking. "It was over the most ridiculous things, too," recalled Forester. "I tried to be oblivious to it, but it hurt." When she learned that her close friend was doping, Forester was shocked. She did not drink or do drugs, and she tried to discourage Taylor from using steroids. "I couldn't believe he was using," she said. "I just didn't think he'd be part of that culture. He was always the one to set the rules, the leader of the pack. I never thought he'd be a follower." Their friendship gradually died.[3]

Liz Krause was more perceptive. She dated Taylor during the fall of their junior year at Plano West and quickly saw that he was "in transition." "I moved to Plano from North Carolina in the summer of 2002," she said. "I really didn't know anybody, until I met Taylor. He had an electric personality, the kind that just lit up a room when he walked into it. He was also very protective of me. If we were at a party and there were drugs or alcohol, he'd insist on leaving. When I had my tonsils out, he'd bring ice cream over to our house and sit with me for hours. He just did sweet things like that." But Krause made it very clear to Taylor that she wanted to be her own person. While she wanted exclusivity in their dating relationship, she expected to make other male friends. "Most of Taylor's friends were female," she recalled. "So, I told him it goes both ways and that he shouldn't get mad at me if I had other male friends. At the same time, if we were dating, I wanted to be able to trust him."

As the fall semester unfolded, Taylor began circulating with a much "faster crowd." They were kids who came from very wealthy families and were using steroids. Krause, on the other hand, began hanging out with kids from another local high school, most of whom came from modest financial circumstances. There were also things that disturbed her about Taylor. He became very jealous of her other male friends and tried to get her sympathy by sulking or becoming agitated. Krause also did not like Taylor's obsession with his physical appearance. "He was always working out, always talking about his body," she said. "It became pretty clear to me that he wanted to fit in with the jocks, many of whom were doping."

One night, Krause and a group of friends stopped at Wendy's, the local hangout. She saw Taylor's pickup truck in the parking lot and went over to say hello. When she opened the door, she found him "making out" with another girl. "That was it," she said. "In my mind, we were done. I already didn't like the kids he was hanging out with, and once I caught him cheating, I ended it."[4] Taylor moved on to a "higher class of female."[5]

Taylor's steroid use had a dual purpose. He wanted not only to enhance his performance as a baseball player but also to build a more chiseled physique to increase his popularity with the opposite sex. The two motives are not mutually exclusive among those who abuse anabolic steroids.

Media attention has focused almost entirely on APEDs used by elite athletes to gain a competitive advantage in sports. In reality, the vast majority of APED users are not athletes but rather "nonathlete weight lifters" "primarily focused on personal appearance, in that they simply want to look leaner and more muscular." In fact, "lean mass builders" are the most frequently used APEDs. Generally, these are anabolic drugs, a man-made synthetic derivative of the male sex hormone, testosterone, that increase muscle mass or reduce fat mass.[6]

Competitive athletes, on the other hand, tend to use several other PEDs in addition to anabolic steroids. Some competitive body builders, for example, use diuretics (e.g., furosemide and thiazides) to improve muscle definition on stage. Similarly, some boxers or wrestlers use diuretics to reduce body weight so they can compete in a lower weight class. Diuretics may also dilute the urine, which can reduce the concentration of the PED to below the limit of detection. Some athletes who engage in endurance competitions use blood boosters (e.g., EPO and transfusions) to improve their performance in such events as cycling, long-distance running, and skiing. Still other athletes combine anabolic steroids and EPO to train harder and recover faster. Similarly, anabolic steroids can be combined with tranquilizers (e.g., benzodiazepines and opiates) to reduce anxiety in events that require steady nerves, such as archery, and opiates can mask pain during competition.[7]

The use of PEDs in sports is not a recent phenomenon. The athletes of ancient Greece and Rome used a more primitive form of anabolic steroids not only to improve their athletic performances but also to enhance their physical appearances. As early as 776 BCE, the Olympic athletes of ancient Greece experimented with herbal substances and strychnine to gain a competitive edge over their opponents. Greek athletes also worshipped their bodies and often engaged in homosexual activities because of this obsession. Similarly, Roman gladiators used hallucinogens and consumed animal hearts or testicles to increase their strength and endurance in competition as well as to improve their musculature to attract both males and females.[8] Centuries later, sports, drugs, and science became more closely linked, as exercise physiologists began experimenting with various hallucinogens and ergogenic substances. In the public mind, their academic credentials made the use of such substances "innovative" or "experimental" rather than controversial.

Perhaps the most significant—and foolhardy—experiment occurred in 1889, when Dr. Charles-Édouard Brown-Séquard, a 72-year-old French physiologist, injected himself with the extract of dog and guinea-pig testicles on the assumption that these organs had "internal secretions that acted as physiologic regulators" that could eliminate pain in the human body.[9] This and other experiments led to the discovery of hormones in 1905 and the subsequent isolation of testosterone in 1935.[10] Other PEDs became popular during World War II, when American soldiers took amphetamines to keep them alert on the battlefield. The German military went even further, using anabolic steroids to increase the aggressive behavior of its soldiers.[11] While these practices provided the impetus for the increased use of drugs, they also resulted in a new framework of ethics, one that defined doping as "cheating" to gain a competitive edge. Olympic athletes were the first to test the boundaries of the new code.

During the early 1950s, Soviet weight lifters, aided by testosterone supplements, routinely defeated their American opponents at the Olympic Games. Suspicious of their success and not wanting to be left behind, U.S. coach John Ziegler unearthed their secret. Shortly after, Ziegler and a team of chemists produced an anabolic steroid, now known as Dianabol, for the U.S. weight lifters.[12]

Over the next decade, several deaths and allegations of drug use led the IOC in 1967 to establish a Medical Commission, which banned the use of drugs and other performance-enhancing substances. Small-scale testing was introduced at the 1968 Mexico City Olympics, followed by full-scale testing at the next Olympics at Munich in 1972. Although anabolic steroid use was banned three years later, blood doping continued for the next few decades due to the lack of a reliable test and the ability of East German, Russian, and American athletes to avoid detection through the development of new compounds.[13] And Olympic athletes were not the only ones juicing.[14]

The use of PEDs and anabolic steroids dates back to the late 1960s in the National Football League (NFL). Lyle Alzado, a former defensive lineman for the Denver Broncos, exposed doping among NFL players in a July 8, 1991, *SI* article, contending that "a number of players on a number of [NFL] teams were heavy users" during the late 1960s and 1970s. Alzado believed that his steroid use was "mentally addicting" and that it led to the brain tumor that eventually claimed his life at the age of 43.[15] Former NFL player and coach Jim Haslett confirmed Alzado's contention in 2005, stating that "half of the players in the league used some type of steroid" in the 1980s, including "all the offensive and defensive linemen and linebackers."[16] Body builders, arguably the vainest users, became even more closely associated with steroid use.

Body building had been popular since the 1950s because of the emergence of Olympic weight lifting and gymnastics champions and the simultaneous popularization of muscle training. Joe Weider, the Canadian-born publisher of *Muscle and Fitness* magazine, built a California-based supplement empire by convincing millions of young readers that the key to improving their physiques was taking his ergogenic supplements. Many of the body builders featured in Weider's magazine used steroids and other APEDs rather than his food supplements, a fact that was conveniently omitted. Weider was also instrumental in cofounding the International Federation of Bodybuilding and Fitness (IFBB) and bringing a young Arnold Schwarzenegger to the United States in 1968.[17] Schwarzenegger, more than any other figure, was responsible for the popularity of body building beginning in 1977, when he starred in the film *Pumping Iron*. The docudrama focused on the previous year's competition between Schwarzenegger and Lou Ferrigno, one of his primary competitors for the title of "Mr. Olympia." While Schwarzenegger did not admit to using steroids at the time, in a 2005 interview with CBS, the former seven-time Mr. Olympia did admit to the practice, insisting that he had "no regrets about it" because he "did it under doctors' supervision."[18] Predictably, the use of anabolic steroids was openly discussed among body builders in the 1970s, in part because they were legal. In 1986, in hopes of joining the IOC, the IFBB introduced doping tests for steroids and other banned substances.[19] Despite this fact, the majority of body builders continued to use steroids for competition.

Noting the competitive advantage that steroids gave body builders and NFL players, other athletes began doping. By the end of the 1980s, anabolic steroid use was common in most sports, both in the professional and the collegiate ranks. Finally, in 1990, Congress passed the Anabolic Steroid Control Act, placing the drug into Schedule III of the Controlled Substance Act. According to the law, steroids, like other Schedule III substances, are defined by (1) a potential for abuse, (2) a currently accepted medical use in treatment, and (3) the possibility of moderate or low physical dependence or high psychological dependence.[20] Three years later, the NFL made testing for PEDs part of its collective-bargaining agreement with the Players Association. At the international level, the World Anti-Doping Agency (WADA) was established in 1999 by the IOC with the support of other international organizations and governments to promote and coordinate the fight against drug use across all sports on an international level.[21] Yet despite these preventative actions, a large number of doping offenses continued among American professional and amateur athletes as well as in Olympic competitions in several sports.

If professional and collegiate athletes relied on anabolic steroids to compete successfully and/or improve their body image, it was inevitable that these practices would eventually be adopted by high school athletes. Pro athletes, in particular, are role models for the young, although many would gladly abandon that responsibility. The media reinforces that heroic status by displaying their chiseled physiques on everything from cereal boxes to the latest virtual games. The message is clear: *If you want to be like your sports hero, you'll use this product.* Unfortunately, star athletes are sending out the same message with their steroid use. Teens are extremely impressionable. The top three reasons for doping cited by first-time adolescent users are (1) to improve physical appearance/body image, (2) to improve self-esteem, and (3) to improve athletic performance.[22] At the same time, teens are careful to hide their use because of the health risks involved and the stigma of "cheating" that became associated with doping in the 1990s. Still, the adolescent user considers those factors "obstacles" to be overcome rather than deterrents.

Taylor Hooton had certainly heard about the dangers of steroid use by age 15, but in his mind, the benefits were well worth the risks. Improving one's physical appearance was extremely important in the upscale culture of Plano, Texas. Male and female students at Plano West were impressed by chiseled physiques, and many went to great lengths to maintain their cut bodies. If weight training and supplements proved ineffective, doping was not an uncommon "next step," even if it cost much more than the safer alternatives.

In late February 2003, Taylor asked his mother if he could sell his prized drum set. "Why would you want to do that?" asked Gwen, taken aback by the request. "You love playing those drums." In fact, Taylor's personal identity had once been based on his drum-playing ability, as evidenced by his preferred nickname, "Stud Drummer."[23]

"I need the money to pay for gas and to get my truck repaired," he replied, referring to the dent he had recently put into the side of his pickup while backing into the garage.

"Dude, that drum set is yours," she said. "If you want to sell it, that's fine."[24]

That night, Taylor put the drums up for sale on eBay and found a buyer within twenty-four hours. The income from the drum set, his weekly allowance, and the money he made through his part-time jobs netted him $450, enough to purchase another eight-week supply of steroids from the Frisco dealer. This time, Taylor took Emily Parker with him to the parking lot of a 24-Hour Fitness Center and made the deal in broad daylight. She thought nothing of it. "It wasn't like, 'Let's go somewhere secret where no one can see us,'" she told Gregg Jones and Gary Jacobson of the *Dallas Morning News*. "It was, 'Where's the closest place to get them?'" Besides, the couple had dozens of acquaintances—athletes and nonathletes—who were doping. "They were good kids," insisted Parker. "They were popular and cool. They were going somewhere in life." Whenever they went to a party or gathered at the local Wendy's, steroids were a part of their casual conversation. "I was around it so much, it wasn't like a drug to me," she admitted. "It was literally a way of life for these guys."[25]

Taylor continued to be obsessed with his physical appearance. Rarely did he pass a mirror or a storefront window without flexing and stealing a glimpse of his biceps, or "guns," as he referred to them. He acted as an adviser to his best friend, Mark Gomez, who also began doping in the spring. To increase muscle mass as quickly as possible, Taylor and Mark were using two steroids at the same time, a process known as "stacking." They went on an eight-week cycle, injecting Deca 300 and taking Anadrol orally. Sometimes they even gave each other their weekly injections. Unsure of how to read a syringe, they guessed at the dosages. Gomez quickly packed 25 pounds of lean muscle onto his slight frame and increased his bench press by 30 pounds. The ball was jumping off his bat, and he entertained hopes of making Plano West's varsity baseball squad.[26]

Another friend, Callahan Kuhns, a basketball player, also took Taylor's advice. Kuhns purchased a 10-milliliter bottle of Deca 300 for $200 from the same Frisco dealer who was selling to Taylor and a vial of Test 400, a synthetic testosterone, for $150 from a friend on the Plano West football team, who had been using steroids for more than a year. Since Kuhns was "freaked out" by injecting the steroids, he asked Taylor to inject him for the first four weeks. Every Sunday afternoon, Kuhns drove over to the Hootons' house, and the two friends would slip upstairs to Taylor's bedroom. They would lock the door, Kuhns would drop his pants, and Taylor would inject him with 1 milliliter of each steroid. In less than a month, Kuhns improved his bench press by more than 50 pounds. The two boys were so impressed with themselves that they even invented a secret handshake that concluded with each one jabbing his index finger into his butt, as if injecting steroids. "Every time we passed each other in the hallway [at school], we would start smiling," said Kuhns. "We thought it was the coolest thing ever." And when friends commented on the boys' dramatic increase in size, neither one denied his steroid use.[27]

Taylor's workout routine became more rigorous as the spring baseball season approached. In early March, Billy Ajello walked into the weight room at the YMCA and watched in amazement as Taylor did triceps extensions with an 85-pound dumbbell. "He was doing three sets of ten reps, three sets of twelve reps, and he's doing them like it was nothing," he recalled.[28] Just two months earlier, Ajello saw his friend struggling with the 60-pound dumbbell as he tried to do one set of five reps of the very same exercise. Taylor's ability to do the same exercise with ease suggested to Ajello that his friend was doping.[29] He debated whether he should confront Taylor but decided against it. Instead, he turned around and walked out of the weight room. "The last thing you want to do is accuse someone of being on steroids," said Ajello after his friend's death. "You just don't want to make their work ethic look bad."[30] But the following week, Taylor's erratic behavior removed any doubt of steroid use in Ajello's mind.

During chemistry class, Taylor handed in an assignment that was nearly a week late. The teacher, who had a reputation for rigidness, informed him that he would receive "a zero for tardiness." The words cut him to the quick. Trying hard to control his anger, Taylor turned his back to the teacher and mumbled, "I'm about to rage." He then walked to the door, punched it as hard as he could, and left the room. Ajello, who witnessed the scene, thought, "This is not the Taylor I know."[31]

Jason Wade, another teammate and close friend, tried to discourage Taylor from doping. Wade, the shortstop on Plano West's varsity baseball team, said Taylor was one of the most likeable kids on the team. He had the instincts of a natural leader. "It wasn't an 'in-your-face' kind of thing," explained the shortstop. "He just had an uncanny way of picking teammates up with a quip or an inside joke. Taylor was exceptional that way. He could sense when you were down on yourself and knew just what to say to snap you out of it. He did that for me many times."[32] Wade became concerned when he learned about his friend's steroid use and repeatedly tried to get him to stop. "I had a reputation for 'walking the straight and narrow,'" he said. "I knew that some teammates were using steroids to get a competitive edge, though I never felt the pressure to juice. But Taylor wanted to be accepted, and that's one of the reasons he started using." Wade also contended that "doping was so widespread" among the athletes at all the North Dallas high schools that "if you weren't doing it, you were at a disadvantage." "In all honesty, if using steroids would've taken me to the next level, I can't say that I wouldn't have done it," he admitted. "But that wasn't the case. I knew I'd hit my ceiling as a ballplayer, so I wasn't going to do steroids. In fact, when I went on to play in junior college, I was told that if I wanted to keep my position, I'd have to bulk up. That was code for 'doping.' When I refused, I lost my spot."[33]

Taylor was different, because he believed that he could go on to the "next level," that being drafted by a major league team and/or Division I school was well within his reach if he used steroids. "Taylor was good," said Wade. "There's no doubt about it. He was a big kid who could throw somewhere in the mid-80s."[34] At 6'3" and 205 steroid-induced pounds, Hooton had the body type that pro scouts and Division I recruiters were looking for in a pitcher. If he could manage to top 90 m.p.h. with his fastball, he had a real chance of attracting some major interest—and he knew it. According to Wade, Hooton "worked his butt off to get to the next level, and he was extremely competitive." "You could tell when Taylor wasn't performing up to his own expectations," said the shortstop. "He wore his emotions on his sleeve. If he was getting hit or the umpire wasn't calling strikes, his body language showed his frustration and anger."[35]

Taylor's rigorous weight training and his intense anger were clear signs of doping. Steroids are essentially synthetic testosterone, or an artificial means of increasing the primary male sex hormone necessary for maintaining androgenic and anabolic effects. While the androgenic effects stimulate the development of masculine traits and reproduction, the anabolic effects stimulate the development of muscle tissue, muscular strength, bone density, and sexual desire. These effects occur naturally when the testes produce their own testosterone and spermatozoa, a process that is dependent on the secretion of luteinizing hormone (LH) and follicle-stimulating hormone (FSH) from the pituitary gland. When the body produces testosterone naturally, it maintains a chemical balance that allows the individual to perform at a normal level. However, steroids inhibit the pituitary secretion of the LH and FSH hormones, disturbing the body's natural ability to produce testosterone. In other words, doping creates a negative "feedback loop" that results in the intensified behavior of the user, including a remarkable physical endurance and heightened aggression.[36] Taylor was exhibiting these excessive behaviors, and he was educated enough about the doping process to know that steroid use could inhibit his sex drive.

Emily Parker, his girlfriend, soon began to make the connection between Taylor's steroid use and both his drastic change in behavior and his obsession with his physical appearance and sexual performance. Parker was often the recipient of her boyfriend's violent mood swings. As spring approached, the couple would "fight all the time."[37] "Before he started using steroids, Taylor was funny and happy, sweet and lovable," she observed. "He had a million friends and didn't have any quarrels with anyone. Then, during the steroids, he was really mean. He became insanely jealous, getting mad at the smallest things and cuss me out."[38] He had also become extremely egocentric, obsessing over his looks and caring little about the damaging side effects of his doping. In fact, the only concerns for Taylor and his friends were maintenance of their chiseled physiques and whether "they could still have sex." To alleviate those concerns, they bought Viagra to overcome a lack of sexual performance and the female fertility drug, Clomid, to prevent a sudden loss of size and strength at the end of a cycle.[39] Gradually, Parker came to detest the steroids culture and what it had done to her boyfriend. Perhaps she began to distance herself from the sordid culture when she accompanied Taylor for the second time to make a purchase and was repulsed by the "disgustingly huge" dealer who sold him the drugs.[40] Or it might have been a month later, when she was "creeped out" by all the empty vials and syringes she saw on the kitchen counter of a friend's house, or by the knowledge that Taylor was injecting kids who were too afraid to do it for themselves.[41] Whatever the case, Parker had serious reservations about Taylor's doping and about continuing their relationship. But neither she nor Ajello had the courage to inform the Hootons about their son's growing problem with steroids.

To be sure, Don and Gwen realized that Taylor had become increasingly aggressive and irritable since January. He would suddenly fly into a violent rage and then just as quickly become tearfully apologetic.[42] Once he hurled a phone through the sheetrock wall of his father's study and tried to hide the damage by hanging a painting over it. And it was not unusual for him to punch walls, doors, fences—even his own prized pickup truck—until his hand bled.[43] "We'd already gone through the adolescent stage with Mackenzie and Donald," said Gwen, who now cannot believe she missed all the warning signals of steroid use. "We knew about hanging out with the *wrong* crowd, the rebelliousness, and the mood swings, though we'd never seen anything as drastic with our older children. Then again, Taylor was always very emotional. He was a sensitive kid. So we thought that his erratic behavior was because of us, because we spoiled him being the youngest, or because we moved around so much when he was younger."[44]

Looking back, Gwen realized that Taylor demonstrated all the signs of a steroid user. His face broke out with acne, and he would use her makeup to hide it when going out on a date. When she found capsules in his bedroom, she asked her son why he had them, unaware that steroids could be taken orally. Taylor quickly dismissed the inquiry, promising to throw them out. "Another time, I found a syringe wrapper in his room, and he told me that it was for a class project," she recalled. "Only later did I find out that Taylor was injecting his friends when they'd come over on a Sunday afternoon. Then he'd flush the needles down the toilet to get rid of them."[45]

While the Hootons tried to respect their son's privacy, Gwen's discovery of the capsules and the syringe wrapper created enough concern to confront him. When they demanded to know whether he was using drugs, he denied it, so they insisted that Taylor agree to a screening. When the test came back clean, he said, "See, I told you I hadn't been doing drugs."[46]

In 2003, drug testing was not as sophisticated as it is today. Most screening at that time was done to identify recreational drugs, not steroids. Even if Taylor had been given a test to determine steroid use, the results would not have been full-proof because no single test can detect all one hundred twenty different types of steroids that exist.[47] What's more, screening is extremely expensive. A basic urinalysis test costs on average $200; if they are administered to an entire team, especially multiple times per year, the cost becomes prohibitive.[48] Even then, the testing is hit or miss. In 2005, when Texas attempted to implement steroid testing in the public schools, it targeted ten of the one hundred twenty steroids and did so with just an 8 percent accuracy rate.[49] In addition, athletes at any level tend to stay ahead of the testers by using designer steroids, such as tetrahydrogestrinone (better known as THG, or "the Clear"), which cannot be detected at all.[50] Other drugs, like Clomid, used by women to increase fertility, can also be used to avoid steroid detection.[51] In fact, athletes do not even have to resort to steroid use to achieve the same results. Instead of anabolic steroids, they can take HGH, which increases lean muscle mass and allows the athlete to recover more quickly from injury, although it may not increase strength. HGH is not a steroid but belongs to a class of organic chemicals called "peptide hormones." It is also produced naturally by the body, specifically in the pituitary gland. In 1979, researchers developed ways to mass-produce artificial HGH to treat patients with hormone deficiencies, such as dwarfism or the muscle loss associated with AIDS. Since then, HGH has become hugely popular on the black market for body builders and athletes, especially since it does not have the stigma associated with steroids and is not easily detectable. Current technology can detect HGH only within hours of its use, allowing the athlete to pass a drug test administered just a day later.[52] Viagra is also used as a substitute for steroids, as it increases endurance and energy during athletic competition as well as in the bedroom.[53] Considering all the variables, testing for adolescent steroid use is a weak deterrent at best.

When Taylor tested negative for steroids, the Hootons were back to ground zero without any explanation for his violent outbursts. Don and Gwen realized that Taylor's behavior went beyond the normal moodiness and irritability of adolescence, but they did not know whom to consult or where to go for an answer. Only after their son's death did they learn that steroids were the cause of his downfall and that the screening they had demanded was designed to identify recreational drugs, *not* APEDs.

5

"IT'S JUST A BIG LIE!"

On Tuesday evening, September 8, 1998, Rob Garibaldi and his parents sat in their living room watching the nationally televised game between the St. Louis Cardinals and the Chicago Cubs. Like baseball fans across America, the Garibaldis were glued to the TV, anticipating Mark McGwire's sixty-second home run of the season, which would break Roger Maris's single-season record.

In many respects, the evening was a sentimental journey for the family, as McGwire was Rob's first baseball hero. He had idolized the Cardinals' slugger from the time he began playing Little League baseball. McGwire was with the Oakland A's then, but signing with St. Louis did nothing to diminish his status in Rob's eyes. McGwire represented all the traits that he admired: hard work, modesty, and perseverance. If those qualities paved the way for "Big Mac's" success, Rob believed they could do the same for him, fueling his own obsession to become a major league ballplayer. Furthermore, Rob's infatuation with Big Mac was so strong that it had even rubbed off on his parents, who referred to the St. Louis first baseman as "Mark."[1] Thus, for McGwire, the Garibaldis, and thousands of his fans across the nation, 1998 was a special, if not magical, season.

Balls were jumping out of major league parks at a record pace. Attendance was up, as were the owners' profits. Fans shed the ill feelings caused by the players' strike of four years earlier. All of it was due to the home run, arguably the most difficult skill to achieve in all of sports. Hitting a home run is the true measure of a ballplayer's brilliance. It is a science

By 1999, Rob had distinguished himself as one of the top junior college players in California. He turned down scholarship offers from Vanderbilt University and the University of Tennessee to enroll at the University of Southern California. *(Courtesy of the Garibaldi Family.)*

that takes exceptional hand-eye coordination, quick wrists, and timing—abilities that have been bestowed upon an individual at birth. You either have them, or you don't. But hitting home runs on a consistent basis also relies on exceptional strength. That is why the home-run hitter evokes such awe and excitement. With one swing of his bat, he can decide a game or a season.

Since the beginning of the "Lively Ball" era in 1920, Babe Ruth of the New York Yankees set the standard for home-run hitters. He hit 60 in 1927—a record that stood for thirty-four years until Maris, another Yankee, broke it with 61 in 1961. During the 1998 season, McGwire and Sammy Sosa kept fans on the edge of their seats as they vied for Maris's record. The rivalry, however, was only part of the season-long drama.

No two sluggers were more different in temperament, personality, and background. McGwire was an All-American athlete. Raised in a middle-class family, he proved to be a gifted hitter at an early age and earned a baseball scholarship to the University of Southern California. Before he was drafted by the Oakland A's, the native Californian anchored the line-up of the 1984 U.S. Olympic team, which lost to Japan in the final round, 6–3.[2] Once he entered the majors in 1987, McGwire quickly established himself as one of the game's premier power hitters. At 6'5" and 250 pounds, Big Mac generated towering, prodigious shots that traveled well over five hundred feet. Afterward, he would jog around the bases with his head down, almost apologetic for showing up the pitcher.[3] It was not an affectation, either—McGwire was a modest man who consciously avoided the media glare. A gentle giant with a bright red goatee, the A's first baseman once wept while announcing at a news conference that he would be donating $1 million a year to child-abuse charities.[4] In 1998, at age 34, he enjoyed the distinction of being the only player in history to compile 400 home runs in fewer at-bats than Ruth. His 58 homers the previous year were the most in a single season since Maris had set the record in 1961.[5]

Sosa, on the other hand, craved the spotlight and unabashedly chased it. Born and raised in the Dominican Republic, Sosa came from modest financial circumstances. His childhood was cut short by his father's sudden death when Sosa was only 7 years old. Compelled to support his family, Sosa worked several odd jobs until 1986, when he came to the United States to play baseball. His success was not immediate, though. The Dominican toiled in the minor leagues for three years before making his major league debut with the Texas Rangers. Traded to the Chicago White Sox in 1989, Sosa gave no indication of the slugger he would become. Not until 1993, after he was traded to the Cubs, did he hit more than 15 homers in a single season. But Sosa took his game to a whole new level in 1998.[6] That summer, he entertained fans across the nation with his prodigious power hitting as well as his demonstrative style—swinging from his heels, taking a spirited jump on his way to first base after hitting a home run, patting his chest and looking up into the heavens to thank the Lord after crossing home plate. In Chicago, Sosa quickly became a folk hero, giving a "V" sign after every home run he hit that season and dedicating each to the memory of Cubs' beloved broadcaster Harry Caray, who had died earlier in the year.[7] At age 29, Sosa was still maturing as a hitter. His 36 home runs ranked him among the NL's top 10 the previous season, but his 174 strikeouts set a Cubs' record and ranked first in the league. Like McGwire, Sosa played hard, and he played every day. His quick wrists and sweeping swing were the natural assets of a pure home-run hitter, and the fact that he played his home games in hitter-friendly Wrigley Field significantly helped his quest to break Maris's record.[8]

McGwire and Sosa represented as great a reflection of the changing dynamics of baseball as could be found during that seemingly magical 1998 season, when each man chased after one of the most cherished baseball records of all-time. White and Hispanic, the two ballplayers represented the past and the future of the national pastime and did so with a grace and élan that rejuvenated public interest in the game. Unbeknownst to most fans, however, the two sluggers enjoyed an advantage that Maris did not have—performance-enhancing anabolic steroids.

Rob Garibaldi was not fooled by the season-long spectacle, though; he had heard rumors among other players about McGwire and Sosa's dirty little secret. So it was with mixed emotions that Rob sat glued to the TV, watching his childhood hero on the verge of making baseball history on that balmy evening of September 8, 1998.

The record-breaking home run came with lightning quickness in the bottom of the fourth inning, on a first-pitch sinker from Chicago Cubs right-hander Steve Trachsel. McGwire ripped a low, searing line drive 341 feet down the left-field line that just cleared the outfield fence by inches. Jogging down the first-base line, Big Mac watched to see whether the ball stayed fair. When he saw first-base coach Dave McKay celebrating, McGwire thrust his right fist into the air and circled the bases. At home plate, he was greeted by his Cardinal teammates, and then he hoisted his son up into the air before Sosa charged in from right field to give his friendly rival a celebratory hug.[9] It should have been a personal highlight for Rob. Instead, he shook his head in disgust, got up, and left the room.

The St. Louis Cardinals' Mark McGwire (*right*), one of Rob's heroes, and the Chicago Cubs' Sammy Sosa (*left*) captured national attention in 1998 when they launched a friendly competition to see which player would break baseball's single-season home-run record. (*By Bill Greenblatt / Polaris Images.*)

Denise Garibaldi was unsettled by her son's response. She could not understand why Rob was not elated that his childhood hero had set an all-time record, one that would ensure his place among the immortals at Cooperstown. Confused, she walked into his bedroom to make sure everything was all right.

"Rob, what's wrong?" she asked. "Mark just broke Maris's record, and you look like you're disappointed."

Silence filled the room. Undecided about speaking his mind, Rob restrained himself.

"This whole thing is a lie," he blurted out. "It's just a big lie!"

Now Denise was even more confused. What exactly was the "lie"? Who was lying to whom? Why was Rob so disturbed by the lie if it did not involve him directly?

"No one really knows what's happening here!" added Rob, looking his mother straight in the eye.

"Rob, what are you talking about?" asked Denise. "Who exactly is lying? What don't I understand here? Is it about McGwire? Are you saying that the home-run race was fixed?"

Her attempt to draw him out was futile. Rob had said everything he intended to say. If he had entertained a discussion, he might have incriminated himself, revealing his own use of steroids. Instead, he remained silent.[10]

To be sure, Rob was struggling with the concept of doping. On the one hand, he realized that it was cheating. He still maintained the ideals of a purist, just like the youngest of baseball fans who understand that steroid use gives a ballplayer an advantage that the nonuser does not enjoy.[11] What Rob had difficulty accepting was that his childhood baseball hero would cheat to break Maris's single-season home-run record, arguably the most hallowed record in all of baseball. This was the side of Rob that believed in the straight and narrow way of doing things—that hard work and perseverance, not shortcuts, were the keys to success. This was the Rob who would never take drugs, because he knew they were bad for his health and would compromise his ability to play the game at his best.

On the other hand, Rob had deluded himself into believing that steroid use was a "healthy" way to build muscle and stay at the top of one's game as well as a "healthy" means of achieving his goal to become a major league baseball player. That is why he purchased the drug the summer after his graduation from high school, why he might have already begun to dope, and, if not, why he would certainly adopt the practice in the near future. It is also why he could accept McGwire's use of steroids. No doubt, the Cardinals' slugger was still Rob's role model, but he had taken a step off the pedestal.

Denise Garibaldi also believed that the "home-run race between McGwire and Sosa served to confirm her son's belief that the only way to achieve his goal to hit with power was to do steroids." "As far as Rob was concerned," she added, "McGwire and Barry Bonds, his other hero, gave him the permission to dope."[12] If his heroes engaged in the seedy practice, he was certainly justified in following their lead. Such a philosophy enabled Rob, along with his natural ability, to become Northern California's best junior college baseball player in 1999 when he attended Santa Rosa Junior College (SRJC) in Sonoma County.

SRJC, founded in 1918, is the tenth-oldest of California's 109 publicly funded two-year colleges. It was modeled as a "junior" version of the nearby University of California, Berkeley, and intended to be a feeder school for the University of California system. In the late 1990s, SRJC was also considered one of California's most distinguished community colleges, with a talented faculty, an innovative online studies program, and a strong General Education program for students planning to transfer to four-year colleges and universities.[13] What distinguished the college, however, was its presence in and commitment to Santa Rosa. Faculty, administrators, and students not only lived in the community but were also involved in its daily activities. Public meetings and affairs were often conducted in college facilities. Adult learners who took courses for their personal enjoyment could frequently be found on campus in day and evening classes. In all these ways, SRJC and the local community were inextricably bound. Predictably, the college has long been regarded as the "crown jewel of Sonoma County."[14]

SRJC's warm, friendly atmosphere was a soothing balm for Rob after the tumultuous events of the previous two years. It allowed him to regroup from the deaths of his high school coach and two close friends as well as from his frustrating semester at San Mateo. "There were many things about our college that benefited Rob," said Ron Myers, who was SRJC's head baseball coach in the 1990s. "He was able to take advantage of our educational support services, since he struggled with a learning disability. He was also near home and family, which was important to him. I'd also like to think that the teachers and coaches here take a genuine interest in the students, and that there is at least one faculty member who will have a strong impact on each student who comes through here. I know that Rob loved to hit, so he and Damon Neidlinger, our hitting coach, spent a lot of time together during the 1999 season, and they struck up a close friendship."[15]

Neidlinger, who succeeded Myers as SRJC's head baseball coach in 2004, remembered meeting Rob during the summer of 1998, when he was running a baseball camp at the college. "I looked down the foul line, and I saw this young guy shagging fly balls," he said. "I knew I hadn't hired him to help with the camp, so I was impressed by his obvious love of the game. After camp ended that afternoon, I went up and introduced myself to him. He told me that he was interested in enrolling at SRJC and playing ball for us. Not long after, we began working together on his hitting." Neidlinger described his friendship with Garibaldi as a "very strong, respectful" one. He was easy to coach because he "had a deep passion for the game and especially for hitting."[16]

To be sure, Myers and Neidlinger were very different coaches than Bob Leslie had been, but Rob made the adjustment. According to Rob, Leslie offered his players "constant positive reinforcement." Myers, on the other hand, "hardly ever said, 'good job' because a good job [was] expected." But the Bear Cubs head coach did teach him to "let the game come to him, not to allow self-doubt take hold." "Coach Myers taught me that if I second-guessed myself on the playing field, I was done," Rob explained in an essay for psychology class. "So I learned to play relaxed but aggressive."[17] Neidlinger further cultivated Rob's already impressive work ethic. "His philosophy," wrote Rob, "was that the great ones become great when no one else is around." "Just show up, be a sponge, put in the extra time and work."[18] Rob bought into SRJC's program quickly. And the Bear Cubs' success spoke for itself.

Members of the Big 8 Athletic Conference, SRJC teams are consistently ranked among the best junior college teams in the nation. The Bear Cubs fielded winning teams year after year, turning out dozens of Division I players. Some graduates have gone on to play MLB, including Jason Lane, 1997 (Houston Astros); Jonny Gomes, 2001 (Tampa Bay Rays); and Clint Pridmore, 2007 (Washington Nationals).[19] Quite fittingly, the 1999 Bear Cubs were a very good team with a lot of returning players. SRJC went 25–3 in the Bay Valley Conference and hit .340 as a team. Most of the starters went on to play at the Division I level.[20] "Rob was the perfect fit," said Neidlinger. "He was the missing piece that made a very good team a great one, so great that we went on to play in the state championship that year."[21]

Rob was not a leader in the traditional sense of the term: a very gifted ballplayer who motivates teammates by the force of an outgoing personality. Instead, he was a "quiet leader" who led by example. He allowed his work ethic and game to speak for itself. According to Neidlinger, Rob "played hard, he played tough, and he was a good teammate." He added, "It wasn't usual, for example, for Rob to work one-on-one with a teammate who was having trouble at the plate. He'd make suggestions on how to improve and actually show him how to do it."[22] But Garibaldi was not a "five-tool player," the complete package who can throw, run, field, hit for average, and hit for power. In fact, Myers claimed that "it wasn't like Rob had a cannon for an arm": "He had a good arm. He ran well, but he wasn't the fastest player on our team. I wouldn't call him a power hitter, either." What impressed Myers was Rob's ability to "hit the ball hard," hard enough to earn a starting job in left field and hit third in the batting order as well as set an example for Gomes.[23]

Gomes and Garibaldi knew each other as teammates at Casa Grande High School and shared an interesting history. Both ballplayers were close friends of Adam Westcott, the Gaucho first baseman who was killed in a May 1997 car accident; in fact, Gomes was a passenger in that car. Like Garibaldi, he was profoundly affected by his friend's death, going so far as to have Westcott's initials tattooed on his right bicep.[24] Also like Garibaldi, Gomes earned all-league honors as a scholastic baseball player. After graduating in 1999, Gomes matriculated to SRJC. According to Myers, "Jonny was raw, not nearly as developed a player as Rob was." "He struggled that first year," he added. "You could see he had a lot of talent, but he had a lot of growing to do before he could harness it. He only began to realize his true abilities during his second year with us."[25] Gomes was an understudy to Garibaldi during the fall 1999 season. "Rob was two years older than Jonny," recalled Paul Maytorena, who coached both youngsters at Casa Grande. "At SRJC, Jonny learned a lot from Rob. If you went on talent alone, Rob was an outstanding player. But he just didn't have the body type to attract a major league club. At the time, the average corner outfielder in the majors was 6'2" and 225 pounds. Rob was only 5'11" and 165 pounds. Scouts knew they'd be taking a huge chance with any player of such a small body type. But Jonny had both the talent and the body type. That's why the Tampa Bay Rays signed him."[26]

Small body type or not, Rob put together one of the finest seasons of any college baseball player in America in 1999. In 170 plate appearances, he batted .459 with 14 home runs and 77 RBI. He also set SRJC single-season records in RBI, hits (78), runs (70), and triples (6),[27] Those statistics earned Garibaldi not only recognition as "Northern California's Junior College Player of the Year" but also a full scholarship to the University of Southern California and the interest of the New York Yankees, who selected him in the 41st round of the June amateur draft.[28] "Rob was the most dominant offensive player on our team in 1999," recalled Myers, who is still in awe of his remarkable hitting more than a decade later. Once, in an away game against archrival Sacramento City College, the Bear Cubs found themselves down by six runs in the second inning. SRJC kept chipping away at the lead, finally pulling ahead by one run in the sixth. Then, in the seventh inning, with two runners on base and two outs, Rob, in one quick stroke, put the Bear Cubs ahead for good. "I can remember that home run to this day," said Myers. "Rob hit that ball so hard and so far out of their park that it just took my breath away." Sacramento was the perennial leader of the Bay Valley Conference's Eastern Division, while SRJC was the toast of the Western Division. "But that home run was like putting the final nail on the lid of a coffin," he added. "I thought to myself, 'We just showed them who the dominant power is in this conference.'" Another one of Myers's treasured memories of Garibaldi's hitting prowess came during a cold April contest against Solano College. The Bear Cubs were down 10–1 early in the game but came back to win, 15–10. "Rob was right in the middle of that comeback," said Myers. "He hit a grand slam and a three-run homer that game. I don't think he realized just how good a hitter he was. Rob just didn't have that kind of conceit."[29]

One can only speculate on how much of Garibaldi's prodigious power hitting was due to natural ability and how much was the result of doping. Both Myers and Neidlinger were adamant that they saw no sign of steroid use. "Rob was a lean athlete, not a muscle-bound one," explained Myers. "There was no erratic behavior, no indication that he was using steroids

Santa Rosa Junior College coaches Damon Neidlinger (*above left*) and Ron Myers (*above right*) built a nationally ranked baseball program with players such as Rob. In 1999, Rob batted .459 and collected 14 home runs and 77 RBI, earning him recognition as Northern California's Junior College Player of the Year and a full scholarship to the University of Southern California. *(Left photo: Courtesy of Damon Neidlinger. Right photo: Courtesy of Ron Myers.)*

whatsoever."[30] Neidlinger also did not "suspect steroid use, because there was no rapid weight gain." "Rob was slight and lean, so you saw muscle definition," he added. "But there was nothing to indicate he was using steroids."[31]

At the same time, erratic behavior, rapid weight gain, and increased muscle mass are not the only signs of steroid use. Just as indicative are exceptional endurance and an obsession with weight lifting. Rob exhibited both of those tendencies and even boasted about them in an essay for a psychology class that spring. "One can push a body to do so much more than one thinks," he wrote. "Last summer, I worked construction all day in the heat. I could have called it a day, but I had to go to the gym. As much as I wanted to go home and sleep, I went straight to the gym and lifted for two hours. I did that six days a week."[32]

Rob placed a lot of pressure on himself at SRJC. He realized that he had to improve not only his game but also his grades if he hoped to attract Division I interest. Although SRJC prepared him for the more rigorous academics of college, Rob admitted that he "still had to make extensive use of educational specialists and tutors" as well as "alternative learning methods" to succeed.[33]

He also admitted to "being stressed about next year, not knowing where he would be attending school."[34] One of the ways he dealt with the pressure was to start drinking. It was an easy step for him to take, because many of his teammates had already adopted the habit. Rob, the team's most successful player, was expected to join the others whenever they partied. If not, his absence would be interpreted as a purposeful snub by a teammate who believed himself to be better than the others. Although recreational drugs were just as accessible, Rob continued to reject them. Interestingly, he was a bit more curious about marijuana. "Drugs are not for me," he wrote in a journal entry in the spring of 1999. "Once I smoked weed and had the worst anxiety attack ever. Instead, I drink because it helps me cope with my anxiety."[35]

Rob's drinking probably increased as the spring semester came to a close. He was being pressured on a daily basis by several Division I coaches as well as pro scouts for the Minnesota Twins, New York Yankees, Oakland A's, and Texas Rangers. Because he was attending a junior college, Rob was eligible for the June amateur draft after both his freshman and sophomore years. In fact, the Yankees were interested in him as a "draft-and-follow" prospect. They would draft Rob after his freshman year and own his rights to sign up until the next MLB amateur draft in 2000.[36] Both Myers and Neidlinger discouraged Rob from going pro. Instead, they advised him to play Division I baseball and use the additional time to increase his physical size, which would increase his chances of being selected higher in the draft after his junior year.[37] With that thinking in mind, Rob turned his attention to the Division I recruiters, who were only adding to his anxieties. "They all say the same thing: 'This is going to be the most important decision of your life,'" he wrote in a personal reflection essay:

> I have out-of-state schools telling me to go out-of-state so I can see the country and play where the competition is better. Then I have in-state schools saying not to listen to the out-of-state schools because I will have to pay more tuition being an out-of-state resident.
>
> I used to believe all this garbage, but I've learned from my mistakes. I first went to the College of San Mateo because the coach gave me every line he could think of to sell me on the school. He

told me how good the learning disability program was. He sold my dad on that, so he could talk me into going there. He promised to get me my own place. I heard all these promises about the competition, about playing time, about being recruited by Division One schools. I never saw one of those promises kept once I was there. So I left and came to SRJC and that was the best thing I ever did.[38]

Although Rob wanted to go to Arizona State University, their coaches did not express an interest in him. As a result, he narrowed his choices to the University of Tennessee, Vanderbilt University, and USC.[39]

In the end, Rob settled on USC for three reasons: (1) Mark McGwire, his hero, had attended the school; (2) John Savage, the Trojans' recruiting coordinator, had pursued him so doggedly; and (3) he would be closer to home than he would be at either of the other two schools.[40] Savage had pitched in the Cincinnati Reds organization for two seasons before turning his attention to college coaching. Between 1992 and 1996, he served as assistant coach at the University of Nevada, helping lead the Wolf Pack to the Big West Conference title in 1994. Hired by USC head coach Mike Gillespie in 1996, Savage served as the Trojans' pitching coach and recruiting coordinator until summer 2000, when he secured his first head coaching position at the University of California, Irvine. His impeccable reputation as a recruiter preceded him. In 1998, Savage earned *Collegiate Baseball*'s Assistant Coach of the Year honors after helping USC capture that season's College World Series Championship. The following year, *College Baseball* acknowledged his efforts for facilitating the top-ranked recruiting class in Division I.[41] Rob was part of that recruiting class.

Savage first took notice of Rob when he was a junior at Casa Grande High School. His interest peaked during Rob's remarkable 1999 season at SRJC. "USC had already recruited Jason Lane out of Santa Rosa," explained Ray Garibaldi. "[Jason] Lane became an All-American outfielder for USC when they won the College World Series in 1998, and he went on to play for the Houston Astros and San Diego Padres. So Savage knew about the quality of SRJC's program."[42] The Trojans' recruiter also knew how to strike the right chords with prospective families. When he learned that Rob had a learning disability, he convinced the Garibaldis that USC had the academic support network that would enable Rob to succeed. In fact, the school did have one of the strongest learning support programs in California's colleges, so it did not take Savage much effort to win over Ray and Denise Garibaldi. "We were convinced that there would be tutors to help Rob with his studies as well as academic monitors to make sure he was getting his

Rob's decision to attend the University of Southern California was inspired by the fact that the St. Louis Cardinals' Mark McGwire had played college ball there. *(By Tom Dipace / Polaris Images.)*

course work done," recalled Ray.[43] Denise also believed that USC was the "right" school for her son based on its learning support system. However, she has since admitted that there was a "red flag" in the school's recruitment of her son that she did not recognize at the time: when the Garibaldis visited USC, Rob was told that he needed to add 20 pounds before the spring of 2000 if he hoped to achieve his hitting potential. The families of other recruits must have also been told something similar, because all the recruits left with containers of supplements.[44] "Ray and I discussed our concern about those supplements," Denise admitted, "but it was more from the standpoint that we couldn't imagine Rob putting on 20 pounds of weight in just three or four months' time. We just went along with the program, because everything we were told on that trip was so amazingly positive. And we believed all of it. Now I realize just how naïve we were."[45]

Savage made a different appeal to Rob. He told him that USC was in a rebuilding phase and that the class he was recruiting for 1999–2000 had some remarkable talent. In fact, the coach predicted that by Rob's junior year, the Trojans would be competing for another College World Series Championship.[46] He did not have to say anything more—Rob was sold. In his college application essay, he wrote that USC would allow him to "achieve that exceptional balance between receiving a good education and developing a baseball career."[47] In truth, Rob viewed USC as a vital step to realizing his dream of becoming a major leaguer.

When Savage learned that Rob was on MLB's 1999 amateur draft list, he immediately phoned the Garibaldis. "Don't let him sign with anyone," he told them. "We want Rob very badly." To sweeten the offer, Savage offered Rob a full baseball scholarship for his sophomore and junior years and a 70 percent scholarship for his senior year. "It was an offer that we just couldn't refuse," said Ray. "His tuition, books, and all of his living expenses would be picked up by USC. In addition, Rob would be given $900 a month for apartment rent. It amounted to $100,000 for two years. In fact, there was only one other player who was given a full ride in that recruiting class."[48] Savage's offer was *very* exceptional. Like other major Division I baseball programs, USC is allotted 11.7 full scholarships. Although NCAA regulations permit the program to carry a maximum roster of 35 players, athletic aid can be divided among only 27 student-athletes. The minimum award for those 27 players receiving athletic aid is a 25 percent scholarship. Full rides are extremely rare. For most top players, scholarships of 40 percent, 60 percent, or, in rare cases, 80 percent are more realistic. These student athletes either have to pay the balance of the tuition or find other sources of aid.[49] To be sure, Rob would have been foolish to turn down an offer like that. Together with the university's strong learning support services, the full scholarship and USC's impressive baseball tradition addressed all of his needs and interests. Not surprisingly, when the New York Yankees drafted Rob in the 41st round, Rob followed Savage's advice and turned them down.[50] When asked by the local media why he declined to go pro, he said, "They have their body types, and I'm not quite big enough."[51]

SRJC's head baseball coach Ron Myers was elated for him. "I remember sitting down with Rob and his father after our season ended and telling them that, in terms of baseball, Rob didn't have anything more to prove at this level," he said. "The key was whether he was ready to move on in terms of his maturity and academics, and only he could make that decision."[52] Because Rob needed to complete his associate degree before matriculating to USC, he abandoned his plans to play in a wooden bat baseball league in Alaska that summer and remained at home to take courses at SRJC. In the fall, he took a demanding twenty-two-unit course load to complete the degree, which eliminated any possibility of playing on the baseball team. Instead, he practiced with the Bear Cubs on a regular basis.[53] "What was so awesome about Rob that fall was his work ethic," said Damon Neidlinger. "Here's a young guy who is Northern California's Junior College Player of the Year, he's accepted a scholarship to USC, a top Division I program, and he's working as if he's trying to make our team. There wasn't an ounce of prima donna in Rob. Even during the spring season when he was putting up huge numbers, there was absolutely no arrogance in him. It was always about staying the course with Rob, about hitting the ball hard, about helping the team win. He truly loved the game. He was a special kid."[54]

That "special kid" was honored by the Bear Cubs before he left Santa Rosa. Speaking at a team banquet, he reminded his audience that "baseball is more than just a game, more than making it to the 'bigs.'" For Rob, the game was about "dreaming big and setting high goals, working as hard off the field as on it, picking up your teammates when they need it most, and staying away from the bad things in life." He concluded his talk with his personal motto: "Take care of the game, and the game will take care of you."[55] Denise called the speech "Rob's Manifesto," because it "contained all the values he held dearest in his life."[56]

6

"ONLY GOD CAN HOLD ME NOW"

Mackenzie Hooton was finishing up a master's degree in special education at the University of Pittsburgh in the spring of 2003. Five years earlier, she had entered Pitt as a freshman and had not lived with her family on a regular basis since then. She had never developed much of an attachment to Plano, Texas, visiting only once or twice a year on holidays. It really was not home for her; it was where her parents and youngest brother had established a new residence after relocating from the Philadelphia area in 1999. But now, at age 23, Mackenzie felt a strong need to be near her family again.

Taylor, who was six years younger, was going to be entering his senior year of high school soon, and she did not want to miss all the highlights—his final baseball season at Plano West, the prom, graduation. Mackenzie was a romantic at heart, but her desire to be with family was more than nostalgic sentiment. She had always been very protective of Taylor, almost as if she were a surrogate mother. The fact that both of them could be equally stubborn fueled her protective instinct, too.

To be sure, there were times during her childhood when Mackenzie had resented the freedom both her younger brothers enjoyed. During high school, her parents held her to a strict 9:30 P.M. curfew. Riding in a car full of teenaged girls was forbidden, as was dating. Neither one of her brothers was saddled with such restrictions, especially Taylor, who Mackenzie believed "could do anything he wanted" with the tacit approval of their parents. "Being the first child, I guess my parents started out strict

The Hooton family is shown here in 2002. *Left to right:* Don Sr., Gwen, Taylor, Donald Jr., and Mackenzie. *(Courtesy of Taylor Hooton Foundation.)*

and became more lenient when Donald and Taylor came along," she said. "I think the other reason they were so strict is because I'm female. My father didn't have any sisters growing up, just two brothers. So he wasn't familiar with girls. My mom grew up with a brother and two sisters, but she felt responsible for raising me, because my dad was traveling for work so much. She didn't want to mess up. But they were much more strict with me than [with] my brothers, especially Taylor."[1]

Perhaps that's why Mackenzie stayed away from Plano during her summers in college; being there would only make her more resentful of the considerable freedom her baby brother enjoyed. She did not speak to Taylor on the phone very much while she was at Pitt, either. But now she felt a deep sense of remorse over all that she had missed in his life. It was time to make amends. She was determined to renew her relationship with him and hoped to become more of a friend than a "big sister." Mackenzie's need to reconnect with Taylor became painfully clear after she received a phone call from her brother Donald during the second week of April.

Donald was living in Philadelphia, finishing up a degree in business administration at Gwynedd Mercy University. Yet the physical distance seemed to make the two brothers even closer than they were when they lived together at home. They were best friends and each other's most trusted confidant, speaking over the phone on a regular basis. That winter, Taylor confided in Donald, telling him that he needed to get bigger if he hoped to make Plano West's varsity baseball team. He also told his older brother that he was considering steroids and that he wanted to find out what Donald knew about them. "I told Taylor that I really didn't know much about the drug, aside from the fact that many of my college teammates were using it and getting bigger," recalled Donald. "The only suggestion I made was that he go and ask a physician about it before putting something like that into his body." Whatever Taylor decided to do, Donald promised not to tell their parents.[2]

In late March, Taylor phoned again, this time complaining that he was constantly feeling angry or depressed. Donald asked Taylor whether he was doping, and his younger brother admitted he was. Now Donald was in a precarious position. He had done some of his own research and knew that his brother was struggling with 'roid rage and needed help. At the same time, he had given Taylor his word that he would not say anything to their parents. If he went back on his promise, Taylor would never trust him again. Mackenzie, with her strong protective instincts, was his only hope. Donald called his sister and explained the situation, knowing that she would take immediate action. Mackenzie phoned a college friend, then playing for the NFL's New York Giants, to find out all she could about anabolic steroids. Although her friend was not a user, he was very familiar with the signs of doping and warned Mackenzie of the dangerous side effects. "I immediately phoned my parents and told them that Taylor was using and how to identify the signs," she admitted.[3]

Don and Gwen confronted Taylor in early April. Seated at the kitchen table, they asked him point blank, "Are you using steroids?" Their son looked them directly in the eye and said, "No."[4] It was a blatant lie. Taylor was in the middle of a second eight-week cycle of stacking Deca 300 and Anadrol after first purchasing the drugs in January. Although he should have taken a thirty-day break between cycles, he had waited only half that time to begin the next cycle, believing that he could increase his strength more rapidly.[5]

As tension filled the room, Gwen noticed that Taylor was absentmindedly shaving the skin off his clenched knuckles with a serrated-edged knife.

"What are doing to yourself?" she cried, alarmed by the sight.

Taylor immediately put down the knife but remained silent.

Trying to restore calm, Don changed the subject. "Are you aware of how dangerous steroids are?" he asked his son.

Again, there was no response. Don, growing more impatient by the minute, was determined to get answers, so he decided to approach the steroids issue from a different angle.

"Your mother told me that she was $450 short in her bank account," he said. "Do you know where that money went?"

Taylor's face was turning red as he felt the rage pulsing through his body. He had known they would discover the missing money sooner or later, and now he was caught. Would it be better to admit that he had stolen the money and ask for forgiveness or to deny it altogether? Realizing that an admission would imply that he was also guilty of buying steroids, Taylor lied again.

"No, Pop," he finally replied. "I have no idea what happened to that money, and I sure don't understand why you're asking me about it."

There was no sense in accusing his son of stealing the money. Don expected that his guilt would eventually surface. Instead, he offered a possible solution, one that would satisfy his concerns and not incriminate his son.

"Okay, Taylor, here's what we're going to do," said Don. "Mackenzie has a college friend who plays in the NFL. He's familiar with the dangers of steroids. We'd like you to speak with him."

It was a shrewd idea. Don hoped that if Taylor agreed, perhaps he would be scared away from doping. Instead, his son flew into a rage. "Well, you know what?" he snapped. "I'll just take a knife and end it right now!"

Don was shocked, and Gwen was on the verge of tears. This was *not* the son they had raised. Taylor had never spoken that way to them before. They realized that he was severely depressed. The illness ran in their family, but they did not know the extent to which steroids could worsen the problem.

Gwen, stunned by the outburst, tried to calm her son, who had risen from the table and headed for the door.

"Listen, Dude," she said, trying to stop him. "Papa and I think you need some help. Please, for our sakes, let me make an appointment for you with a psychiatrist."

It was too late. Taylor had already made it outside the house. He climbed into his pickup truck and headed off to see his girlfriend, Emily Parker.[6]

At school the next day, he struggled with feelings of guilt, shame, and remorse. Knowing that his father had left town on an extended business trip, Taylor was relieved that he would not have to answer any more questions. But he certainly did not have the courage to face Gwen. So when he returned home that evening, he went upstairs to his bedroom and closed the door. Before he turned in that night, the teen typed an e-mail to his mother, admitting his guilt:

> I wanted to get something off my chest. It's time for me to grow up and be a man for once, and deal with the consequences. Last night, y'all asked me about the money that was missing, and I denied taking it. I want to be up front and honest with you and tell you that I did [take it]. The only reason I [lied] is because I'm afraid of Pop. I hate telling him things because I know it's always for the worst. I know that we can't keep this between you and me, as much as I wish we could. I know what I did was wrong and I have to deal with the consequences. But I'd rather be honest with you than have you look down on me even more than you already do.
>
> I don't know why I [took the money], and it was stupid. But I'm going to pay it off this summer, and double what I took. It feels good to be honest with you. . . . I feel a little relief that I told you this and I want you to know that I love you very much, Mom.

Taylor also shared some of the pressures he was feeling, both at home and at school. "I've been really down lately, and overwhelmed with stress," he wrote. "I want to be the best son I can be, but it's just so hard because y'all have such high expectations of me." He also admitted that he was "tired of school, of baseball, of [his] friends," because "all of those things feel so pointless."

At the same time, Taylor insisted that he "didn't need a therapist" to help him. Instead, he attributed his sadness to depression, because it "runs in the family." "I know that I am a strong person," he concluded. "I can deal with this, and I'm going to be OK. It's just going to take some time."[7]

Now convinced of her son's need for therapy, Gwen contacted psychiatrist Dr. Babette Farkas and made an appointment for him. To appease his mother, Taylor met with the psychiatrist on a regular basis.

Farkas slowly drew him out. What she learned was that Taylor was struggling with low self-esteem and that to measure up, he believed he had to make certain adjustments in his life and do things that were popular among his peers. Most of the changes dealt with his physical appearance—bleaching his hair, wearing an earring, getting a tattoo, and

especially getting bigger. When the psychiatrist had earned his uncon-
ditional trust, Taylor admitted that he had been injecting himself with
Deca 300 and taking Anadrol orally. "That's when I put him on low doses
of Lexapro," Farkas said in a 60 Minutes interview after her client's death.
"I realized that there was depression from his steroid use as well as the
probability that he'd become even more depressed as he was coming off
the steroids."[8]

The temptation to continue doping must have been overwhelming.
Taylor had been promoted to the varsity team in April due to a rash of
injuries on the pitching staff. Now throwing in the mid-80s, he would be
used in relief on a trial basis.[9] "He was bringing heat," recalled his catcher, Billy Ajello, "and you could count on him to throw strikes."[10] If Taylor
proved to be successful in Class 5A's highly competitive District 9, perhaps
Plano West could launch a formidable challenge for the conference title
against rivals Plano East and Rockwell. A successful performance would
also increase his chances for a spot in the starting rotation in his senior
year. Then there was the pressure of wanting to fit in with his new varsity teammates, many of whom were juicing. But Taylor's growing concern
about his violent mood swings and the negative effect they were having
on Parker and his parents provided sufficient motivation to stop his steroid use.

In early May, at the urging of Farkas, Taylor admitted to his parents
that he had been doping but insisted that he was now clean. He also
told Parker and Ajello of his decision to stop using.[11] The next few weeks
proved to be an especially critical period as Taylor experienced the painful
difficulties of withdrawal.

When a user goes off steroids, his testosterone level is low, because
the drug suppresses his body's natural ability to produce the hormone. It
takes weeks and sometimes months for the body to produce testosterone
at its natural level again.[12] Under these circumstances, the body's chemical imbalance often results in depression. Donald A. Malone, MD, of the
Cleveland Clinic first identified the link between depression and steroid
withdrawal in the 1990s in a study of 170 body builders. He found that
severe depression occurred when the user quit "cold turkey," going from
one extreme to the other. The body is left in a state of shock because of
the absence of steroids.[13] In addition to depression, other researchers,
including Harrison G. Pope Jr. of Harvard Medical School, have found
other problems associated with steroid withdrawal, especially when a user
stops abruptly instead of cycling off the drug by lowering the dosages
in the final weeks of use. The effects include increased irritability and

agitation, resulting in 'roid rage; excessive remorse, exhibited by periods of uncontrollable weeping; and suicidal thoughts and/or tendencies. If depression runs in the family, the user is more likely to take his life during withdrawal.[14] Teenagers are especially prone to these effects because of the inevitable hormonal and biochemical changes that occur in the body during puberty. Under normal conditions, adolescents experience emotional and behavioral swings. When steroids are added to the equation, such excessive behaviors are magnified.[15] Even body builders recognize the significant dangers of adolescent steroid use and discourage it.[16]

Taylor exhibited many signs of serious depression after he stopped doping. With Parker, he would often behave in a melodramatic fashion, saying that he "couldn't go on without her," and he would become gripped by periods of uncontrollable crying.[17] Although he never spoke of suicide to her, Taylor did mention it to his friend Callahan Kuhns in an e-mail that read, "Dude, I laid in bed with a knife last night."

"Shut up," replied Kuhns. "Don't say stuff like that."[18]

There were incidents of rage as well. One Sunday afternoon when Mark Gomez visited the Hootons' home, the two friends were upstairs in Taylor's bedroom when he "just snapped." "I watched him punch the headboard of his bed for a good ten seconds at least," recalled Gomez, still stunned by the memory. "When he finally stopped, he was like, 'Damn it.' Then he looked at his hand and it was bleeding pretty badly. It was intense. Definitely, raging."[19]

The 'roid rage climaxed one Friday night in early June. That evening, Taylor and Parker drove over to the local Wendy's to hang out with a group of some thirty friends. Someone mentioned that their parents were out of town, and they were going to throw a party later that night. As the teens made plans, Parker's former boyfriend drove up and parked his Jeep. When she saw him, Parker said hello and gave him a warm hug. Such public displays of affection were not uncommon among Plano West's couples, who tended to remain friends after a breakup. Extremely jealous of Parker's male acquaintances, Taylor snapped. He started screaming at Parker's ex-boyfriend, who remained silent and began walking away. But before he could climb inside his Jeep to leave, Taylor grabbed him in a headlock and began punching him until he fell to the ground.

A crowd of kids encircled the two teens and began to cheer, fueling an already dire situation. Some pulled out cellphones to record the brawl, which was clearly one-sided.

"C'mon!' screamed Taylor, who stood over the bloodied youth, egging him on. "Get up! I'll give you more!"

Parker was beside herself with fear. She saw that Taylor was out of control, the veins in his neck pulsing with anger.

"Please!" she begged him, "Stop! He didn't do anything to you!"

The former boyfriend was barely moving at this point. Parker, fearing for his safety, pleaded with friends to get him to the hospital, where he later received nine stitches.

Taylor showed no remorse. "God, I wish I'd been on steroids," he told Parker, with unabashed bravado. "It would've been way worse."

What could she say? Taylor's behavior had become so ghastly that she did not even recognize the bully who now stood before her. Picking up her belongings, Parker walked home in stunned disbelief. Unfazed, Taylor went to the party alone. When he was shown images of the beating by friends, he continued to boast that it could have been "way worse."

The incident was never reported to the police.[20]

Patrick Burke, who saw the fight, believed that steroid withdrawal was only part of the problem. "Even before Taylor began using, it was not uncommon for him to talk about fighting," he recalled. "It was typical for a lot of kids to talk about wanting to get into a fight. It was part of the macho adolescent culture we belonged to. After the steroids, it became more than 'just talk'—it became something very tangible. So, for Taylor, once he began juicing, it was easy to cross the line from talk into action."[21]

The next day, Parker issued an ultimatum—stop using steroids or we're through. Taylor apologized repeatedly and swore that he was not doping any more. "There was no more yelling," recalled Parker. "He was going to strengthen his relationships and stay away from steroids for good." Taylor kept his promise for the next few weeks. But his depression also worsened as he continued to go through withdrawal. "He'd just cry all the time," she said. "We'd be on the phone for hours and he'd just be crying."[22] No one knew exactly what was upsetting him, although there were several possibilities. He might have felt remorse over disappointing his girlfriend and his parents. Perhaps his baseball season was not working out the way he had hoped. Taylor's pitching was not meeting his own high expectations after he was promoted to varsity. He had become a swing player, pitching strictly in relief for the varsity but mostly for the JV. And he was not pleased with his body.

Although he still carried about 20 pounds of the muscle he had gained while using steroids, he had lost his boyish face and looked much older than his 17 years. Afraid that he would lose more mass the longer he went without cycling, he told Parker that he was desperate to return to doping and promised to stop "right away" if he "started raging again."[23] But she remained firm. "No, Taylor," she declared. "I don't want to go through that again." She hated the Taylor who was on steroids, the one who alternated between anger and tearful remorse, violence and depression. She was frightened by that person. She wanted the kind, funny, happy-go-lucky Taylor she had begun dating a year earlier. Once again, he asked her to reconsider, and again she said, "No"—this time with a finality that cut him to the quick.[24]

Despite the fact that he was on antidepressants and continued to meet with Dr. Farkas on a regular basis, Taylor's mental health was extremely vulnerable. He was losing the body mass he valued so much as well as the false sense of self-confidence that came with it. He finally buckled. In mid-June, Taylor stole another $400 from his mother's bank account and, along with Gomez, purchased another eight-week supply of Deca Durabolin from the Frisco dealer.[25] But this time, he was more careful to hide his use.

In addition to the steroids, Taylor purchased Azo, a detox readily available through the black market that masks evidence of doping in the urine, as well as Clomid, an estrogen pill. Designed for women with fertility problems, Clomid tends to limit mood swings in steroid users by balancing out the additional testosterone produced by doping.[26] The combination of the two drugs appeared to achieve his intended purpose.

Blake Boydston, Plano West's varsity baseball coach from 2000 to 2005, certainly saw no indication that Taylor was doping. Although the teen was swinging between the varsity and the JV, Boydston saw him on a daily basis that spring. Even on those occasions when he was pitching for the JV, the teams stretched and warmed up together during the first part of practice.

"Taylor was a good kid, very personable, very approachable," recalled Boydston. "He always came to the field in good spirits. When we spoke, it was 'Thank you,' 'Yes, sir,' or 'No, sir.' You could talk with him about anything, too." The coach noted that Taylor never displayed any troubling behavior, and if it seemed that he was gaining weight, it was natural, because "he had room to grow." But as far as steroid use was concerned, Boydston "didn't see anything," and he "didn't suspect anything." In fact, he does not believe that the school's student body ever had a serious problem with steroids.

"I've never seen a problem in the past or now," he insisted in an interview, being careful not to use the word *steroids*. "Is there stuff that goes on? Yes, I'm sure there is. But for me to see it on a day-in-day-out basis? No, I never did."

Instead, Boydston, still an elementary physical education teacher in the Plano Independent School District, attributed sudden increase in body

Taylor, a first baseman and pitcher, believed that he had the ability to become drafted by a major league club or to play at the Division I level by his junior year in high school. (*Courtesy of Taylor Hooton Foundation.*)

mass among teens to better conditioning and diet. "Sure, you see some kids who are bigger, or stronger, or faster," he said. "But I don't look at that as them doing something illegally. For the most part, they're good individuals who are making the right choices. They're taking care of their bodies by eating the right foods, and they're getting stronger and faster because of all the training opportunities and facilities they have. I just don't look at it as cheating."[27]

Don Hooton has questioned that theory but not Boydston's contention that he never suspected his son's steroid use:

I'm extremely reluctant to accuse anybody of knowing and deliberately denying that there's an anabolic steroids problem among teens. I still give Blake the benefit of the doubt that he didn't know of Taylor's use and that he honestly believes there was no doping problem at Plano West. At the same time, Gwen and I learned after Taylor's death that at least seven of the fifteen kids on the varsity baseball team and half the players on the football team were juicing. How do we know? Because Taylor's friends told us in the days following his death. They were so consumed by grief that they wanted to confess everything they knew. We also found out from parents who asked Gwen and me to counsel their families. They were concerned that their sons were juicing, having found anabolic steroids in their bedrooms. Some of those kids later admitted it. So when I say that half the boys on Taylor's varsity baseball team at Plano West were doping, it's not idle speculation.[28]

After school let out in late June, the Hootons took a two-week family vacation to England. One of those weeks was spent in the rustic countryside, far from satellite television and Internet reception. They took periodic day trips to visit nearby historical sites but returned to their rented cabin each evening. The trip offered the family a rare opportunity to reconnect, free of the busy lives they led back in the states. That was important, especially for Gwen. She did not know how many more family vacations they would take. Although Mackenzie had recently moved to Plano, she was 23 years old and embarking on her own career as a schoolteacher. Donald Jr., age 22, was finishing up college at Gwynedd Mercy in southeastern Pennsylvania. Taylor was already 17 and had just one more year at home before going off to college. Gwen treasured every moment of that vacation. "We were always laughing," she remembered fondly. "Everyone was happy, and Taylor was the life of the party. He seemed to be his regular self, joking around and trying to be cool."[29]

The "joking around" was easy for Taylor, especially while being crammed into the back seat of the family's rented Rover sedan with his two older siblings. When he and Donald Jr. were not trading lines from Will Ferrell movies, Taylor kept the family in stitches with his wisecracks. Once, en route to a castle, he turned and looked at Mackenzie, who was scrunched beside him, and said, "Boy, you is UG-G-G-L-Y!" Everyone broke up, except for Mackenzie, who retorted, "If I'm ugly, you're ugly, too, because we look exactly alike!"

On another occasion, Taylor's efforts at "being cool" backfired when the family decided to go swimming at a local beach. While they were setting up a blanket and umbrella, the boys discovered that many of the female sunbathers were going topless. Of course, Taylor took special note of two well-endowed—and bare-breasted—co-eds nearby. Mustering the courage to get a better look through his sunglasses, he coaxed Donald Jr. into taking a stroll in their direction. Just as the two brothers got within striking distance, Taylor, doing his best to act cool, lost his footing in an inconspicuous hole someone had dug. Much to the amusement of his family and the two topless girls, he fell head first and ended up with a face full of sand. It was such an uproarious mishap that just the thought of the episode evoked laughter for the remainder of the trip.[30]

Yet when Gwen looked back in later years, she recognized that there were also signs of Taylor's worsening depression and even indications that he may have been contemplating suicide. Near the end of the vacation, for example, Don Sr.'s obsession with picture taking had become so tiresome

Taylor viewed his dad as a disciplinarian, but he also had a special love for him that is evident in this photo taken in the summer of 2003. *(By Cindy Fox. Courtesy of Taylor Hooton Foundation.)*

that the family refused to accompany him on any excursion, realizing that they would have to pose for more photographs—that is, every member of the family except Taylor. When Don Sr. asked whether anyone wanted to "go take pictures," Taylor would pipe up, "Okay, c'mon, Pop, I'll go and take pictures with you."[31] It was as if he were saying, "I know how important this is to you, Dad, and I want to show you that I love you, so I'll go. I want to show you that whatever happens, I'll always love you. That's the way I want you to remember me."

During the last few days of the vacation, Taylor also had a tattoo of a crucifix etched onto his back. Located on the right shoulder blade, the tattoo read, "Only God Can Hold Me Now."[32] Only Taylor knew the true meaning of that phrase and his reason for having it tattooed, but the way he had lived his life offered some pretty good clues. He had always been religious, a genuinely good human being who wanted to do right by others, by his family, and by God. He had dedicated his life to Jesus Christ at the age of 14 and had renewed his commitment in the waters off the Florida shoreline two years later during summer Bible camp. The tattoo may very well have symbolized an outward sign of the deep and abiding spiritual relationship he had with his God. Perhaps Taylor also suspected that he was fighting a losing battle with steroids. Whatever the case, he kept the tattoo a secret from his parents, sharing it only with his brother and Parker.

Doping had become an addiction. He was already planning his next purchase. In London, he stole a laptop and two digital cameras from the hotel, intending to pawn the items when he returned stateside so he could buy another eight-week supply of anabolic steroids.[33] He could not help himself. Nor could he control the intense mood swings that were distancing him from those he loved most—his parents, his siblings, and Parker. Only God could help him, and he knew it.

Then there was the letter he wrote to Parker on the plane ride home from England. He had learned from a mutual friend that she was "seeing someone else."[34] Whether that meant she had moved on from Taylor, unable to deal with his erratic behavior, or that she was simply spending time with another male friend is unclear. What is certain, however, is that Taylor was struggling with a wide range of feelings over her. He was desperate to hold on to her, jealous of her other male friendships, and remorseful over the altercation with her ex-boyfriend:

> Hey Baby!! How are you? I'm OK. I'm about one hour into the flight home and figured I'd write you a note. Can't wait to see you. It's been too long . . . and I was thinkin' about you every step of the way.
>
> It's weird how almost everything reminded me of you. Last night (morning for you) [it] really hit me to know how much I missed you when we talked on the phone. I felt like I wanted to cry, sad enough to say. I didn't mean to sound jealous, but you know how I am. I trust you. I just got scared b/c you'd been hanging out with [a mutual male friend] a lot, but I know you're still my girl. Always will be. I wasn't threatening to kick his ass, just being protective. (You know me). . . .
>
> I got a tattoo in London. I made it myself, and I think it's cool. My bro said it was "badass," lol, but knowing you, you won't like it. . . . [I]t didn't hurt too bad. I kinda get a kick out of physical pain. . . .
>
> I love you with my whole heart, Emily Christine Parker!!
> Always,
> Tay[35]

Taylor also wrote a poem that offers some insight into his mental state the day before he took his life. The sonnet underscores his infatuation with Parker, including numerous professions of love. More telling, however, is Taylor's emphasis on the *long-term* commitment he has to Parker and the assumption that she shares that same commitment:

> This poem was written to and for the one I love,
> The girl in which all my dreams are made of.
> The one who has truly filled that empty space in my life,
> And the one who is soon to be my future wife.

I am so in love with you, and to you I give my heart,
And if the day came that we were ever to split, it would surely be
    ripped apart.
When I am close to you, no other can compete,
Your breath is so soft, and your voice so sweet.

Beyond the gems in your eyes, I can see your shining soul,
Which is a part of you that makes me feel whole.
A day without you is like a day without air,
And to not be with you seems so unfair.

When I look into your eyes, I see a glance of hope,
Reassurance that you're the one for me, and the one [with] whom
    I'll elope.
Your name to me even means something great,
Each letter meaning something which surely does translate.

E stands for eternity, the time you'll spend with me,
M is for model, which shows me your stunning beauty.
I stands for impossible, which is the chance of us being apart,
L is for the love we share, what fills the center of my heart.
Y stands for the years we will happily spend together
And "us" is a term that will surely be used forever.

You are the only girl who has successfully won me over,
I thought I was a brick wall, but I must be a four-leafed
    clover.
Because I am the luckiest man on the face of this earth,
You indeed were made for me since the very day of your birth.

If someone were to ask me, "How much do you love her?"
"More than words can express," would surely be my answer.
God answered my prayers that night I wished upon a star,
And it was definitely the best dream come true by far.

The night I asked and wished for someone to fill that hole,
You [came] just in the nick of time and captured my soul.
I love you with my whole heart and definitely always will,
A kiss from you is such an unexplainable thrill.

Until the day I die, my heart will eternally be yours,
For every other girl, I've already closed the doors.
I truly love you Emily, and forever you'll be mine,
Forever and always, until the end of time.

I LOVE YOU![36]

The poem reflects a sensitivity that is rare among adolescent males. Taylor was, at heart, a romantic who could express his feelings in a creative and articulate manner. What distinguishes the poem, though, is the passion that informs it. His professed love for Parker is so strong that he views it as the result of God having "answered [his] prayers," a love that "fills the center of [his] heart," making him "feel whole."

On the other hand, Taylor's admission of a personal dependency on Parker is dangerous at a time when he was struggling to find emotional and mental stability in his life. His seemingly confident assumption that he would eventually marry Parker contradicts the insecurity he expresses over the possibility of a breakup with her—something that he says would result in his heart being "ripped apart." Taylor also rules out any alternative for a meaningful relationship with another female, as he reveals in the line "For every other girl, I've already closed the doors." What is so troubling is the contradiction in the final stanza of the poem, which begins, "Until the day I die, my heart will eternally be yours." To be sure, there is no limit to eternal love: it goes beyond the grave or, as Taylor writes in the last line of the stanza, "forever and always, until the end of time." It begs this question: Is Taylor's assurance of eternal love for Parker a veiled message that he plans to take his life?

Such remarks go well beyond typical teenage romanticism when they are written by someone dealing with a chemical and hormonal imbalance brought on by steroid use. If Parker was, in fact, considering a breakup, that could push Taylor over the edge. Only two people know whether that was the case; one of them is dead, and the other declined to be interviewed for this book.

Regardless, Gwen Hooton has decided that all the "missed signals" added up to one inescapable conclusion. "I think Taylor knew he was going to take his life," she conceded. "I think he knew after he did that, all his troubles would be gone. He'd be with Jesus, and that God was going to take care of him."[37]

On July 14, before the Hootons left London, Donald Jr. told his father that Taylor had stolen the laptop and digital cameras. Because he was flying back to Philadelphia, while the rest of the family was going to fly into Dallas, he wanted to give his parents a heads-up so they would not be detained by customs officials. Fortunately, Taylor cleared customs.[38] But when the family got home, Don and Gwen, at the urging of Dr. Farkas, confronted their son. The family intervention took place around the kitchen table. Mackenzie, invited to join, sat next to Taylor.

"Did you steal a laptop and two cameras when we were in England?" Don asked, cutting to the chase.

When Taylor denied it, Don asked about the tattoo. Again, he refused to admit that he had had any body art done. So Don demanded that his son remove the wool sweater he was wearing so he could examine his back. Once again, Taylor refused.

"I can't believe you," Mackenzie said, disgusted by her brother's act. "You are lying through your teeth. Dude, you can't just take something you want without paying for it. That's just wrong!"

Realizing that he had been caught, Taylor confessed.

"What were you going to do with the laptop and the cameras?" asked Don, intent on getting the whole truth.

"I was going to sell the stuff to get a nasty stereo for my pickup," he replied, hoping to deflect the conversation away from his true intention of buying more steroids.

Don realized that he was pressing his luck if he thought he was going to get the truth from his son. What's more, the discussion had become too painful for Gwen, and he did not see any purpose in prolonging it.

"Okay," he said abruptly. "Your behavior has become unacceptable to this family. We just can't tolerate stealing. You are grounded for the next two weeks. Give me the keys to the pickup and your cellphone."

Taylor was stunned. He had just gotten back home and desperately wanted to be with Parker. But there was no use in appealing the decision, as his father had already walked out of the room. So he turned to his mother.

"Please, Momma!" he begged. "Please don't ground me. I hate myself for this. I am really sorry and I really hope that y'all can forgive me. I will do anything, I mean ANYTHING, not to be grounded. I will mow the yard, clean the house, walk the dogs ten times a day. Anything, Mom, anything."

Gwen sat across the table, tears streaming down her face. Her heart was breaking with each and every word, but she had to remain firm. Although she largely refused to give in to her son's pleas, Gwen did allow him to visit Parker so he could give her the presents he bought in England and tell her of his punishment. It would be inhumane not to allow such a small conces-sion. She also knew that if she refused to allow him the visit, he would just wait until everyone fell asleep and sneak off to see Parker anyway.[39]

Mackenzie offered to drive her younger brother over to Parker's. She saw how upset he was and felt horrible for the way she had confronted him during the intervention. Again, her protective instincts took over. En route to the Parkers' house, she attempted to have a heart-to-heart talk with Taylor.

"Dude," she began. "You're going to get through this, I know you will. It's just a bump in the road. One day, you'll look back on this and say it was nothing."

Taylor remained silent. There was nothing to say as far as he was con-cerned.

"Look, I'm sorry for what I said at the table," she continued. "But you know me. I've always looked out for you. I can't help it."

There was no response.

If Mackenzie was hoping for forgiveness, she was sorely disappointed. Her heart-to-heart had become a monologue. Frustrated, she was silent for the rest of the drive.[40]

When they arrived at the Parkers' home, Mackenzie remained in the car while Taylor sat with his girlfriend on the front porch and told her everything: that he had stolen a laptop and two cameras, that he had con-fessed, and that he would not be seeing her for the next two weeks because he had been grounded. He also gave Parker the gifts he had purchased for her in England—a teddy bear, a key chain, T-shirts—as well as the letter and poem he had written for her on the flight home. Aside from his confession, Taylor was mostly quiet when he was not crying. Parker had become used to the melodrama by now. If she was considering a breakup, this was *not* the time to do it—that would be heartless. Instead, she told Taylor that he had been grounded before and that everything would be all right.[41]

Forty minutes later, Taylor got into his sister's car and returned home to begin serving his punishment. It would be the last time he saw his girlfriend.

Taylor Hooton's desperate behavior suggests that he had an addiction to APEDs. Body builders recognize the "potential for addiction with ste-roid use" that can be "both physical and psychological in nature." Physical addiction occurs when the drug alters the body's chemistry to the extent that the user cannot function properly without it. Thus, the body's normal state becomes the "drug state." Psychological addiction or dependence occurs when the user experiences an intense craving for the drug and believes that he or she cannot survive without it. Closely related to addiction is the issue of tolerance. Once the body grows accustomed to a certain dosage of drugs, including steroids, the user must take ever-increasing dosages to achieve the same effect. If the user stops, he or she will experience withdrawal symptoms, which may include depression, intense irritation, hallucinations, sleeping disorders, and fatigue.[42]

Although the medical profession contends that APEDs are not addictive, several studies suggest otherwise. As early as 1989, the *Journal of the American Medical Association* reported one study involving a 24-year-old male weight lifter who exhibited several criteria for drug dependence, including continued use of steroids for longer than planned, unsuccessful attempts to taper off the drug, continued use despite negative effects on his social life, a developed tolerance to the drug, withdrawal symptoms after stopping usage, and continued use of steroids to avoid withdrawal symptoms.[43] A 2001 study revealed that a subgroup of individuals who practiced sports intensely and made use of both addictive drugs and PEDs appeared to be at increased risk for developing a dependence.[44] A 2013 study conducted by the Biological Psychiatry Laboratory at Harvard Medical School suggested a surprisingly high prevalence of anabolic-androgenic steroid (AAS) use and dependence among Americans. Based on data from American surveys of school and youth populations, the study used mathematical models to estimate the lifetime prevalence of AAS use. The analysis estimated that 2.9 to 4 million Americans have used AAS at some time in their lives.[45] What is important to note is that the study took into account the fact that anonymous surveys of American high school students almost always overestimate the prevalence of AAS use. Students erroneously answer that they have used "steroids" when they have actually used corticosteroids rather than AAS or have used over-the-counter supplements that they incorrectly believe are steroids.[46] The same study sought to estimate the number of Americans who had experienced AAS dependence. To do so, the investigators combined the data from 10 studies that collectively diagnosed AAS dependence in 1,248 AAS users.[47] The analysis yielded an estimate that 32.5 percent of users developed AAS dependence. Applying this proportion to the above estimates of the overall American AAS-using population, the researchers hypothesized "that in the U.S. alone, about 1 million men have experienced AAS dependence at some time."[48]

Still another study, conducted by Harvard psychiatrist Harrison Pope, explored the reasons for AAS dependence. "AAS, unlike conventional drugs of abuse, may induce dependence via at least three separate pathways—the *anabolic, androgenic,* and *hedonic*," he explained.[49] First, users obsessed with "body image" who believe that they are not adequately muscular may become dependent on AAS for the *anabolic* effect of building muscle. These individuals often become extremely anxious if they stop cycling and lose even a little muscular size. When this happens, they resume their use, which contributes to the AAS dependence syndrome. Second, users who experience "hypogonadism" (the functional incompetence of the testes with an inability to produce testosterone or sperm) during withdrawal may become dependent on AAS for the *androgenic* effect of stimulating greater sexual performance. Although illicit AAS users often take Viagra to minimize this effect, many still experience profound hypogonadism for weeks or months after discontinuing use. The associated symptoms of fatigue, loss of libido, and depression may prompt some to quickly resume their AAS use. Third, users who mix steroids with other addictive drugs, especially opiates, may experience *hedonic* effects, which promote dependence. Unlike most addictive drugs, which typically deliver an immediate "reward" of intoxication, AAS produce few intoxicating effects and are instead taken primarily for the delayed reward of increased muscle mass and decreased body fat. But the combination of steroids and addictive drugs may lead the user to believe that the steroids also produce an intoxicating effect, increasing the desire to resume use.[50] Taylor exhibited at least two—anabolic and androgenic—of the three dependencies.

The morning of Tuesday, July 15, was bright, sunny, and swelteringly hot—typical summer weather in the Lone Star state. Taylor Hooton woke up around 9:30 A.M. but remained in bed, thinking of ways to be excused from the two-week grounding imposed on him the night before. His mother, Gwen, was downstairs, unpacking from the family's two-week vacation in England and waiting for her daughter, Mackenzie, to arrive. They planned to retrieve the family's two dogs from the kennel where they had been housed during the vacation. Don, her husband, had left for work two hours earlier.

At about 10:00 A.M., Taylor came downstairs and cozied up next to his mother on the family room sofa. He was ready to put his game plan into action.

"Momma, please forgive me," he began. "I really feel terrible about the stealing, and I promise never to do it again."

Gwen was very familiar with the routine. Her son would butter her up by asking for forgiveness and then play on her conscience to get what he wanted. Fully expecting Taylor to ask for his freedom, Gwen was not going to give in this time—he had gone too far. Stealing was just plain unacceptable in the Hooton family. Besides, what would she be teaching her son if she failed to make him accountable for his actions? Nope, not this time. She had already granted the concession to visit his girlfriend the night before. That was as much as her conscience would allow.

"Momma, can Tommy still come visit next week?" he asked, sheepishly.

The request took Gwen by surprise. She had forgotten that Tommy Odea, Taylor's good friend and former next-door neighbor, had been invited to visit the next week. Although the Odeas had moved to Kansas City two years earlier, the boys remained close and visited each other over the summers. Still, Gwen was unmoved by the plea.

"No, Taylor," she replied. "We'll have to phone Tommy and tell him that he can't come."

Stunned, he asked, "You mean, you really aren't going to let him visit?"

"No," repeated Gwen, firmly.

"Then I guess I'd be wasting my time if I asked if you'd unground me," he muttered.

Gwen's heart was breaking. She wanted to forgive but could not. Instead, she forced herself to assume the uncomfortable role of disciplinarian, which had always been Don's job.

"You'll have to wait until Pop comes home this afternoon," she replied. "We can talk about it then."

Taylor finally realized that he had gone too far. He could accept the grounding from his father. He expected it. Fathers are to be both feared and loved by their sons as a matter of respect. Taylor knew that his father would never lift the punishment. But his mother? She was his soul mate, the one person he loved and trusted above all, the *only* person who truly understood him. She had forgiven him countless times before, but not this time. This time, he had disappointed the one person who loved him most. The guilt must have been unbearable.

Devastated, Taylor looked at his mother with puppy-dog eyes, took her hand in his, and squeezed it. It was their special way of saying, "I love you." Then, he picked himself up and returned to his bedroom.[51]

No one knows for certain what Taylor did during the next few minutes. Perhaps he took a long hard look in the dresser mirror. For months, he had been taking stock of his life, reflecting on the person he had become. There must have been times when he loved what he saw in that mirror—the ripped body with the impressive biceps, the handsome smile, and the movie-star good looks. But considering the emotional roller coaster he had been riding since the late spring, there must have been other times when he despised the monster he had created.

Juicing had robbed him of his honesty, his humility, his carefree spirit, his compassion for others, and now, it seemed, his will to live. If he did, in fact, take a look in that bedroom mirror, he may have believed that the Taylor who stared back was an egocentric bully. That Taylor lied to those who loved him most, stole to get what he wanted, and thought of only himself, even at the expense of others. He might well have thought about the phrase "Only God Can Hold Me Now" that he had recently had tattooed on his back—and how prophetic it seemed.

No one knows what goes through the mind of a person before he or she decides to commit suicide, but the desperation to be relieved of suffering must be overwhelming. By all accounts, Taylor had reached the breaking point. Only God could hold him now.

What is known is that Taylor took a pair of scissors and cut himself out of a group photograph of him, Parker, Gomez, and Gomez's girlfriend. He also wrote a brief note to his family that read, "I love you guys. I'm sorry about everything." Then he repositioned the dresser mirror so it faced his bedroom door. Rifling through his closet, he found two belts and tied one around the doorknob. He attached the two belts together, threw the slack over the door frame, and fashioned a noose at the other end. Taking one last look in the mirror, Taylor Hooton, just 17 and with so much to live for, placed the noose around his neck and jumped. The weight of his body caused the door to crash into the wall with a loud bang.[52]

Downstairs, Gwen heard the noise but quickly dismissed it. "Taylor probably dropped something," she thought. Unfazed, she continued unpacking while waiting for her daughter to arrive.

At about 11:00 A.M., Mackenzie phoned to ask whether her mother wanted some lunch from a local sandwich shop. Standing in the kitchen, Gwen opened the refrigerator to see whether there was an alternative. Realizing that there was not, she placed her order.

"What about Taylor?" Mackenzie asked. "What does he want?"

"Hold on, I'll ask," replied Gwen.

"Taylor!"

There was no response. Perhaps jet lag had finally set in and he had gone back to sleep.

"Hold on a minute," she told her daughter, as she headed upstairs, phone in hand.

When she reached the top step, Gwen was horrified to find her son with a belt fastened around his neck, hanging from his bedroom door.

"Oh my God!" she shrieked into the receiver. "Mackenzie, get here quick!"

Dropping the phone, Gwen rushed to loosen the belt from her son's neck. Grabbing him from the waist, she managed to unfasten the make-shift noose as her son's limp body fell to the floor. His hands were blue, his body pale.

Gwen picked up the phone, called 911, and somehow managed to describe the nightmare that was unfolding before her. She was instruc-ted to begin cardiopulmonary resuscitation (CPR) immediately and to keep the line open for further instructions until the paramedics ar-rived.

Sobbing uncontrollably, Gwen did as she was told. She pleaded with God to save her son as she pumped his chest and forced deep breaths into his mouth. But the only air in Taylor's lungs was her own, which caused the body to make a soft gurgling sound.[53]

Meanwhile, Mackenzie, alarmed and confused by her mother's sudden outburst, pulled over on the side of the road and tried to call her father. There was no answer. Screeching back onto the road, Mackenzie contin-ued to push the redial button until Don finally answered.

"Dad, you have to get home RIGHT NOW!" she screamed. "Something's happened with Taylor!"

When Mackenzie neared the house, she saw an ambulance and rescue squad van in the driveway and a police car with flashing lights parked next to the curb. Her father's car was parked behind it.

Rushing into the house, Mackenzie found her parents in the down-stairs hallway. Don, tears streaming down his face, was trying to comfort his wife, who was barely able to control her emotions. Gwen had yielded to the paramedics, who continued to perform CPR upstairs in Taylor's bed-room.

"What did he do?" Mackenzie demanded, fearing the worst.

Told that her younger brother had hanged himself, she fell to the floor, grief-stricken.

The paramedics placed an oxygen mask around Taylor's face, strapped his body to a stretcher, and carried him out to the ambulance. Appar-ently they still had hopes that the teen would survive, because they took a change of clothes for him with them.

Taylor was rushed to Presbyterian Hospital, where his parents and sister sat helplessly in a waiting room, praying for a miracle. Deep down, they knew they were on a death watch. They did not have to wait long.

About twenty minutes after their arrival, a social worker approached them with the tragic news: Taylor was dead. The official ruling was "death by suicide."[54]

Offered the opportunity to view the body, Don and Gwen followed her into the trauma room. But Mackenzie could not bring herself to view her baby brother's lifeless body. She just did not want to remember him that way. After composing herself, she phoned Donald Jr. in Philadelphia and delivered the horrific news.[55]

Inside the trauma room, Taylor's corpse lay on a hospital gurney, covered to the waist in a white sheet. "My precious baby boy looked like he was sleeping," recalled Gwen. "But I knew he'd never wake up again. I would never hear his laugh or funny jokes or see that wonderful smile of his again."[56]

The Hootons kissed their son good-bye and returned home to prepare for the funeral.

7

USC'S BASEBALL "FAMILY"

In January 2000, the Garibaldis made the six-hour drive to the University of Southern California (USC), where Rob would begin his sophomore year. The family was greeted by two members of the Trojans' recruiting staff, who guided them to the apartment that Rob would be sharing with one of his new teammates, Rick Hellend, a back-up catcher.

The drive from Petaluma was not easy for Ray or Denise. Los Angeles seemed as though it were on the other side of the world, and Rob had never lived that far away from home before. SRJC was a commuter school, and even when he had attended CSM, he had lived with an uncle. Rob had led a sheltered life, never being far from family or the protective eye of his parents. USC was going to be a huge change for everyone. Ray would not be able to attend every one of Rob's games, as he had done in the past. Nor would he ever get to know any of his son's coaches or teammates with the same intimacy that he had with those in high school and junior college. It was not going to be easy for Ray, whose social life over the years had come to revolve around Rob's baseball teams. Denise had larger concerns. She worried that her son would be overwhelmed because of his attention deficit disorder and dyslexia. How would he be able to manage a full course load given the demands of playing a Division I sport? Although John Savage, the recruiting coordinator, had assured her that other members of the baseball team also struggled with learning disabilities and managed to balance their academic and athletic commitments just fine, she believed that her son was different. From the time he had started school,

The Garibaldi family is shown here in 1999. *Left to right:* Rob, Ray, Denise, and Raymond. *(Courtesy of the Garibaldi Family.)*

Denise had been his homework monitor and one of his tutors. She made sure to communicate on a regular basis with his teachers and to familiarize herself with his course work and textbooks. When he matriculated to junior college, Denise reviewed and corrected all of Rob's assignments before he handed them in. Perhaps she was just now beginning to realize how sheltered Rob had been.

Despite their concerns, Ray and Denise did their best to be optimistic. They were certainly excited about Rob's future. USC represented the realization of a dream or, as Rob viewed it, the "first step on the journey to a career in Major League Baseball." Still, their noticeable anxiety gave them away. Before they left, they dropped Rob off at the baseball field for a 4:00 P.M. practice. As Denise gave her son a hug good-bye, she started to tear up. Savage could see that the Garibaldis were lingering. He knew how difficult the experience was for parents, having witnessed it so many times before. Hoping to lessen the heartache, he made his way over to Denise and Ray. "Mr. and Mrs. Garibaldi," said the assistant coach in a polite but firm voice, "don't worry about Rob anymore. We're his family now. We'll take care of him."[1] The couple desperately hung their hopes on that promise. Rob was now part of the USC baseball "family," and by all accounts, it was a family with a hugely impressive lineage.

USC's baseball program has been compared to that of the New York Yankees, the most storied and successful franchise in MLB. Established in 1888, the USC baseball team, a member of the highly competitive Pacific-12 Conference, is by far the most dominant in the history of college baseball. No other Division I school has won as many national championships as the twelve the Trojans captured between 1948 and 1998. A proving ground for professional baseball, USC has produced dozens of major leaguers, including Fred Lynn, Mark McGwire, Roy Smalley, and Barry Zito. Most of the program's success is due to Rod Dedeaux, who coached from 1942 to 1986 and led the Trojans to eleven of their twelve College World Series titles. In 1987, the future of that rich tradition was handed off to Mike Gillespie.[2]

Gillespie was a worthy successor to Dedeaux. He was one of only two individuals to both play for and coach an NCAA-championship baseball team. Gillespie was Dedeaux's starting left fielder on the 1961 College World Series champions, and he coached the Trojans to the 1998 national title.[3] Prior to his arrival at USC, Gillespie was the head baseball coach at the College of the Canyons, a Division II program he built from scratch. Over a sixteen-year tenure, he compiled a 420–167 win-loss record (.716) and won eleven Mountain Valley Conference Championships, including six straight from 1981–1986. Gillespie also captured three California state titles during that period. His success was so impressive that USC hired him to succeed Dedeaux in 1987.

Intelligent, ambitious, and determined to return his alma mater to baseball glory, in just his second year, Gillespie guided the Trojans to the West Regional, where USC fell just one game short of a return to Omaha, Nebraska, home of the College World Series. Gillespie's teams made the postseason every year for the next decade, including two appearances in the College World Series (1995, 1998) and winning the national title in 1998. He was also named National Coach of the Year by *College Baseball* and the American Baseball Coaches Association that same year.[4]

After a disappointing 1999 season, in which the Trojans went 36–26 (.581), Gillespie was desperate to find players who could compete for another national title. "Winning," after all, is the only objective in major Division I baseball programs and the only way a head coach keeps his job. That fact was not lost on Gillespie. He relied on Savage to find players who would restore the Trojans' dominance, and Savage did just that. In 1999–2000, he put together what *College Baseball* ranked as the top recruiting class in Division I.[5] Expectations were great for those who accepted a scholarship and even greater for the select few who received a full ride. Rob Garibaldi inherited such a glorious burden.

USC began the 2000 season on a hot streak, winning five of its first six games.[6] Rob, the starting right fielder who hit either sixth or seventh, was batting .333 with 2 RBI and 2 doubles.[7] Then he made his first error of the season. On Friday, February 11, the Trojans played Texas Tech at Lubbock. The game was a scoreless tie through three innings. In the fourth, USC took a three-run lead on an RBI single by first baseman Bill Peavey and RBI doubles by Garibaldi and third baseman Justin Gemoll. The Trojans held the 3–0 lead going into the bottom of the ninth when the game unraveled.

Texas center fielder Marco Cunningham led off the inning and hit a lazy fly ball to right field. Rob circled under the ball for the catch, but it glanced off his glove for an error, allowing Cunningham to reach first base.[8] A lapse of concentration—taking his eye off the ball at the last minute instead of watching it into his glove—led to the error. Had Rob been hustling after a ball hit in the gap, the error would probably have been overlooked by his coach, but there was no excuse for what was essentially a mental error. Gillespie was understandably livid. "Are you on drugs, Baldi!?" he screamed at the top of his lungs.[9]

The error ignited a four-run rally that ended with a bases-loaded walk by the Trojans' sophomore pitcher, Mark Prior. Texas won the game, 4–3.[10]

Committing the error was bad enough, but Rob just could not let go of Gillespie's insulting remark. "I've been hustling and playing hard every day," he wrote eleven days later, in a February 22 journal entry:

> But I'm making way too many stupid mistakes. . . . I haven't felt this way since my sophomore year of high school. For me, to play well, I have to play relaxed, with a clean head. But the coaches here are telling me so many different things. I know I'm not a head case. To me, drugs are an excuse to be lazy, a way of escaping whatever a person can't deal with on their own. I don't do drugs. What gets me so mad is that I'm not helping the team win, and it's because I always expect to play perfect every time I step onto the field. I just need to get on the same page as Coach Gillespie.[11]

What's so revealing is that Rob took Gillespie's remark about drugs not only personally but literally as well. He actually believed that he had to defend himself, writing, "I don't do drugs." The entry also reflects his angst over his inability to "play relaxed" and being "told so many different things by the coaches," who were trying to change his hitting mechanics. Interestingly, Rob assumed the burden of responsibility for his poor performance; he did not blame Gillespie or the other coaches. Instead, he insisted that he "need[ed] to get on the same page." It did not take long.

On February 22, the same day he wrote the above journal entry, Rob hit his first home run as a Trojan. It was a three-run shot to right center that came in the first inning of a nonleague game against the University of San Diego at USC's Dedeaux Field. Rob also hit a run-scoring double in the fifth to go 3-for-4 in the game. He was responsible for four of the Trojans' seven runs in the 7–3 victory, helping spot starter Mark Prior to his second win of the season.[12]

By mid-March, Rob had regained his confidence. With the Trojans boasting a 14–8 record, he was batting .320, and Gillespie moved him up to the second slot in the batting order due to his ability to reach base consistently.[13] But Rob still felt the sting of his earlier insult. "I will never forget that day," he wrote in a March 15 journal entry. "I know Coach G. yells for a reason. But I wore it like a man, and I never gave him an excuse. Nor will I ever give him an excuse."[14]

Things were not going as well academically. When he arrived at USC in January, Rob had just three weeks to acclimate to the school before baseball season began. Predictably, he was anxious and confused about his classes as well as his course load. Four weeks into the semester, Rob phoned home and asked his mother, "Am I supposed to be taking Russian literature?"

Astonished by the question, Denise asked whether he was joking.

"No," replied Rob. "They have me in Russian literature, and I'm failing. There's no way I can pass this class."

The very next day, Denise phoned Savage and informed him of the problem. Savage agreed that Rob should not have been taking Russian literature and had him drop the class and sign up for a guitar course.

"It was just crazy," recalled Denise years later. "All of the classes were difficult for Rob. He really needed much more support from Educational Resources that first semester at USC."[15] Denise, a licensed psychologist in private practice, had been impressed with the Office of Disability Services and Programs (DSP) when she visited earlier in the year. But she was still unclear about its coordination with the Student-Athlete Academic Services (SAAS). Naturally, Rob's learning disability and his status as a baseball recruit made it necessary for him to receive help from both departments. As it turned out, SAAS was responsible for assisting Rob with course selection and course-related tutoring. On the other hand, his testing accommodations, books-on-tape, learning assistance, and academic-support counseling would be done by the DSP. Denise believed that SAAS was lax in its specific responsibilities as well as in its coordination with the DSP.[16]

When the baseball season began, Rob was even more desperate. The team either practiced or played seven days each week, and some of the away games were as distant as the Pacific Northwest. Such a demanding schedule left Rob with extremely limited time to study or to receive tutoring. Even worse, whenever Rob approached the baseball team's academic monitor about getting tutors, he was told that none were available. As the semester unfolded, he found himself falling farther and farther behind in his classes.[17] At spring break, Denise and Ray drove down to USC to watch Rob play, and she purchased copies of all his textbooks so she could monitor his studies. "I literally wrote Rob's papers for him via e-mail," she confessed. "I also tutored him over the phone, and he was still on academic probation at the end of the semester. I tried to protect him, and it was a mistake."[18] Completing her son's papers, which was a violation of the university's academic regulations, could have resulted in Rob's dismissal.

At mid-April, the Trojans were 26–16 and in the thick of a race for the Pac-10 baseball title. Rob had been instrumental in their success, too. Between March 14 and April 18, he was hitting at a torrid .392 pace with 15 RBI, 9 doubles, and 4 home runs. Rob had especially productive series against Stanford (5 hits, including 3 doubles, a home run, and 3 RBI) and Arizona State (5 hits, including 3 doubles and 4 RBI). Those performances came in the midst of a nine-game hitting streak.[19] On Tuesday, April 18, he hit his fifth homer of the season to seal a 6–2 victory over the no. 2 ranked UCLA Bruins. Rob was responsible for 3 of USC's 6 runs.[20] However, he struggled for the next two weeks, collecting just 5 hits in 26 at-bats with 5 strikeouts.[21] Never had Rob performed that poorly at any level of play. Gillespie dropped him to eighth in the batting order at one point. Some of his difficulty was due to loneliness.

What is known of Garibaldi's relationship with his teammates comes from his parents; from an interview Rick Hellend, a roommate, gave to the *Santa Rosa Press Democrat* in March 2004; and from Rob's own journal entries. Hellend gave mixed reviews, stating that Rob was a "great roommate" in 2000 but that in 2001, his behavior became "scary" and he "feared for [his] own life."[22] His parents did not know what to think, because they believed that Hellend and a later roommate, Anthony Reyes, had been very helpful to Rob in making the adjustment to USC. But they also heard more disturbing things from Rob about the other players.[23] According to one of Rob's journal entries, his teammates "weren't mixing with [him] at all." Instead, they teased him about his 5'11" height and his learning disability, often calling him "stupid." Rob interpreted the teasing as "malicious"—not the kind of repartee that occurs on most teams, which is meant to make the target feel part of the squad. Perhaps there was some jealousy, because Rob was only one of two team members with a full-ride baseball scholarship. Perhaps the other players interpreted Rob's introverted nature as "elitist," as if he thought he was better than they were. For whatever reason, the same people who were supposed to be his "family" were ostracizing him. To make friends, Rob wrote, he "went out to the bars with his teammates" and "got drunk" on a few occasions,[24] but even that did not improve his social situation.

Nevertheless, Rob persevered. For the remainder of the season, he enjoyed occasional performances that were outstanding. On April 29, for example, he hit his sixth homer and collected 4 RBI as the Trojans defeated Arizona State, 12–2.[25] Similarly, on May 13, he hit his seventh homer and picked up another 4 RBI as USC dispatched Oregon State, 16–7.[26] When the Trojans advanced to the West Regional at Fullerton, California, Rob collected another 3 hits and 4 RBI in a 13–5 blowout against Loyola Marymount. By that time, he had reclaimed the no. 2 slot in the batting order,[27] but his "roller-coaster" performance suggests that he was juicing. To be sure, hitters experience slumps, sometimes prolonged ones. However, one of Rob's strengths had been his consistency at the plate, and the power numbers Rob was producing during his hot streak were exceptional for him. Prior to mid-April, he was hitting .333 with just 5 extra base hits, including 1 home run in 71 plate appearances. But during his month-long hot streak, Rob increased his batting average by nearly 60 points to .392 and collected 15 extra base hits, including 4 home runs in 74 at-bats. After the hot streak ended, his average dropped by 94 points to .298, and he collected just 5 extra base hits in 89 plate appearances: 3 homers, a triple, and a double. It was a dramatic change for a player who hit for a high average and whose natural power limited him to doubles.

One of Rob's greatest thrills came on June 3 at the Super Regional College Tournament in Atlanta, Georgia, when USC played Georgia Tech to determine who would advance to the College World Series. Rob came to bat in the third inning with one out and a runner on first and slammed a 2–2 fastball over the right-field wall for a two-run homer. It was his 8th and final home run of the season, and it paced the Trojans to a 6–3 win.[28] Although USC was eliminated by Florida State, 3–2, in the third round of the College World Series, Gillespie had restored the Trojans' winning tradition. USC had gone deeper into the postseason than expected by the prognosticators, going 16–8 in the Pac-10 (44–20 overall).[29] Rob's performances

Rob is shown here on deck at the 2000 College World Series. That year, Rob played the outfield and batted .329 with 18 doubles, 8 home runs, and 44 RBI for the University of Southern California Trojans, who advanced to the College World Series. He also had a .401 on-base percentage and a .977 fielding average. The impressive performance caught the attention of *Baseball America*, which identified Rob as one of the Top 100 college players in the nation. *(Courtesy of Chris Parker.)*

were just as impressive. In 56 games that season, he batted .329 (fourth on the team) with 18 doubles, 8 home runs, 44 RBI, a .401 on-base percentage, and a .977 fielding percentage.[30] Those statistics made him an All-Pac-10 Honorable Mention and, more importantly, caught the attention of *Baseball America*, which identified Rob as one of the Top 100 college players in the nation.[31] Sadly, that season proved to be the capstone of Rob's baseball career and the beginning of the end of his dream to become a major leaguer.

After the College World Series, Ray Garibaldi received a phone call from Gillespie. According to Ray, Gillespie expressed disappointment in Rob's academic performance and warned that he was in danger of having his scholarship revoked. Ray became defensive, insisting that Gillespie's staff did not "do their job" in terms of monitoring Rob's academic needs.

Stunned by the remark, Gillespie did not know how to respond.

"Your coaches promised my wife and me that Rob would get the academic help he needed," Ray continued, the anger in his voice palpable. "We told them that Rob has dyslexia. They were supposed to arrange the proper tutoring, and they dropped the ball. Instead, my wife spent the semester tutoring him over the phone. So now he's in trouble, and you're partly to blame for it."

Gillespie allegedly admitted that he was not aware of Rob's learning difficulties. But Ray insisted, "John Savage, your recruiting coordinator, was aware of the problem, and still nothing was done about it."[32]

Shortly after the phone conversation, Denise wrote Gillespie a letter, reminding him of the baseball program's responsibilities to her son and of Rob's rights under the Americans with Disabilities Act that required the school to provide special educational services. Despite the letter, Rob was placed on academic probation.[33]

In an effort to restore his eligibility, Rob took courses at SRJC that summer instead of competing in the prestigious Cape Cod League in which he had been invited to play.[34] Coming off the high of the College World Series, he was depressed over the fact that he was not playing ball and that a girl he had been dating for almost a year had broken up with him. Denise suggested that Rob see Brent Cox, MD, a psychiatrist colleague of hers. Cox prescribed the antidepressant Effexor, unaware that Rob had already begun a ten-week cycle of Deca Durabolin, the most widespread and commonly used injectable steroid.[35]

Denise and Ray Garibaldi have admitted that they do not actually know when their son began to use steroids. After his death, they learned that he had purchased the drugs the summer after his graduation from high school. But if Rob planned to dope to improve his power hitting, there was no reason to do so after he decided not to play for CSM during the spring of 1998. In addition, his coaches at SRJC insisted that they "saw no sign of steroid use" when Rob played there the following spring. However, they did admit that he worked out in the weight room excessively and compiled 14 home runs and 77 RBI that season—exceptional statistics for a ballplayer whose power hitting had been limited to mostly doubles in high school. What is known is that Rob, after the 2000 College World Series, told his parents that the USC coaches wanted him to become "more of a power hitter in his junior year."[36] Looking back, Ray and Denise believe that is when Rob started his first cycle of steroids. "He might have experimented with the drug before," said Denise, "because we now know he purchased steroids the summer after he graduated from high school. But in terms of sustained use, that's when we think it began."[37]

The combination of steroids, the Effexor that Cox prescribed for depression, and the Provigil Rob had been prescribed earlier for his attention deficit disorder had a volatile effect. One evening, Denise returned home from work to discover that an antique chair she had treasured was shattered. When she asked Rob about it, he told her that he was "so angry," he "[had taken] a baseball bat to it." It was the first time Denise had ever seen the results of such intense anger from her son. "I just never knew he was capable of something like that," she said. "But at that point I didn't know it was steroids. Ray and I thought that Rob was bipolar. He was his normal self one moment, then exceedingly angry the next. I only found out later that it was the first of many rages we'd see in the future."[38]

Rob returned to USC for the fall 2000 semester. Before leaving home, he began another ten-week cycle of Deca Durabolin to ensure that he would impress the coaches with his power hitting during the fall season. Rob was also concerned because Savage, who had recruited him, had left USC to take his first head coaching job at the University of California, Irvine. Savage's departure complicated Rob's circumstances. He would have to prove himself to a new coaching assistant, and no one else in the baseball program was as familiar as Savage with his learning disability and special needs. Whether the former USC assistant had informed another member of the coaching staff of Rob's needs and how to monitor them is unknown.[39]

In October, Denise and Ray paid their son a visit. When they entered his apartment, they noticed that all the furniture in his bedroom was covered with blankets. Denise thought it was strange, because the dresser drawers were inaccessible. Because she did not want to put Rob on the defensive, she waited a day or so to raise the subject. Then, before returning to Petaluma, she sat him down to have a heart-to-heart. "So, what's going on with your furniture?" Denise asked.

Without saying a word, Rob got up and started ripping the blankets off his furniture. Virtually every piece had been destroyed, just as he had done to his mother's antique chair.

"I was just so mad, I took a baseball bat to my furniture," he admitted, embarrassed by the horrific sight.

Taken aback, Denise struggled to find the words to proceed.

"So, things aren't so good?" she finally asked.

"No," came the reply. Rob was noticeably uncomfortable now.

Over the next half hour, Denise drew him out. Rob told her that he was sleeping excessively and that he was concerned that the antidepressant he was taking "wasn't working very well." He also had thought he was "doing well" in all his classes, since the DSP had assigned him a counselor. She was meeting with him "on a daily basis" and "seemed to really care about him." But then he had learned that he had failed a mid-term exam.[40] Rob recorded what happened next in his journal:

> I walked into my apartment and my roommate starts bitching at me. I picked up the first bat I saw and swung as hard as I could, breaking all of my furniture. Then I broke a wood bat over my

knee. Tears started to fall, so I jumped on my bed and asked, "Why am I so stupid?" For once, I thought I was smart and look what happened? I'm just a failure. I'm also under a lot of pressure. If I don't get a 2.4 [G.P.A.] then I'm done with USC baseball.[41]

Depressed, struggling with self-esteem, and unable to control his anger, Rob was exhibiting many of the signs of steroid use.

According to Harrison Pope, a Harvard psychiatrist with expertise in steroids research, 'roid rage is a physical manifestation of a user's irritability, aggressiveness, and sometimes violence, along with a disregard for the consequences of his or her behavior. It often occurs when the user is going through withdrawal, particularly when he or she abruptly stops using rather than lowering the dosage in the final weeks. Among the symptoms are depression, excessive sleeping, disinterest, and, in extreme cases, suicidal behavior.[42] If Rob began his ten-week cycle of Deca Durabolin in early August, he might well have been experiencing withdrawal by mid-October, when he destroyed his apartment furniture with a bat. And the withdrawal symptoms continued.

About a week after his parents' visit, Rob slept through a practice session. When he woke up, one of the assistant coaches was standing over him, asking why he had never shown up. "I was scared to death," Rob wrote in a December 12, 2000 journal entry. "I didn't understand what the hell was going on. Then I was told that Coach Gillespie wanted to see me, and it only got worse. He threatened to kick me off the team."[43] Then Gillespie phoned Ray to inform him of the offense. Ray could not understand it. "Rob was always the first one to practice for as long as I can remember," he said, "and he'd *never* miss a practice. The only thing I could think of was that he couldn't stay awake because of the combination of studying well into the morning hours and the antidepressant he was prescribed."[44]

Although Gillespie was disturbed by the incident, he did not discipline Rob at the time. It is also unknown whether he or any of his assistant coaches attempted to find out why Rob slept through the practice session.[45] In addition, Dr. Edward Roth, the director of USC's DSP, has indicated that there is "no existing record on Garibaldi," because "disability documentation is not maintained longer than seven years."[46] Similarly, the university's SAAS has proven unhelpful, because no one currently affiliated with SAAS was on staff in 2000 and 2001 when Rob played for the Trojans.[47]

Whatever the case might have been, no disciplinary action was taken against Rob. In fact, at the start of the 2001 baseball season, Gillespie praised his right fielder. In an interview for the USC Trojans' Baseball website, he remarked, "Rob is a returning starter who looks to be a key and outstanding player for us. He had a very good season last year and should be a premier college player and an outstanding hitter this season. He's one of the reasons we'll be good this year."[48] Instead, Rob's situation continued to deteriorate during the spring of 2001.

Still doping, Garibaldi was hitting for power through the first ten games of the season, with 2 doubles, a homer, and 8 RBI. But his average was just .277, extremely low for him. And he was not getting on base as consistently as he had in the past.[49] Prior to the final game of a three-game series against UCLA on February 18, Gillespie dropped him from second to eighth in the batting order. It was a cold day, in the high 30s, and Rob, playing right field, made a throw to home to nail a Bruins' base runner in the bottom of the ninth to preserve a 5–4 Trojan victory.[50] "You could see that he hurt his arm as soon as he threw that ball," recalled Ray, who had driven from Petaluma to see the UCLA series. "Turns out that Rob damaged a nerve in his left forearm, and he couldn't throw without pretty severe pain after that."[51] He did not play at all in the next game, a 9–1 drubbing at the hands of Loyola Marymount.[52] When Rob returned to the lineup on Wednesday, February 21, it was as a designated hitter. For the next five games, Gillespie rotated seniors Abel Montanez and Josh Self and freshman Jonathon Brewster in right field.[53] Even when Rob returned to the outfield, his arm had not fully recovered.

In early March, Ray drove to Palo Alto to watch USC play Stanford. As the Trojans ran onto the field to do the pregame warm-up, he noticed that Rob was nowhere to be found. Then, in the bottom of the first, he saw his son run out to right field to take his position. After the game, a 2–0 loss, Ray asked why he had not taken the pregame infield-outfield. Rob replied, "I was told to skip [infield-outfield] to save my arm and not to let loose on any throws unless I absolutely needed to. They wanted my bat in the game, and there was nowhere else to play me."[54] The arrangement continued for the next month until Rob's left arm started feeling better.

Throughout the early spring, Rob was on edge. He was not performing up to his expectations in the classroom or on the playing field, and he was worried about losing his scholarship. Unbeknownst to anyone, Rob was also mixing several drugs. In addition to cycling Deca, he was taking the antidepressant Effexor and Provigil, another prescription medication for attention deficit disorder. He had also started smoking marijuana and drinking more frequently to relax.[55] Then, the bottom fell out.

On Sunday, April 1, Rob's grandfather, Ben Garibaldi, passed away.

The following morning, when Rob informed Gillespie that he needed to return home for a day or two to attend the funeral, the coach became agitated. According to Ray, the coach immediately phoned and asked whether Rob's grandfather had really passed away. When Ray confirmed the news, Gillespie allegedly insisted that the team needed Rob and that he really could not miss the time. Ray interpreted the response as a "hard, cold challenge." "There was no expression of sympathy for our family's loss, just a callous statement of his position," recalled Garibaldi. "The implication was clear: Rob was being *paid* to play for USC. His remuneration was his scholarship, and the commitment was absolute. There were no exceptions made for *any* player to miss a game or a practice during the season, especially for those on a full ride." Ray also stated that a year earlier, Rob had missed his brother's wedding because USC was playing on the same day. So he knew that he had to tread lightly with Gillespie.

"Coach, I'm trying to work the funeral around your practice and game schedule," he explained. "I'll put him on a plane after your practice is over today, and I'll have him back before tomorrow's game against San Diego State."

Ray did exactly as promised.[56]

Even if Gillespie refused to accommodate the Garibaldis, such a refusal would not be uncommon among major Division I head coaches. "Division I sports are a business," said Joe Garibaldi, a nephew who attended San Diego State University on a baseball scholarship. "The head coaches are paid to win. That's the bottom line. It is not unusual for a head coach to deny a request to go home for a funeral or a wedding, especially if it interferes with a game." Nor is it unusual for Division I schools to reevaluate scholarship players. Some of the evaluations are performance-based, others are based on academics, and still others on attitude. Add to that the fact that Division I baseball has so few scholarships compared to football, making the coaches extremely protective of that money. "Head coaches are always moving scholarship money around to reward those players who are delivering in any given year. Sometimes the coaches forget that their players are *student*-athletes who are in college to earn a degree, not just to play sports. I'm not condoning those practices—I'm just saying that they do exist," Joe added.[57]

Rob was an emotional wreck when he returned to USC after his grandfather's funeral. Over the next seven games, he batted just .105, managing only 2 hits in 19 plate appearances.[58] He could not concentrate on his studies or baseball, finding his only relief in sleep. In a few weeks' time, his behavior became increasingly erratic, often deteriorating into rage. It got

Joe Garibaldi, Rob's cousin, who attended San Diego State University on a baseball scholarship, noted that his experience as a Division I pitcher taught him that head coaches at that level are "paid to win" and that they "sometimes forget their players are in college to earn a degree, not to play sports." *(Courtesy of Joe Garibaldi.)*

so bad that his roommates, fearing for their own safety, began sleeping with baseball bats. Hellend even dead-bolted the door to his room.[59] "I don't know what happened," the Trojan catcher told the *Santa Rosa Press Democrat* in a March 24, 2004, interview. "Rob was a great roommate one year, and the next year I had to get a dead-bolt for my door because I was afraid for my life." Hellend admitted that he and Reyes asked the coaches for help when they noticed that kitchen knives were disappearing. "The coaches gave Rob the benefit of the doubt for a long time because he was a starter," he said. "It wasn't until he started acting up on the field and missing practice that they started taking us seriously."[60]

On Monday, April 24, Rob noted in his journal that he was "overwhelmed with school work, depressed and sleeping excessively." He also admitted that he "forgot about a make-up game against Loyola Marymount and missed the team bus." When he met with Gillespie the following day, the head coach told him that the incident represented the only time during his tenure that a USC player had missed a game. After telling Rob that he should have found a way to get to the game after he missed the bus, Gillespie informed him that he was suspended for the next game and that if he missed another game or practice, he was "done with USC baseball." But the next day, Rob, sick to his stomach, excused himself from a morning team workout and arrived late to an afternoon team practice. Consequently, Gillespie suspended him for a crucial three-game series against UCLA, which was vying for the Pac-10 conference title against USC.[61]

"That whole week, Rob just stayed in the apartment," recalled Hellend. "We'd come home from practice, and he'd be sitting on the floor with his back to the wall and just stare at us. It was spooky."[62] He also made the final entry in his journal at this time. It is an almost unintelligible rant, probably written in the heat of a 'roid rage:

> 1st of All Barry Bonds is Dead wrong. He blames Orlando Cepeda's kid for his own personal problems. Orlando Cepeda's kid does not eat cake. Barry Bonds does. Barry is a slap in the face. Ya know what. I thought when Rob Garibaldi read Dusty's book, Barry might have put up better #'s than you. But he is still on 'roids. He even confessed to me at the pool when I was a kid that he likes to impress girls and boys. Why else does he load up on shit. . . . Barry had similar powers as I do now. . . . [M]y point is this—you're not the best athlete of all-time. I, the spiritual leader, Garibaldi, deserves his shot because I am going to be great.[63]

Essentially, the combination of steroids, prescription drugs, and alcohol made Rob delusional. According to the entry, he claims to have met Barry Bonds as a youngster, which his parents have insisted never occurred. Just as telling is his excoriation of Bonds for doping, a practice Rob had adopted. Rob's disappointment with his boyhood idol had now turned into a venomous anger. Finally, Garibaldi reveals his jealousy of Bonds. He writes that he has "similar powers" but has not been given the same opportunity. Referring to himself in the third person, he claims to be a "spiritual leader" who "deserves his shot" because he is "going to be great." Reading the entry, one gets the impression that Rob feels "entitled" not just to a "shot" at the major leagues but to a career at that level, too. His anger at the inequity is reinforced by the near illegible scrawl with which he wrote the vituperative entry, and it is not a coincidence that he did so during a period of desperation.

Rob had always been the "coach's pet." Name the coach: Bob Leslie and Paul Maytorena at Casa Grande High School, Rob Bruno of the NorCal Angels, Ron Myers and Damon Neidlinger at Santa Rosa Junior College—*anyone* who ever coached Rob admired his quiet confidence, exceptional work ethic, innate ability to hit a baseball, and the courtesy he displayed to both coaches and teammates. But now, Gillespie, the coach who would determine whether he had a future in professional baseball, had suspended him from his team, and for misconduct, of all things. Helplessly caught in a self-destructive spiral, Rob knew he was watching his dream slip away.

Relegated to sitting in street clothes on the bench, Rob repeatedly begged Gillespie to play him, but his pleas fell on deaf ears. Now, Rob sought vengeance. According to Hellend, his roommate, Rob began making late-night and early-morning phone calls to the head coach, accusing *him* of misconduct. "It was a very scary time," said Hellend, who never suspected steroids, though he knew APEDs were being used by a lot of college players. "Once, I looked at a bottle of his pills [for attention deficit disorder], and it had a warning label about drinking alcohol. I figured that was the problem because Rob was going out a lot at night and drinking."[64] At wit's end and growing more delusional, Rob threatened to go to the *Los Angeles Times* and tell his side of the story.[65]

Concerned for Rob's mental health, Hellend's mother phoned the Garibaldis on Monday, April 30, and told them that they had to "get down to USC quickly because Rob was blowing up."[66] That same day, Gillespie phoned Denise Garibaldi and informed her of her son's many infractions. "It's Rob's health we're concerned about here," he added. "What's in his best interests." Denise assured the coach that she would talk with Rob and explain the severity of his situation. She did not have to make the call; Rob then phoned home to defend himself, insisting that "Gillespie had it out for him." "I listened to him rant," recalled Denise. "Then I talked Rob through the process of being respectful. I emphasized that this was Gillespie's team, *not* his. Before ending the call, Rob said he felt better and that he would talk with the coach again and apologize. But I understand that when Rob went to him, Gillespie told him that he was going to suspend him for the rest of the year and 'pull his scholarship.'"[67]

Finally, on May 3, Denise, Ray, and Rob met with Gillespie; Janet Eddy, the director of DSP; another individual who was familiar with the DSP as well as Rob's situation; and one of the university's lawyers.[68] Eddy had come to USC in 1984 as a learning disabilities specialist and, seven years later, became the DSP's director. She had served as a liaison between the university's athletic program and disabled student-athletes for most of that time. No one on campus had a better understanding of the Americans with Disabilities Act of 1990 (ADA) than she did. Still, USC arranged to have one of its lawyers attend the meeting to ensure that the university was not culpable of wrongdoing. Eddy would serve as a mediator and ensure that Rob's rights under the ADA were observed.[69]

After introductions and an explanation of the reason for the meeting, Rob was excused so his head coach could speak candidly. According to several people in the room, when the Garibaldis blamed USC's coaches for their son's troubles, Gillespie allegedly exploded: "That's not my problem! I had no idea that Rob had a learning disability. Right now, he is suspended and I'm revoking his scholarship."[70]

A combination of steroids, prescription drugs, and alcohol rendered Rob delusional during the 2001 baseball season. His erratic behavior distanced him from teammates and coaches, and by mid-season he had been benched. *(Courtesy of the Garibaldi Family.)*

"How could you *not* know, coach?" Ray snapped. "The reason we chose USC was because of the learning disabilities department. In fact, we spent hours talking to your recruiting coach about Rob's disabilities. The day we dropped him off at school—his first time living away from home—the coaches told us they would treat him like he was their own son, like part of the family!"[71]

Eddy understood the frustration. She had been in similar meetings over the last ten years and had learned to balance her respect for the university's head coaches with her responsibility as a mediator in such confrontational discussions. She reminded Gillespie that Rob's baseball scholarship—like any athletic scholarship—could not be canceled for nonperformance on the playing field, only for lack of academic performance or violation of team policies. If Rob finished the semester with a 2.4 average, the university would be required to honor his scholarship.[72]

According to Ray and Denise, the frustrated Gillespie implied that Rob was a troublemaker because of his violation of team policies. Gillespie also claimed to have interviewed several team members who were "fed up with Rob on and off the field" and wanted him "off the team." He then identified several infractions dating back to the fall semester (sleeping through practice and missing the team bus for an away game) as well as Rob's repeated phone calls to him, a letter disparaging a member of the head coach's family, and his threat to go to the *Los Angeles Times*.[73] There was some question as to whether these incidents constituted "violations of team policies," "personal harassment," manifestations of Rob's attention deficit disorder and depression, or some combination of the three.[74] In retrospect, the incidents were clearly related to Rob's use of steroids, but no one knew it at the time. Regardless, Rob's behavior indicated that he was in the wrong. Gillespie had a legitimate complaint about the troublesome behavior, but it is still not known whether he pursued the reason for it. Did he suspect illegal drug use? If so, why did he not confront Rob?

To be sure, the concept of *in loco parentis*, which places a legal obligation on an educational institution to assume some of the functions and responsibilities of a parent, has largely disappeared in higher education. Since the Free Speech movement of the 1960s, a student's First and Fourth Amendment rights are much more respected by college administrators and faculty than they had been in previous decades. USC, like all universities and colleges, regards its students as responsible adults.[75] Even if Gillespie suspected illegal drug use, he did not have the legal right or the moral obligation to interfere in Rob's private life. Doing so would not only violate Rob's civil liberties but also breach the implicit trust between a coach and his player that the team policy against the use of illegal substances was being respected. At the same time, Rob's civil liberties ensured that he could not be dismissed from USC or one of its programs without due process. In other words, Coach Gillespie did *not* have the legal authority to revoke Rob's baseball scholarship if he met all the conditions specified by NCAA regulations. Eddy and the lawyer were present to ensure that those rights were observed by the university. Under these circumstances, the May 3 meeting could be viewed as a "due-process hearing."

What is unclear is whether USC and/or its baseball program had a greater legal responsibility to Rob to serve as a guardian because of his disability. Under Title I of the ADA, a government-funded institution is "required to make a reasonable accommodation" for any employee, student, or applicant who has "a physical or mental impairment that substantially limits one or more major life activities."[76] Rob certainly met the criterion for academic accommodations, but did his attention deficit disorder make him a candidate for accommodations involving his participation in baseball—specifically, "guardianship"? For example, if Rob's excessive sleeping were caused by the combination of prescription drugs for attention deficit and depression, did the baseball program have a legal obligation under the ADA to assign a member of its staff to make sure he attended practices and games and did so on time? In other words, could Rob, because of his attention deficit disorder, be held not responsible for his disturbing behavior?

Eddy rejected that possibility. Although she could not recall the particular details of the Garibaldi meeting, she contended that "in all cases," she "reviewed the written documentation on the [learning disabled] student to identify necessary accommodations, met with the student, and agreed on how those accommodations would be implemented." "Never, in all my years working with learning disabled students, did I assume the role of 'parent,'" she insisted, eliminating the possibility that Rob should have been assigned a guardian to help him meet his responsibilities to the baseball program. "When I was director of DSP, our purpose was to level the playing field for students, not to water down the university's academic or athletic standards. That doesn't prepare the student for the real world."[77]

Eddy also emphasized that throughout her career as the DSP director, one of her "most challenging jobs was to get parents to back off." She contended that it is "hard enough" for parents to separate from their children when they go off to college, but when the child has a learning disability, "the process becomes even more difficult." "Often, I had to tell parents to let their child go," said Eddy, "and that they could not protect him in college. If a parent keeps enabling their child, it becomes extremely difficult for the university to help that student, especially if he is struggling with a learning disability."[78] Intellectually, Denise and Ray understood that they had to "let go" of their son, but emotionally, it was a tremendous challenge for both of them. If the Garibaldis had convinced themselves that they had broken the umbilical cord when Rob left home for USC, they were certainly second-guessing themselves now. For them, Rob's situation at USC was both "unexpected and untenable." "We were shocked at the level of need Rob *acquired* while he was there," admitted Denise, years later.[79]

Ironically, Gillespie might have gotten his wish to revoke Rob's baseball scholarship and dismiss him from the team if he had known that Rob was doping. According to Title I of the ADA, disabled individuals "currently engaging in the illegal use of drugs are not covered by the ADA when an employer acts on the basis of such use," and tests for illegal drugs are not "subject to the ADA's restrictions on medical examinations." Accordingly, Rob, who was using an illegal substance, would have been "subject to the same performance standards as other, non-disabled individuals."[80] NCAA regulations ban steroids, and, by affiliation, so must the USC baseball program.[81] Thus, Rob would have been subject to punitive action, including the revocation of his scholarship and dismissal from the baseball program. Still, after Eddy's reminder about Rob's rights, Gillespie realized that he could not legally revoke the scholarship and became more conciliatory. He allegedly admitted that he was not capable of understanding the depth of Rob's learning disabilities and that he needed to act in Rob's best interests. But the coach also insisted that he had an overriding responsibility to maintain a high-quality baseball program. As a result, Gillespie allegedly concluded that Rob should no longer play baseball for USC.[82]

Denise and Ray were stunned. Neither one offered a rebuttal. Instead, Ray sat in stone-cold silence, while Denise took meticulous notes of Gillespie's remarks. Sixteen months earlier, they had been told not to "worry about Rob anymore," because the baseball program "was his family" and would "take care of him."[83] But didn't families, by definition, support their members in times of greatest need? The Garibaldis had placed their trust in the promise that Rob was part of another "family" who would take care of him, look out for his needs, and be loyal to him when he needed that "family" most. Now, the Garibaldis were being told that USC had done everything it could do for their son, legally and ethically—the rest was up to him. It was difficult for these parents to view USC baseball as anything more than a hard, cold business that was more concerned with protecting its own legal interests than their son's. But it was also not until that moment that the couple understood just how erratic Rob's behavior had become. "It finally dawned on me that Rob was really ill and that we had to take him home," recalled Denise, years later. "I think Ray felt that way, too. So mid-way through the meeting, neither one of us were concerned about Rob's baseball career at USC, [but] we were very concerned about his mental well-being."[84]

Another party who attended the May 3 meeting later spoke on the condition of anonymity. That individual, who was familiar with Rob's circumstances as well as the university's learning support network, came to advocate for him. Disputing Coach Gillespie's suggestion that Rob was a troublemaker, the individual identified Rob as a "bright kid, who could also be mischievous but definitely not a troublemaker." While the advocate acknowledged that Rob had "delusions of grandeur" and "periods when he lost touch with reality," he was generally a "very respectful, sensitive, and caring person with a real passion for life." The individual also believed that the baseball program could have done "much more" for Rob by paying closer attention to his academic and emotional needs.[85]

"I don't believe that to be true," said Eddy, more than a decade after the meeting. "I think Coach Gillespie tolerated much more than he should have. I've known him for nearly thirty years and consider him to be a very thorough and compassionate person who knows his players well. He was highly respected at USC, not only by his players but also by the administration." The former DSP director added that Gillespie's reputation is "exceptional, especially when you consider the fact that as a Division I coach, he was hired to win games."[86]

As the meeting came to a close, Eddy informed the Garibaldis that if Rob completed his outstanding school work, passed his final exams, maintained at least a 2.4 grade point average, and acted more respectfully toward his coaches and teammates, he would be eligible to play baseball, and his scholarship would be honored. Gillespie added that under NCAA regulations, Rob had until August 1 to decide whether he wanted to exercise that option. In addition, he offered his "full support" in helping Rob "find another college baseball program that would take him."[87] By that point, the meeting had been going on for nearly four hours. Rob was allowed to return to the room, and Eddy, as mediator, spoke for the group. She told Rob that they "didn't think he was well and that it was best if he went home for the rest of the semester." She also informed him that Gillespie personally did not want him back on the team, but that if Rob wanted to return, he could do so as long as he met the established conditions.[88]

Shortly after the meeting adjourned, Ray and Denise met separately with Eddy, who told them, "This is a crisis of mental and physical health, and Rob is not capable of finishing the season." She also gave them a list of recommendations, including meeting with a psychologist from student counseling services to help Rob recognize his condition and the reasons for USC's actions. The Garibaldis acted on all the recommendations before packing up their son's belongings.[89]

Despite Rob's protestations, Denise insisted on taking him home. Before leaving, Rob asked to speak with Gillespie alone, but Denise would not allow it. She feared he would destroy whatever chance he had of returning to USC and the baseball program.

"But, Mom," he pleaded, "I have something important to share with him."

"You are not well, Rob," replied Denise, "and we are going to take you home."

"But there's something going down in baseball," he protested, hoping to reveal the "open secret" about steroids. "No one is going to believe it. It's about numbers. You know about number theory? I want to show Coach."

"No! That's enough, Rob," said Denise with a sternness that cut him to the quick.[90]

Instead, Rob went to the practice field to say good-bye to teammates— the same people who were supposed to be his "family." When he arrived, he found his gear stuffed in a garbage can next to the dugout. It was the "family's" way of telling Rob he was no longer wanted.

With tears in his eyes, he collected his things, turned around, and headed back to his apartment to meet his parents for the long drive home.[91]

Deep inside, he knew he would never return to USC. His dream had ended.

8

FIGHTING BACK

Taylor Hooton's suicide launched his family's fight against adolescent steroid abuse. It was and continues to be a frustrating battle, one that sometimes feels as though the authorities who should be supporting their efforts are setting up roadblocks.

The odyssey began when the Plano police officers who responded to the 911 call started their investigation. Searching Taylor's bedroom—now considered a "crime scene"—they found four gelatin capsules and two vials of steroids with labels written in Spanish. The items had been wrapped in an American flag and hidden inside a chest of drawers near the bed.[1] As the ambulance carrying Taylor pulled away from the house, one of the officers approached Don Hooton and asked, "Did you know your son was taking steroids?"[2] Don was immediately struck by the question as well as the tone of the officer's voice. "He appeared to be suggesting that steroids had played a role in Taylor's death," said Hooton. "Now, he didn't come out and *say* that, but it was clear to me that that's what he meant."

Don admitted that he was aware of Taylor's doping, but he also indicated that his son had "recently stopped using." When the officer mentioned his discovery of the steroid vials, Hooton was determined to find out whether there was a connection between the steroids and his son's suicide.[3]

To be sure, the Collin County coroner's autopsy report did not show any trace of steroids in Taylor's urine, probably because he was using the detox Azo to mask his use. But the report did reveal the presence in the

Rev. Neil Jeffrey of the Prestonwood
Baptist Church accepted the difficult task
of explaining the meaning of Taylor's death
to the Hootons and other attendees at the
teen's funeral. *(Courtesy of Rev. Neil Jeffrey.)*

bloodstream of the metabolized steroid Nandrolone, which Taylor appar-
ently had begun injecting six weeks
earlier.[4] The autopsy also found Cita-
lopram, an antidepressant prescribed
for depression.[5] Don began to suspect
a fatal connection between the steroids
and his son's suicide.

Taylor was buried on July 18, 2003,
at Ridgeview Memorial Park in Allen,
Texas. More than three thousand people attended the memorial service at
the Prestonwood Baptist Church, a profound testimony to the 17-year-old's
popularity. Several eulogies were delivered by family, friends, and teammates, but it was left to Reverend Neil Jeffrey to explain the meaning of
Taylor's death to those who gathered to remember him. It was not an easy
task.

Crafting his message on 2 Timothy 4:6–8, Jeffrey reminded the
mourners that the deceased teen had "fought the good fight," "finished
the race," and "kept the faith," permitting him to find his eternal reward.
Anticipating that it would be difficult for some to understand why God
would allow Taylor to enter heaven when he had sinned by taking his own
life, Jeffrey explained:

> We, as Baptists, believe that God is a loving God and that He does
> not judge any person on a single act of his life. Suicide is not an
> unpardonable sin for those who have accepted Christ into their
> lives. The only unpardonable sin is not taking Him into our life.
> How we deserve to get into heaven is by grace, and we achieve
> grace by trusting in Jesus Christ, who paid for our sins by dying
> on the cross, and to trust in His righteousness.

The Baptist minister made every effort to lessen the self-inflicted
guilt of family members and friends, yet he was also careful to emphasize
that committing sin was not to be taken lightly:

Does that mean it's okay to commit sin? That it's okay to take your own life, the most precious gift the Lord has given us? No, it certainly isn't. But Taylor, like us all, was human and, like us all, was subject to sin. He may have sinned by taking his life, but God forgave him for that sin on the day Taylor was baptized. On that day, Taylor trusted Jesus Christ as Savior and accepted Him into his heart. That was the day he was granted eternal salvation.[6]

It was a poignant, heartfelt message that gave meaning to Taylor's life and death and lessened the guilt family and friends might have felt over not preventing his suicide.

The funeral procession to the cemetery was a mile-and-a-half long and required an escort from the Plano Police Department. Gwen, who wore her son's no. 10 Plano West baseball jersey, later did not remember much from that day, aside from kissing Taylor's portrait after the memorial service ended. Placed alongside the coffin, the image showed the teen in his Yankees' summer tournament league uniform. "That's always been my favorite picture of him," she said. "It shows [him] the way I want to remember him, with those beautiful bluish-green eyes and mischievous smile, the way he was before he began using steroids."[7]

Don's memories were more vivid. One of Taylor's friends, Dustin Barnes, stood by the coffin during the viewing and explained in detail how local dealers traveled to Mexico to purchase steroids, returned across the border, and sold them at a profit to male students at Plano West. Others told of dozens of kids at the school who were juicing. In fact, Taylor's suicide triggered a wave of confessions from friends.[8] In the days preceding and immediately after the funeral, the Hootons were visited by a steady stream of kids who were "upset and feeling guilty enough" to tell Don and Gwen "anything they wanted to know." "They told us who was selling steroids, how much they cost, and how many other kids were juicing," recalled Don. "They even volunteered to help the police with their investigation."[9] That is, everyone except the one person who could shed the most insight—Taylor's best friend, Mark Gomez.

Both Don and Gwen repeatedly asked Gomez whether he was doing steroids and whether he knew anything about Taylor's doping. He always said, "No." "I thought it would hurt them more if they knew I was doing it, too," admitted Gomez in a later interview. "There was a lot of crap running through my head. I felt partly responsible for Taylor's death, for not telling the Hootons that their son was using steroids."[10] Soon, the guilt caught up to him.

One night, about a week after the funeral, Gomez went into the garage, rifled through the glove compartment of his father's car, and took out his pistol. He was having a difficult time accepting the fact that he had known about Taylor's doping and could have prevented the suicide. His life hung in the balance as he stood alone in the driveway. A myriad of thoughts raced through his mind: "Why didn't I tell the Hootons?" "What kind of a friend was I?" "How can I go on living knowing that I could've saved Taylor's life?" Then, just as suddenly, the teen returned the pistol to the glove compartment and walked back inside the house. The next day, Gomez visited Don and Gwen Hooton, admitted his doping, and told them everything he knew, including the name of the Frisco dealer who sold Taylor and him the steroids.[11] At that point, Don began his own investigation.

Searching Taylor's bedroom for anything the police might have missed, he discovered more vials as well as needles and syringes hidden in his son's jackets. He also found a foil packet of Clomid, a female fertility drug used to ease the loss of body mass between steroid cycles. On the back of the foil packet, written in a black felt-tip pen, was the first name of the dealer Gomez had identified.[12] Shortly thereafter, Chris Jones, a detective for the Plano police, called on the Hootons to follow up on the department's investigation. When Jones asked to see Taylor's bedroom, Don accompanied him upstairs. Jones lay down on the bed, surveying the room. His experience with teenage drug abuse told him that a user would hide his stash within arm's reach. The detective looked under the mattress and rifled through dresser drawers that had already been searched by Don. He even inspected bottles of water, shaking the liquid and smelling it to determine whether Taylor tried to hide the drugs by dissolving them. But he came up empty-handed. Before Jones left, Don gave him the additional vials and the foil packet of Clomid tablets he found. He also told the detective the name of the dealer who sold his son the steroids and gave him the names and contact information for several of Taylor's friends who had volunteered to tell the police what they knew. Jones jotted down the information but explained to Hooton that to arrest the dealer, he would need physical evidence, which meant catching the Frisco teen in possession of anabolic steroids or selling them. Promising to pursue the lead, the detective took his leave.[13]

During the next three weeks, Jones made an earnest effort to arrest the dealer. He conducted surveillance outside the suspect's house, which proved to be difficult, because his parents lived in a gated community. He also set up a sting operation but was forced to abandon it when another undercover agent was called for military duty. When the dealer surren-

For two years, Don Hooton enlisted the support of Taylor's friends and the Plano Police Department in his struggle to find answers about his son's suicide. *(Courtesy of Taylor Hooton Foundation.)*

dered to the Collin County sheriff, pleading guilty to a recent burglary, the investigation was suspended altogether.[14] Frustrated, Don phoned Jones and asked why he could not simply arrest the dealer and try him based on the testimony of the teenaged eyewitnesses. The detective repeated his earlier statement—the police would have to witness a sale to bring the suspect to trial.[15]

After a year passed with no further developments, Don, convinced that the Plano Police Department had abandoned the investigation, wrote to the alleged dealer's father on September 9, 2004. In the letter, he explained how several of Taylor's friends identified the man's son as the dealer, with some having witnessed one of the sales. Don described how he had gone to the police with the information, hoping to make the son accountable for his actions in selling illegal drugs. And he had consulted with researchers, who confirmed a strong connection between steroid use, severe depression, and even suicide. Don admitted to the father that the Plano Police Department's narcotics team appeared "to have given up on proving" his son's guilt. "Your son is one lucky young man," wrote Don, "because he got away with it this time. But my family didn't 'get away with it.' We have suffered the most serious loss that I can imagine any parents anywhere having to bear." He continued:

> As a father, I don't think I need to tell you how painful our loss has been. I've been waiting for the right time to send you this letter in order that you will know what role it looks like your son played in the death of my 17-year-old son, Taylor.
>
> If you would like to talk, I'd be pleased to do so. I have friends who know you, and they tell me that you are a good man.

Good luck with your family and take a moment to give the
Good Lord thanks that you have them all with you today.[16]

The letter resulted in a phone call from the father, who expressed his
sympathy for Taylor's death but was careful to avoid any discussion of his
own son's alleged dealing of anabolic steroids.[17]

In June 2005, the Plano Police Department told the *Dallas Morning
News* that the Taylor Hooton investigation was "not closed, but [was] inac-
tive pending the development of any further leads or information" and
that "it would be inappropriate for [them] to discuss the specifics of the
suicide and the subsequent investigation."[18] It is the same position they
maintain today, more than fifteen years later.[19]

The Plano Police Department's response to the Hooton investigation
is consistent with the reluctance of law enforcement officials nationwide
to bring steroid dealers to trial. Law enforcement officers face significant
challenges in their efforts to investigate, prosecute, and deter anabolic-
steroid traffickers. The challenges include (1) the foreign origin of many
illegally sold steroids, (2) the widespread use of the Internet in steroid
trafficking, (3) the volume of mail that must be screened to prevent the
entry of anabolic steroids into the United States, (4) the relatively low
sentences given to dealers as a result of the federal sentencing guidelines, and (5) the use and abuse of anabolic steroids by police officers
themselves.[20]

Prior to 2005, most anabolic steroids sold illegally in the United States
came from abroad. Significant quantities originated in Mexico, where steroids can be sold legally without a prescription. Because Mexican distributors were not violating their nation's laws, U.S. law enforcement agencies
found it difficult to secure assistance from their Mexican counterparts in
their investigation of the distributors. In 2005, however, the U.S. Drug
Enforcement Agency's (DEA's) Operation Gear Grinder took down eight
large Mexican companies along with numerous drug traffickers; various
Chinese companies then stepped in to fill the void.[21] Today, China fun-
nels the largest amount of raw steroid powder into the United States, and
underground labs in this country have become a much larger source for
illegal steroids, according to the DEA. The black-market trade comes in
the form of kits to make steroids at home, steroid products, and many
chemical derivatives. Like in Mexico, the production and distribution of
steroids are unregulated in China and thus legal. Unlike in Mexico, Chinese steroids are of a dubious quality, many being contaminated. Some
have been found to contain lead, arsenic, baby oil, cooking oil, and even

horse urine, which makes them far more dangerous than the more expensive unadulterated steroids used by pro athletes.[22]

Complicating matters is the smuggling of anabolic steroids across the U.S. border, a critical part of the illegal distribution network. For example, American smugglers can take orders from steroid customers in person, over the phone, or via e-mail. After obtaining advance payment from their customers, the smugglers will travel to the source country to purchase the steroids. To avoid arrest, they may pay someone else to carry the drugs across the border or enlist a foreign source to ship the steroids to the United States. Some smugglers protect themselves by shipping the steroids to a partner in the United States, known as a "remailer," and providing the remailer with addresses of specific U.S. customers. The remailer repackages the steroids and sends them to the customers in return for cash or payment in steroids. The customer may then use the steroids or resell them to others, usually at gyms or body-building contests.[23]

Still, the Internet is the most popular means of buying and selling steroids. Distributors use foreign-based websites that cater to young, inexperienced buyers. They typically require advance payment through Western Union, PayPal, credit cards, or bitcoins. After receiving payment, the seller will ship the steroids through international mail or an express carrier. The advantage of this approach is anonymity. To prosecute illegal steroid dealers, law enforcement officials must identify them and gather evidence of their trafficking activity. But this is extremely difficult to do because Internet sites can be installed, moved, or removed easily and quickly, preventing law enforcement agencies from identifying, tracking, monitoring, or shutting them down. Sending steroids via international mail also presents a significant challenge.

U.S. Customs and Border Protection (CBP) has a mandate to inspect all mail entering this country through the U.S. Postal Service and private carriers at the fourteen international mail facilities and twenty-nine express consignment carrier facilities located nationwide. The CBP inspects for illegally imported controlled substances, such as anabolic steroids, contraband, and other items that are banned from the United States. Considering that the international mail and carrier facilities process hundreds of millions of pieces of mail and packages each year, the failure to detect steroids is fairly common, especially when dealers conceal the drugs in books or small pieces of electrical equipment.[24]

Even if a distributer is arrested, the penalties faced under the federal sentencing guidelines do not reflect the seriousness of the crime or provide adequate deterrence. Sentences are determined by drug quantity, and the quantity of anabolic steroids necessary to secure a long-term sentence is considerable. Anabolic steroids are categorized as a Schedule III controlled substance, or those accepted for medical use in the United States but with the potential for abuse and addiction.[25] Schedule III substances are based on a unit system. In this case, a unit is "one pill, capsule, or tablet or, if in liquid form, 0.5 milliliters." Thus, an offender responsible for selling forty thousand pills or twenty liters of a Schedule III controlled substance would face a sentence of thirty-three to forty-one months.[26] Prior to 2006, the sentencing guidelines treated anabolic steroids differently from all other Schedule III controlled substances. At that time, one unit of an anabolic steroid was fifty pills, capsules, or tablets; in liquid form, one unit equaled a 10cc vial of injectable steroid. Thus, under the old sentencing guidelines, an offender convicted of selling forty thousand pills of an anabolic steroid would have faced a sentence of just up to six months in prison.[27] Under the current sentencing guidelines, steroid-related offenses carry the same sentencing guidelines as other Schedule III controlled substances. Federal officials made the revision in the wake of the BALCO scandal that brought down several major league baseball stars. The amendment also added stricter sentences for athletes using masking agents to hide their steroid use, for coaches pressuring athletes into experimenting with the drug, and for individuals distributing to athletes.[28]

Finally, the use and abuse of anabolic steroids by police officers themselves make it extremely difficult even to apprehend a dealer. "Cops have long been a hush-hush subset of anabolic steroid users," according to Pennsylvania State University sports-science professor Charles Yesalis, author of *The Steroids Game*. "Most of the police officers I've known who have used these drugs consider them a tool of the trade."[29] Anabolic steroids appeal to officers wanting a tactical edge or an intimidating appearance. Some of the police officers even claim they need AAS to do their jobs effectively or to improve their job performance.[30] This is not a new problem. The Federal Bureau of Investigation (FBI) anticipated it as early as 1991, when it stated that "anabolic steroid abuse by police officers is a serious problem that merits greater awareness by departments across the country."[31] Within the last decade, however, the problem appears to be growing. In 2007, for example, DEA officers engaged in Operation Raw Deal discovered several links to current or former law enforcement officers.[32] More recently, police officers in nine states were accused of steroid-related crimes, including a seventeen-year veteran of the Arlington, Texas, Police Department, who was arrested by the FBI for buying anabolic steroids for himself and other officers. The juicer cop also accessed confidential government databases to tip off a steroid dealer who was under police surveillance.[33]

"I've heard many, many accounts of police officers taking steroids," Harrison Pope, MD, a Harvard steroid specialist, told Sabrina Erdley, a journalist for *Men's Health Magazine*. "But it's impossible to put a number on it. Even if I got a federal grant to study this, I wouldn't be able to get that number, because of the veil of secrecy."[34] Quantification is impossible. Policemen who use steroids are a secretive subculture within a secretive subculture.[35] None would dare to arrest a steroids distributor, especially if he were being supplied by the dealer. To do so would not only incriminate the officer but also invite the wrath of other juicing cops.

Considering the extensive amount of time and resources that is required to locate, charge, and convict criminal anabolic steroid dealers, not to mention the minimal sentences they received prior to 2006 and the subculture of juicing policemen, there was no incentive for the Plano Police Department to go after the Frisco teenager who sold steroids to Taylor Hooton. Perhaps the only reason the department gave as much attention as it did to the Hooton case was because of all the publicity it received. To do nothing would have been bad public relations for the police.

PISD officials were also feeling the pressure. Eight years earlier, the PISD had been at the center of an embarrassing drug scandal when a dozen teens overdosed on heroin. The incident made national news when the *New York Times* ran a story on the drug-related deaths, and MTV, the music cable channel, followed up with a documentary titled *Fatal Dose*.[36] The school district could not afford more negative press, let alone the possibility that the Hootons might file a lawsuit for negligence. When Don proposed a partnership to educate teens, parents, teachers, and coaches on the signs and dangers of steroids, PISD officials quickly accepted the offer. "I thought if I didn't know about Taylor's steroid use, then our coaches, school officials, and parents might not know about it," explained Don, who never considered litigation against the school district. He remembered the idle chatter among parents seated in the bleachers at Plano West's baseball games. "Some would comment on the sudden weight gain or muscle mass of one of the players and joke about steroids," he said. "Others would just snicker, completely ignorant of the dangers anabolic steroids present to teens. Just like 99 percent of them, I didn't know any better."[37]

Plano school officials agreed to let Hooton organize steroid-awareness seminars at the district's three senior high schools. The first one was held at Plano West in September 2003. More than six hundred parents, teachers, coaches, and students attended, including Taylor's friends, who sat tearfully listening to descriptions of the dangers of anabolic steroids. Physicians from Southern Methodist University Hospital discussed the drug's side effects. Mike Long, a Texas high school football coach and former user, talked about the effects of steroids on his body, including a serious bout with cancer. Principle Phil Saviano "could not have been any more sympathetic or nicer," recalled Don. Reporters from the *Dallas Morning News* also attended and ran a story a few weeks later on Don's campaign to educate others on steroid use.[38] The seminars at the other two schools were not as encouraging, in part because the students and coaches did not know Taylor. Although the seminar at Plano Senior High School drew about three hundred people, some of the coaches appeared sullen, seated with their arms folded as if they had been required to attend. One even had the impudence to fall asleep. And the football players, the group most vulnerable to steroid abuse, had not been told of the seminar. Only a few dozen attended the final seminar at Plano East.[39]

Discouraged, Don considered abandoning his plans for similar programs at other Dallas-area high schools. But Dr. Gary Wadler, an expert on drug use in sports and an adviser to the WADA who advised Hooton, encouraged him to continue his educational efforts. Insisting on the importance of "putting a face" on the issue of teenaged steroid abuse, Wadler contacted *New York Times* journalist Jere Longman and urged him to do a story on Taylor's suicide and his father's efforts to help others. Longman flew out to Plano and spent three full days with the Hootons, interviewing Taylor's closest friends; his varsity baseball coach, Blake Boydston; and his psychiatrist, Dr. Babette Farkas.[40] The story, titled "Drugs in Sports: An Athlete's Dangerous Experiment," headlined the *Sports* section of the *Times* on Wednesday, November 26, 2003.

In the story, Don and Billy Ajello, one of Taylor's close friends and a catcher on Plano West's varsity baseball team, said they doubted that PISD was taking the dangers of steroid use seriously. If it did, the district would have begun testing students for PED use. Ajello's remarks were especially damning. He insisted that steroid use at the high school was "extremely widespread" before Taylor's death and that school officials "don't want to talk about it." When coaches were asked about the 18-year-old's statement, they insisted that Plano West did not have a serious steroids problem. Boydston, the varsity baseball coach, ranked steroids "at the bottom of the list" of the school's problems. Mike Hughes, the head football coach, told the *New York Times*, "I have been in the district for 21 years and I have not known of a kid who was on steroids." He also insisted that no one at the school was "trying to brush [the steroids issue] aside." "We hurt," admitted Hughes, "but we have to move on and continue to educate kids." Both coaches admitted that they had advised players to get bigger and stronger, but they insisted that they do it through better nutrition and weightlifting and that they had cautioned against steroid use. One school official suggested that Taylor's case was an exceptional one; it was that administrator's first encounter with steroids.[41]

When asked about the possibility of implementing a testing program for steroids, Cliff Odenwald, PISD's athletic director, said the district could not "afford to do it with the financial situation we're in." Longman questioned this claim, pointing out that the school district had recently built a $15 million stadium and indoor practice fields for the three senior high football teams. But Odenwald explained that those facilities were built through bond issues approved by voters and that the money for drug testing would have to come out of an annual district budget that was "already stretched to the limit."[42]

The *New York Times* story was only the opening salvo in Don Hooton's fight against teen steroid use. The article was so compelling that it captured the attention of Amiel Weisfogel, an associate producer with *60 Minutes* on CBS, who arranged a future episode on Taylor's suicide and the dangers of adolescent steroid use. In the program, aired on March 3, 2004, Don went on the attack. He accused Plano's coaches and school officials of ignoring the steroids issue. Larry Gwyn, PISD's Health and Athletics director who was appointed by the district to speak on its behalf, questioned the severity of the steroids problem and stated that Plano West and its coaches provided "an easy target for blame." Instead, Gwyn suggested that the blame for Taylor's death rested with his parents and their inability to identify his steroid use. When journalist Jim Stewart asked whether he thought that the coaches "bore an especially particular responsibility for keeping kids off steroids," Gwyn replied, "I think they do, and I think our coaches exercise that responsibility, and our athletic director makes sure that they do."[43] When told of the school official's remarks, Don said he "didn't disagree." "Taylor's death was our responsibility, and I'll take the blame for it," he declared. "But at the same time, the guy who makes the decision on who makes or doesn't make the team, if a kid is going to play or not play—that guy has a lot more influence on my kid, on how he works out, and what's important to him from an athletic standpoint than Mom or Dad ever will."[44]

After the airing of the *60 Minutes* episode, Don's efforts to educate others on the dangers of steroid use were no longer welcomed by PISD. "We were viewed as 'enemies' by the school district," he said. "Looking back, I can see why the coaches viewed us that way. Feelings were pretty raw then. I'm sure some of the heat [school officials and coaches] were feeling was real. They took it as though I was saying this was just a Plano problem. Unfortunately, they missed the whole point. What got lost was the educational message."[45]

In March 2004, PISD Superintendent Dr. Doug Otto released a statement acknowledging that Taylor's death was "a tragic event" and that he "appreciated [the Hootons'] efforts to make the issue [of anabolic steroid use by teens] more of a front-burner issue for schools." But Otto also insisted that steroid use across the district was "minimal because of the work of our teachers and coaches." To defend his assertion, Otto cited a poll done by the Public Policy Research Institute of Texas A&M, which indicated that only "2 percent of students in grades 7–12" said they used anabolic steroids.[46] After that, PISD officials and Plano West's coaches remained silent, refusing to address any more criticism.

On August 12, 2004, the *Dallas Observer News* reignited the controversy when it ran a story titled "All the Rage," written by investigative reporter Paul Kix. "That 2 percent number is a joke," Ajello told Kix when reminded of Otto's statement about the percentage of students using steroids in the district. "A lot of kids who do steroids won't tell a single [adult]. But I know so many people who have taken steroids and still take them." According to the teen, students at Plano West spoke openly to other kids and even bragged about steroid use before Taylor's death.[47] Emily Parker was just as adamant about widespread steroid use at Plano West. "I just don't understand how all these kids are saying, 'Look—we're around [steroid users],'" she told Kix. "We know it's a problem. We're friends with these people. We go to school with them. You don't know [about the problem].' And then [school officials] don't even acknowledge it? They're totally dismissing it. They don't want to have anything to do with it at all." Parker told Kix that after Taylor's suicide, some students were scared away from steroid use. She was happy to hear that, but she insisted that "not nearly enough [users]" had come forward. "Like ten," she said, "out of the hundreds of guys who took steroids."[48] Gomez echoed her remarks, declaring that PISD officials "just don't take [steroids] seriously." "They don't know what it can do to you," he added. "It's still a problem."[49]

Of all of Taylor's friends, Patrick Burke, a member of the Plano West cross-country team, was the most outraged by Otto's statement minimizing the extent of the steroids problem. "It's the elephant in the corner," insisted Burke, who told Kix that he had actually seen kids doping at Plano West. "They'd mostly do it in the locker room showers," he said. "They'd just carry the stuff in their shower bag, take a shower and, when no coaches were around, just quick," he explained, sticking an imaginary needle in his behind. "Some kids wouldn't have the nerves to do it themselves, so they'd have others do it for them. It's an everyday thing. I'd say 80 percent of the athletes either have used or are using in . . . wrestling, some track, a lot of football and baseball."

When Burke heard about Otto's "2 percent" estimate, he wrote the superintendent a letter to tell him that he was mistaken. "In my personal experience," he began, "steroids as well as other illegal drugs have been readily available and at our students' fingertips since I have attended high school in Plano. To deny that such a situation exists is a cowardly and irresponsible approach to dealing with this deadly problem." Burke also disputed Otto's remark about the efforts of the faculty to prevent steroid use among students. "As a student," he wrote, "I can only recall one section on steroid awareness that was buried within one chapter of one textbook in Plano's one required health class. I would call this effort mediocre, at best." The teen believed that the district's administrators and coaches were either "blind" to the steroids problem or "[had] their heads in the sand." "Taylor Hooton's death brought national attention to our community," concluded the letter. "The eyes of the nation are upon us. Failure is no longer an option."[50]

Hoping to learn Plano West's side of the story, Kix tried to get interviews with Superintendent Otto, Principal Saviano, and coaches Boydston and Hughes, but they failed to return his repeated phone calls, e-mails, or written requests.[51] Today, more than fifteen years later, the school and PISD officials refuse to comment on the issue. Their silence only served to strengthen Don's resolve to launch his own crusade.

In 2005, Don left his job as an executive at Hewlett-Packard and dedicated himself to educating others about the signs and dangers of APEDs. Inspired by their Christian belief that God has a purpose for all the things that happen in life, Don and his family established the Taylor Hooton Foundation to honor his younger son's memory.[52] "He's gone," said Don, explaining his decision to create the foundation on *60 Minutes*. "It's devastating. We'll never get over it. The only way I know how to deal with it is to find out exactly what happened and then to ring the warning bell so that nobody else has to go through what we've gone through."[53] To his credit, Don redefined the steroids debate in this country, focusing on the desperate need to eliminate doping among America's adolescents.

"When I began doing educational outreach, I was afraid of making mistakes," he admitted. "I'm not a physician, and the impact of anabolic steroids on the human body and mind is a highly clinical subject, so I didn't want to lose credibility." Don's fears were put to rest, however, when he spoke before the American Association of Family Physicians in 2005. More than five hundred doctors were in the audience, and after his presentation, literally dozens of them made their way to the microphones at the front of the auditorium to ask questions. Now his heart was pounding. "'Here it comes,' he said to himself. 'I'm going to be schooled now.'" "Mr. Hooton," began the first questioner, "you began your presentation by saying that we, as physicians, were really the experts on steroid abuse. I think you need to understand that we were not trained on this subject in medical school, nor has there been much research completed on it. We aren't the experts—you are!"[54]

From that point on, Don has never questioned his own credibility. Instead, he conducts himself like a gentleman-scholar. His research is meticulous and thorough, and he presents his knowledge in a manner that is not only informative but also intellectually insightful and engaging. He also listens carefully to the remarks of others—supporters as well as critics—and answers questions in a thoughtful, compassionate manner. But Don suffers no fools. Those who patronize him or attempt to exploit his cause for selfish interests incur his wrath, regardless of their power, wealth, or influence.

Working through the nonprofit Taylor Hooton Foundation, Don; his son, Donald Jr.; and a handful of employees educate students, parents, teachers, and coaches about the symptoms and dangers of APEDs through online and outreach programs. Today, the Taylor Hooton Foundation, based in McKinney, Texas, is the nation's leading organization in the fight against APED use by young people thanks to the financial support of MLB. During the 2005 congressional hearings on steroids, Commissioner Bud Selig was so moved by the stories of Taylor Hooton and Rob Garibaldi that he committed MLB to become a founding partner by donating $1 million to the foundation to help educate youngsters, parents, and coaches at the prep, high school, and collegiate levels about the dangers of using APEDs. In 2008, Selig insisted that MLB donate another $1.5 million and agreed to other forms of support, including a Web page created by MLB.com that linked to the foundation's website and the use of MLB ballparks by the foundation to present its "Hoot's Chalk Talk" program on an annual basis in conjunction with the Professional Baseball Athletic Trainers Promoting a Lifetime of Activity for Youth (PLAY) program. The talks provide kids with information about how to improve their athletic performance, build their strength, and enhance their conditioning without the use of steroids or other PEDs.[55]

More recently, the foundation launched the "All-Me League," which will showcase the support professional athletes and teams are giving to the fight against APEDs. Again, MLB has taken the lead, with thirteen role models joining an advisory board for the initiative: Jay Bruce (Cincinnati Reds), John Danks (Chicago White Sox), David DeJesus (Tampa Bay Rays), Brian Dozier (Minnesota Twins), Brett Gardner (New York Yankees), Dillon Gee (New York Mets), Clayton Kershaw (Los Angeles Dodgers), Jason Kipnis (Cleveland Indians), Mark Melancon (Pittsburgh Pirates), Anthony Rendon (Washington Nationals), Max Scherzer (Detroit Tigers), C. J. Wilson (Los Angeles Angels), and Brad Ziegler (Arizona Diamondbacks). The website, which is available at www.allmeleague.com, encourages youngsters to join the "All-Me League" along with these major leaguers, who have each taken a pledge to play clean. Kids can also submit videos explaining how they intend to make the world of sports a better place by joining the initiative to play clean and fair.[56]

Since 2005, other professional sports organizations have joined MLB in sponsoring the Taylor Hooton Foundation, including Little League Baseball International, the New York Yankees, the Texas Rangers, the NFL, and the National Hockey League. In addition, the foundation boasts a highly accomplished board of advisers, including Randy Levine, the president of the New York Yankees; Neil Romano, the assistant secretary of Labor for Disability Employment Policy during the administration of President George W. Bush; James Whitehead, the CEO of the American College of Sports Medicine; Stratton Nicolaides, the CEO of Numerex Corporation; Gary I. Wadler, MD, an associate professor at New York University School of Medicine; Gene Gieselmann, the former head athletic trainer for the St. Louis Cardinals; Ron Arp, the president of Amplify Group, Inc.; Matt Butkus, an insurance broker for the Horton Group; Jeff Cooper, MS, ATC, the former head athletic trainer for the Philadelphia Phillies; Pat Fox, the managing member and general counsel for the Rockpoint Group; Mike Guidry, CEO of the Guidry Group; Jake Schroepfer, the president of Crowdsourcing at the Marketing Arm; and Mark Thompson, the president of Smith Thompson Home Security.[57]

According to Donald Hooton Jr., who coordinates the organization's educational programs, the foundation has served more than one million people through seminars across the United States, Canada, and Latin America since its establishment in 2004. Countless others have benefitted from the organization's online resources. With a staff of five full-time employees and an annual operating budget of $850,000, the Taylor Hooton Foundation has been remarkably successful in achieving

Donald Hooton Jr., pictured here
in 2004 as a pitcher for the
University of Texas at Arlington,
once inspired younger brother
Taylor's baseball dreams. Today,
Taylor inspires Donald's mission to
educate parents, teachers, coaches,
and especially student-athletes
about the dangers and symptoms
of steroid abuse. *(Courtesy of Taylor
Hooton Foundation.)*

its mission, and yet the staff
believes it can do more. "We
barely scratch the surface in
terms of the number of kids
and adults we need to reach,"
Donald Jr. has insisted. "Currently, our limited resources
don't allow us to address the
nearly sixteen million high
school students in this country. In order to do that over a
four-year period, our organization needs to become significantly larger
than it is right now. That doesn't include the resources necessary to reach
middle schoolers or college students, either."[58] Although Donald Jr., who
left a successful career in real estate to join the foundation, admitted the
long hours and constant travel can be exhausting at times, he "wouldn't
trade his position for all the money in the world." "Taylor was not only my
brother; he was my best friend," he said. "I think he would be so proud to
know that we are doing all we can to prevent other families from losing
their sons and daughters to steroid abuse. And the reward I get from that
is immeasurable."[59] There have been disappointments, though.

In 2006, Don was contacted by Texas Lieutenant Governor David
Dewhurst, who wanted to increase awareness of steroid use and its dangers in the state's public schools. Don recommended the implementation
of a testing program, among other suggestions. Dewhurst jumped on the
idea, promoting it among state legislators. A year later, Texas lawmakers
passed a bill mandating the steroid testing of high school athletes beginning in the 2007–2008 school year, with an annual budget of $3 million.
According to the measure, named "Taylor's Law," any athlete who tested
positive or broke protocol would be suspended from sports for thirty

school days. The state's University Interscholastic League estimated that Drug Free Sport of Kansas, Missouri, the agency hired to do the testing, would test twenty thousand to twenty-five thousand students (roughly 3 percent of Texas's more than seven hundred thousand student-athletes) in the first year. It was a huge undertaking, considering that similar testing programs in Florida and New Jersey affected only five hundred high school student-athletes annually.[60]

Over the next three years, 51,635 tests were done, resulting in 21 positive tests, 2 unresolved, and 139 not passing for procedure violations, such as unexcused absences. Governor Rick Perry indicated that the funding might have been excessive and cut the annual budget for the program from $3 million to just $750,000 for the 2010–2011 school year. The budget reduction was due, in part, to an economic downturn. But Don also believes that state politicians do not fear steroid use as much as they did when the bill was enacted. In addition, he insists that the results of the testing did not accurately measure steroid use among the state's high school athletes.[61] In retrospect, Don contends that the testing program was "poorly operated," because it "only tested for 10 kinds of steroids when there are 120 types, meaning that a user only had an 8 percent chance of getting caught." In addition, there was no "supervised collection of urine samples," so the "[student-athlete] being tested could have turned in another kid's sample." At the same time, Don has pointed out that the primary reason for the testing was to "deter users, not to measure usage rates": "If the testing accomplished that goal, it was successful."[62]

A more personal disappointment came in 2010, when it was reported that New York Yankees third baseman Alex Rodriguez had been using steroids while making guest appearances for the foundation.[63] It was the second time A-Rod had been caught. In February 2009, Rodriguez admitted to using testosterone, HGH, and insulin-like growth factor-1 six years earlier while playing for the Texas Rangers.[64] Commissioner Selig considered whether to discipline the Yankee star but decided against it, because there were no punishments for steroid use at the time of the testing.[65] Later that month, in an interview with ESPN, A-Rod explained that he had used the steroids testosterone and Primobolan because of an enormous amount of pressure to perform. He also said that he hoped to use the incident in a constructive way by discouraging kids from using anabolic steroids.[66]

When Don heard the interview, he felt sorry for A-Rod. The Yankee All-Star had been Taylor's baseball idol when he was growing up, so Don had a soft spot for him. He phoned Levine, the president of the Yankees, and proposed a partnership between his foundation and Rodriguez. "Randy got very excited about the idea," remembered Don. "So was Alex. Within twenty-four hours, we negotiated a three-year agreement in which he would visit schools with us and talk to kids about the dangers of steroid use. He also offered to make an annual financial contribution to the foundation."[67]

The agreement was formalized at a February 17, 2009, press conference held at the Yankees' spring-training facility in Tampa, Florida. Don joined sportswriters, photographers, and current Yankees under a huge tent at George M. Steinbrenner Field to witness A-Rod's confession and pledge.[68] Seated at a banquet table between Yankees' manager Joe Girardi and general manager Brian Cashman, Rodriguez implicated his cousin, Yuri Sucart, for bringing him a "mysterious Dominican substance." He also blamed his "lack of a college education" for his being so vulnerable as to take the substance. Then, after pausing for thirty seconds, seeming to cry, A-Rod pointed at Hooton and said, "I hope that kids would not make the same mistake I made, and I hope to join Don Hooton, who has done some incredible things, who's sitting right over there."[69]

Don was ecstatic. What better way to spread the word about steroids than having Taylor's boyhood idol serve as a spokesman for the foundation that bore his name? During the next four years, A-Rod made about a dozen appearances annually for the Taylor Hooton Foundation. "I truly believed that Alex was a fine role model for kids," Don said. "Whenever we did programs, the kids would go nuts. Alex would talk about the mistakes he made by using steroids and [say] that he wished he'd had the opportunity as a youngster to attend our program so he could avoid those mistakes. He'd always end with an extremely positive message: 'God has given you everything you need to succeed in life. While you might not have what it takes to be a third baseman with the New York Yankees, he's given you the ability to do something real special with your life. Use that ability. Don't resort to shortcuts, like doing drugs.' Those were some of the most memorable programs our organization ever did."[70] But there were also red flags.

On February 28, 2010, the *New York Times* reported that Rodriguez had received treatment from Anthony Galea, a Canadian physician who was providing patients with unapproved and mislabeled drugs, including HGH and the PED Actovegin. Galea confirmed that he had treated Rodriguez but said that he had prescribed only anti-inflammatories.[71] Don gave A-Rod the benefit of the doubt and continued their partnership. Then, on January 22, 2013, the *Miami Times* obtained documents indicating that

In 2009, Don Hooton and the New York Yankees' Alex Rodriguez joined efforts to fight teen steroid use. Over the next year, A-Rod served as a speaker for the Taylor Hooton Foundation, addressing school groups and encouraging youngsters to use their innate abilities to achieve their dreams. The relationship ended in February 2010, when the *New York Times* reported that the Yankee third baseman was using steroids. *(Courtesy of Taylor Hooton Foundation.)*

Rodriguez was one of several star players linked to Biogenesis, an antiaging clinic in Coral Gables, Florida, that distributed HGH and other PEDs to major league ballplayers as well as high school students.[72] Still, Don remained loyal to his son's hero, believing his repeated denials of any relationship with the clinic or its director, Anthony Bosch. Not until August 5, when MLB suspended Rodriguez for the remainder of the 2013 season and all of the next season, did Don cut his ties to A-Rod.[73]

Stunned by the news, Don feared that the foundation would lose credibility among the very people it was trying to serve—the kids. According to the Commissioner's Office, Rodriguez not only had "used numerous forms of prohibited performance-enhancing substances, including Testosterone and Human Growth Hormone" but had done so "over the course of multiple years."[74] The words were painful to read. It was clear that the Yankee third baseman had betrayed thousands of kids by lying to them during educational outreach programs. What was truly unconscionable, however, was Rodriguez's enlistment of the Taylor Hooton Foundation as an unwitting accomplice in "cover[ing] up his violations of MLB's drug policy." In other words, the Hooton family—and Taylor's memory—had been exploited by A-Rod in a selfish effort "to obstruct and frustrate the Office of the Commissioner's investigation."[75] Instead of seeking retribution, Don issued a brief statement that read, "I am disappointed and saddened by the decisions Alex has made that led to this ruling. The Taylor Hooton Foundation fully supports the efforts made by Major League Baseball to eradicate illegal anabolic steroids and other appearance- and performance-enhancing drugs from the game."[76] Not until 2016, when Rodriguez left the Yankees, did he apologize to Don.

Don is a strong Christian, though. His faith teaches forgiveness, even for those who have committed the most unpardonable sins. He has also learned to turn a tragic loss into a meaningful legacy. Thus, he views the work of the Taylor Hooton Foundation as nothing less than a calling, which he practices with the fervor and commitment of an evangelist. Don hopes that a forthcoming feature film being produced by Andy Meyer of Aunt Max Motion Pictures will give greater public exposure to the foundation. Occasionally, he allows his ambitions to take over—his desire for greater financial resources, the goal to provide more extensive outreach to kids and their parents, and the desperate need to reform the way high school and collegiate sports train their athletes. That is when his wife, Gwen, intercedes and keeps him grounded.

"This is not *your* foundation; it's God's," she reminds him, with the loving firmness of a soul mate. "He opens the door, not *you*. And He will open that door in His time, not *yours*. If we can help just one family avoid the loss of their child, then Taylor's legacy will truly have meaning."[77]

Don and Gwen Hooton are the perfect couple. Together, they act from the head and the heart in a mutual quest to do God's work on Earth.

Taylor would be proud.

9

LOSING A SON,
REBUILDING A FAMILY

hortly after returning to Petaluma from USC, Rob Garibaldi admitted to his psychiatrist, Dr. Brent Cox, that he was doping. Although Cox advised him to stop the practice, Rob refused, saying he wanted to gain another 10 to 15 pounds. Rob also admitted that he had reduced his dosage of Effexor and intended to stop taking the antidepressant altogether, because its interaction with the steroids was interfering with his ability to gain muscle mass. "The irony is, he is telling me all this with the mind-set of a warrior," said Cox in a December 19, 2004, interview with the *San Francisco Chronicle*. "He was like a warrior going into battle, and he had to go through this sacrifice in order to sculpt his body into the perfect specimen."[1]

Still, the psychiatrist laid the groundwork for a resumption of Rob's academic and baseball activities by writing a letter on his behalf. Stating that Rob had been his patient for more than a year, Cox wrote that he met the "equivocal diagnostic criteria for attention deficit hyperactivity disorder complicated by a major depressive disorder." He stated that Rob's severe depression came in the "aftermath of his traumatic departure from the USC [baseball] program" and that "ongoing intensive psychotherapy" should "steadily modulate" the symptoms of the depression. In turn, Cox believed that the psychotherapy would "permit this highly promising fellow to continue his academic and athletic training." He closed the letter with a request for "any accommodations that might be offered to Mr. Garibaldi around his co-existing learning and emotional difficulties."[2]

However, nowhere in the letter did Cox mention Rob's ongoing use of steroids. Not until months after Rob's suicide did Cox finally disclose that he knew of his doping. Although Denise Garibaldi, Rob's mother, acknowledged that there was doctor-patient confidentiality, she was angry with Cox for not providing the information. "By the time Rob left USC, he was no longer responsible for himself," she said. "He was delusional and may well have been suicidal from the combination of all the drugs he was taking."[3]

There is no doubt that Rob's experience at USC was emotionally and psychologically devastating. At SRJC, he might have struggled academically, but he persevered and succeeded in the classroom, probably because he was doing so well on the baseball diamond and, if he was doping, being conservative about the dosages. Rob's mental outlook was heavily influenced by his playing performance and his ultimate goal of becoming a major league ballplayer. Under those circumstances, academic success, no matter how minimal, was just another challenge on the road to that goal. It was a challenge he believed he could meet with the very same work ethic he applied to baseball. John Daly, an academic adviser for athletes at SRJC, confirmed that Rob was a conscientious student. Although he could not by law discuss Rob's academic performance, Daly did say that before Rob left for USC, he was focused and attentive, someone who "always took care of business."[4]

Sixteen months later, after leaving USC, Garibaldi was an emotional and psychological wreck. Cox, his psychiatrist, was astonished by the change. "This was someone who, despite a learning disability, was highly functional socially and very adaptive to his environment," he said. "Rob had great friends and was absolutely a sweetheart of a kid, and now he had trouble focusing and was very worried about his future."[5] Convinced he was a failure, Rob struggled to regain a sense of normalcy, but it was too late. His steroid use, combined with other prescribed medications, severely compromised his natural intelligence as well as his ability to behave as a rational adult. In fact, when Rob, in anticipation of applying to other colleges, took an intelligence test for learning disability eligibility services, Denise was shocked to learn that his I.Q. had dropped by 24 points.[6] "Rob was a shell of the person we knew when we brought him home from USC," recalled his father, Ray Garibaldi. "He was severely depressed, more than I had ever seen before. All he wanted to do was to get back to USC, take his exams, be reinstated on the team, and play in the College World Series again. But we knew he was not capable of doing that." Rob exhibited such drastic mood swings that his parents believed he was bipolar. There were other issues, too. "He couldn't seem to remember anything, and he didn't appear to be as intelligent," said Ray. "We still had no idea that he was using steroids."[7] For many years, the Garibaldis blamed themselves for not knowing the signs and dangers of steroid use. Severe depression alternating with extreme anger or rage, symptoms often associated with bipolar disorder, are also telling indicators of doping, as are the loss of memory and intelligence. Rob was exhibiting all of these signs.

Since the early 1990s, various studies have established that anabolic steroid use can result in "hypomanic or manic symptoms," such as "irritability, aggressiveness, hyperactivity and psychotic symptoms" as well as "depressive symptoms during withdrawal, including depressed mood and hyper-somnia and suicidality."[8] But the loss of memory and intelligence was not linked with AAS until very recently. According to the Endocrine Society, the world's largest and most active organization devoted to research on hormones and the clinical practice of endocrinology, recent studies involving animal and human neuronal cells "raise[d] the ominous possibility that long-term users of high-dose AAS might develop potentially irreversible cognitive deficits." Memory loss, in particular, was found "to be associated with a total lifetime burden of AAS exposure."[9]

Despite his cognitive difficulties, Rob returned to USC to take his exams during the summer of 2001, and he managed to maintain the 2.4 grade point average necessary to play baseball and retain his scholarship. Throughout the summer, Coach Mike Gillespie phoned the Garibaldis, hoping to find out whether Rob had made a decision about returning to USC. According to Ray, the coach phoned him in early July to remind him that Rob still had a full scholarship at USC and that he needed to know whether to hold it for him or to redistribute the money if he was not going to return.

"We'll let you know by August 1," replied Ray, reminding Gillespie of the deadline. Before ending the conversation, the head coach informed Ray that he had been getting a lot of phone calls about Rob's availability and assured him that he would not stand in the way if his son wanted to transfer to another Pac-10 school.

Ray was surprised by the concession, realizing how difficult it was for a transfer to remain in the same conference.

"Thanks, Coach," he said, ending the conversation. "We'll let you know by August 1."[10]

According to Denise, Gillespie phoned again in late July, hoping to learn of Rob's decision. She told the USC coach that her son "was still ill" and "couldn't make up his mind yet" but that they would "let him know on

August 1." Frustrated, Gillespie reminded her that if Rob was not returning to USC, he needed to know so he could offer his scholarship to another
player. Denise acknowledged the remark and thanked him for his concern
before hanging up.[11]

Rob was still undecided about returning to USC. His cousin Joe Garibaldi asked him on several occasions to consider "the bigger picture." "I
told him to look beyond the baseball program," recalled Joe. "I said that if
he stayed at USC, he was going to graduate from a highly reputable institution with one of the wealthiest, most respected alumni groups in the
nation. I also pointed out that he was going to get a great job and have
opportunities that most people could only dream about." But Rob barely
heard a word. Instead, he insisted that he was "going to play major league
baseball" and that "nothing else really mattered." Joe discouraged that
thinking. He had been a successful Division I pitcher who was drafted by
the Texas Rangers, and he knew that less than 3 percent of those who play
at the collegiate level make it to the majors. Joe had used his education at
San Diego State to get a well-paying job in public administration. "But Rob
just couldn't understand that the overwhelming majority of players who
leave college early for pro ball see their careers end in the low minors, and
they have no alternatives because they didn't earn a degree."[12]

Eventually, Rob realized that he could not return to USC and that he
would have to pursue his big league dream elsewhere. "Once Coach Gillespie makes his mind up about you, it's over," he told his parents.[13] As
it turned out, Rob had several options: Texas Tech and Louisiana State
had contacted USC about his availability and later made offers.[14] But Rob
wanted to live at home. So Paul Maytorena, the head baseball coach at
Casa Grande High School, contacted John Goelz at nearby Sonoma State
University (SSU). Maytorena, a graduate of SSU, had played for Goelz
and thought that Rob would benefit from the more relaxed Division II
program. "I knew Rob wanted a new beginning," said Maytorena. "I felt
that being closer to home would be better for him. Goelz wanted to help
out. He had had several [Division I] throwbacks who made a comeback at
Sonoma, so Rob wouldn't have been the first kid to get a bad break. And it
wasn't like Goelz was taking a risk on him either."[15]

To be sure, Goelz was familiar with stories like Rob's. They were kids
who came from high schools and junior colleges where the coaches were
close to their players, kids who had lived at home all their lives and were
surrounded by the same support system they had known since birth.
Many of those kids experienced culture shock when they went away to
school at a major Division I university. "At the Division I level," said Goelz,

"*winning* is the primary emphasis. Sometimes the coaches lose sight of what's truly important, like developing good people as well as good players. While winning is also very important at the Division II level, and our teams at Sonoma State have done extremely well over the years, our coaches give the kids more individual attention, and we are proud that our kids go on to do good things with their lives."[16]

On Maytorena's recommendation, Goelz sent a release form to Gillespie, asking to speak with Garibaldi, and was granted permission. Goelz met with Rob and his father and learned of the difficulties he had had at USC with coaches and teammates. He also learned of Rob's erratic behavior. It did not take long for Goelz to understand that Rob did not enjoy the same individual attention or emotional support at USC that he had had earlier in life and that as a full-scholarship player, he was expected to perform well on a consistent basis. "The pressure on Rob must have been overwhelming, especially when he was dealing with a learning disability," he said.

At the same time, Goelz could appreciate Gillespie's position. He knew Gillespie fairly well from his years as head baseball coach at College of the Canyons, a community college in Valencia, California. In fact, Goelz had recruited many of Gillespie's players. "Mike's a great coach," he said. "He did a wonderful job at USC, and he continues to do a great job now that he's at Cal-Irvine. I also believe that he would never condone doping."

"What you also have to understand though, is that at the Division I level, every head coach is under tremendous pressure to win," Goelz added. "He doesn't have much job security unless he wins on a consistent basis." Thus, Goelz was not surprised when he learned that Gillespie had dismissed Rob for constant harassment and his threat to complain to the newspapers. "It's easier to dismiss a player who's causing problems and move on to the next guy," explained the SSU coach. "Not that I condone it, but I understand it, considering the pressure a Division I coach has to win."[17]

Rob enrolled at SSU in the fall of 2001. Despite the sharp drop in his I.Q., he managed to do well academically and batted over .440 in the fall season.[18] Then the erratic behavior resurfaced. "Rob was on a roller-coaster," said Goelz. "He had problems being on time, got confused about times, dates, and places. It got to a point where I'd write practice and game times on his wrist with a Sharpie marker so he wouldn't forget. Once, he showed up for a Saturday morning game at 6:00 A.M. so he wouldn't be late for batting practice, which began at 9:00 A.M. But he fell asleep in his car in the parking lot and woke up at 9:15 A.M., so he was still late. If it wasn't so sad, it'd almost be funny."[19]

Again, Denise tried to protect her son. "I became his superego that semester," she admitted. "I told him where he had to be and at what time. I would write everything down for him. I put Post-Its in his car. I'd ask his instructors about his assignments and make sure he was handing them in."[20] Ray was in denial. For years, he had lived vicariously through Rob and his baseball successes. Ray not only shared his son's dream but also did his best to help him achieve it. For years, coaches had told him that Rob was a "can't-miss" prospect destined for major league stardom. Even after his son decided to leave USC, Ray refused to let go of that belief. Returning home was just a brief setback.

Although it was a Division II school, SSU also turned out ballplayers who attracted pro scouts. Some were "D-I Throwbacks," an insulting reference to those transfers who could not cut it in major Division I programs. Others had matriculated from reputable junior college programs. Rob represented both, and Ray knew it. But he had invested too much of himself in the dream to let go. In the process, he had distanced himself from his eldest son and namesake and abandoned whatever interests and social life he had once enjoyed outside Rob's baseball circles.[21]

Two months into the spring of 2002's baseball season, Rob's behavior became surrealistic. Once, he almost sent a teammate to the hospital after giving him some of his attention deficit disorder medication for heat cramps. It was not a cruel prank—Rob was genuinely trying to be helpful.[22] Other times, he would lash out at a teammate for no apparent reason and storm off the field.[23] Perhaps the strangest incident occurred when he painted his black baseball shoes gold before showing up for a game. By that point, Rob's teammates were already disgusted with him, but Goelz, known for his compassion and his sense of humor, decided to make light of the situation rather than blow up. Escorting Rob into his office, the good-humored coach asked, "Rob, you know that our team wears black baseball shoes, so why are you wearing gold ones?"

"I really like these shoes, Coach," he gushed. "I stayed up late last night painting them gold. I know they are going to help me play great. You won't believe it!"

Goelz, bemused by the reply, tried to draw him out. "Tell me how great you're going to play, Rob."

"I'm going to get on base every time up," he said without missing a beat.

It was difficult to take seriously. After all, even the very best major league players do not reach base every time they go to bat. But Goelz humored his troubled player.

Sonoma State University coach John Goelz, who has the reputation of being a players' coach—one who strikes a good balance between his commitment to each player and his commitment to the team—gave his all to help Rob achieve his dream of becoming a professional baseball player. *(Courtesy of John Goelz.)*

"Okay, Rob," he said. "I'll tell you what I'm going to do. I'll respect your belief that those gold shoes are going to make you play better. I'll allow you to wear those shoes as long as you get on base 3 of the 4 times you go to bat. But if you go 2-for-4, or 1-for-3, you have to lose the gold shoes and go back to the black ones."

Rob agreed, so Goelz went out to the dugout and informed the rest of the team of their deal. After the initial feelings of disgust and disbelief passed, the players actually looked forward to Rob's plate appearances.

The first time up, he walked. Jogging down to first base, Rob looked over at Goelz, who was standing in the third-base coaching box, and smiled, as if to say, "I told you so." His second at-bat produced a hit. Now Rob was really proud of himself, smiling from ear to ear and looking at his teammates as he was standing on first. Everyone—coaches and teammates—was laughing. The "game" was actually becoming pretty fun.

But Rob's third at-bat resulted in a strikeout, and despite the encouragement of his teammates, he grounded out during his fourth and final at-bat. Realizing that he had lost the deal, Rob entered the dugout, removed the gold shoes, and threw them in the garbage can, muttering, "These shoes suck!"[24]

Goelz was not trying to embarrass Rob—he genuinely cared about his welfare. He had always prided himself in being a "player's coach," one who made every effort to balance his commitments to the individual and to the team. "Rob was a great kid who was having problems," he recalled in an interview. "I couldn't give up on him. We don't do that in our program. If the kid makes a commitment to us, we make a commitment to him. So it wasn't just me. Our coaches were constantly communicating with Rob, trying to find something that would work. It was as if we were trying to reprogram his behavior, but we couldn't get at the root problem, which, in the end, we discovered was steroids."[25]

The extent of Garibaldi's steroid use at SSU is unclear. Maytorena had learned about Rob's doping and repeatedly urged him to quit. Maytorena believes that the ex–Casa Grande star did at least two cycles during his time at SSU and increased the dosage as the June amateur draft neared. "Rob was not only using Deca Durobolin and Sustanon at the same time, but he would back up cycles," Maytorena said. "It got to the point where he didn't even cycle off, just go back to back. You can't do that with steroids. You have to cycle on and then cycle off. But Rob thought, 'If I do back-to-back cycles, I can get a little stronger.'"[26] Rob also confided in his mother.

On Mother's Day 2002, Rob told Denise that he was doping and made her promise that she would not tell his father. "He knew that Ray strongly disapproved of drugs and that if he knew Rob was using steroids, he'd make him stop," she explained. "To be honest, I was also afraid of how Ray would react." There were other reasons she agreed to keep his trust. "Rob made it sound as if this was something new that he was trying, not that he'd done it in the past," said Denise. "He couldn't even tell me the exact dosage. Instead, he told me, 'This much,' extending his left thumb and index finger about half an inch apart. That convinced me that he hadn't used before." In addition, Denise believed that she could "talk freely with Rob about the potential dangers of steroids" after doing her own research. Insisting that steroids were "safe," Rob told his mother that he needed to take them, because June was his "last chance" to be drafted by a major league team, but he promised that he would stop if she believed his behavior was becoming "too weird." Wanting to believe her son and fearing the confrontation that would occur if her husband found out, Denise took Rob at his word. She has since admitted it was a "huge mistake." What she did not know was that her son not only was using steroids but was "addicted to the drugs."[27]

Rob's need to continue doping reflects the definitions of "physical" and "psychological" dependencies described by body builders as well as the "anabolic," "androgenic," and "hedonic" dependences described by Harvard psychiatrist Harrison G. Pope Jr. in his extensive research on steroid use.[28] The hedonic combination of substances Rob was using made him especially dependent on steroids. That volatile combination included the prescription drugs Effexor, an antidepressant, and Provigil for attention deficit disorder; the anabolic steroids Deca Durabolin and Sustanon; and the increasing use of alcohol. Although they are legal, antidepressants and alcohol are addictive substances that, according to the research, can potentially trigger an additional dependency on steroids.

On June 4–5, MLB held its 2002 amateur draft. Rob spent those two days holed up in his bedroom, while Denise remained downstairs, listening to the draft on the radio and fearful of what her son might do if he was not selected. She checked on him when he did not emerge from the bedroom and found her son under the covers.

"I didn't make it," groaned Rob.

"Yes, I know," replied Denise, as she attempted to console him. But Rob recoiled. He just wanted to be alone. Heartbroken, Denise left the room.[29]

Goelz did not need to hear the draft to know that his center fielder was bypassed. Several pro scouts had approached him about Rob during the spring, but Goelz admitted that his behavior had become "so unpredictable by June" that he "couldn't recommend him." Instead, the SSU coach phoned several independent teams, hoping to get him a tryout. Goelz believed that "if Rob could straighten himself out and play for one of those teams, he might still have a shot at organized baseball." But he even doubted that, once he learned in early July that Rob was using steroids. Instead, he did the only thing a responsible and compassionate person could do—he told Rob's parents.[30]

Goelz's phone call put an end to the secret Rob and his mother had been keeping since May. Now Ray knew about his son's doping, and, just as Denise had predicted, there was a confrontation. Ray demanded to know which drugs his son was taking. Rob erupted. Grabbing his father in a choke hold and throwing him to the floor, he screamed:

> I'm on steroids, what do you think!? Who do you think I am!? I'm a baseball player. Baseball players take steroids. How do you think [Barry] Bonds hits all his home runs!? How do you think McGwire and all the others hit homers!? You think they just do it from working out normal!?

Shocked by the outburst and gasping for air, Ray struggled to break loose. Finally, Raymond, his eldest son, came to the rescue, pulling Rob off and pinning him down on the floor until he was too exhausted to fight back.[31]

"It was a huge reality check for my parents, especially my dad," recalled Raymond. "All this time, he thought that he was protecting Rob from all the dangers that could happen to him. Now, this happens." In fact, Raymond had long predicted that something terrible was going to happen to his younger brother, because his parents had placed Rob's baseball career above so much else in their lives.

Raymond had always been the responsible son, a hard worker who took the initiative to learn a trade and find rewarding, gainful employment as a mechanic for the Golden Gate Bridge Transportation District. Rob, on the other hand, was a romantic who invested all his energies in baseball, with the dreamlike goal of reaching the major leagues. "Once, I told my mom, 'You and Dad are setting Robbie up for failure,'" Raymond remembered. "'What happens if he doesn't make it in professional baseball? He has no work experience. He's never had to work in the real world a single day of his life.'"[32]

During the last three months of his life, Rob, according to Ray, was like an "out-of-control freight train that nobody could stop." He was "up all night, pacing the house like a lion trapped in a cage," and then he would "sleep for most of the day." His behavior became more unpredictable. After supper, for example, Rob would sit down with his father in the living room and they would be having a good conversation. Suddenly, he would "storm out of the room, return two minutes later, and be screaming" at him.[33] There were other incidents of 'roid rage. Once, Rob took a wood bat and destroyed all his baseball memorabilia and high school and college awards. Another time, he attacked his father and accused him of being "overinvolved," adding that he should have "stayed out of my affairs." The incident was so unnerving that Denise called the Petaluma police for help. On still another occasion, Rob threatened suicide, screaming that he was going to "blow his brains out."[34] Concerned for his safety, Ray took away his car keys.

Rob was also delusional. He thought he was Jesus Christ. He told his parents he was dating actress Cameron Diaz. He insisted that burglars were building tunnels under the house to steal his clothes. He watched San Francisco Giants' games on television and believed that Barry Bonds was speaking directly to him. Perhaps the most surreal incident occurred when Rob was invited to try out for the Sonoma County Crushers of the independent Western Baseball League. Raymond drove him to the ballpark and could not believe what transpired there.

When Manager Kevin Mitchell, a former outfielder for the San Francisco Giants, greeted him, Rob exclaimed, "Hey, Kevin! What's up, man? I want to play for your team. I've come to show you how to hit home runs. I've hit more home runs than you ever hit!" Mitchell, initially shocked by the shameless boast, figured that Rob was just trying to be funny. Dismissing the insult, he guided the brothers into the ballpark, where Rob took batting practice. He hit fairly well, too, driving several balls into the gaps and sending a few other balls over the outfield fence. Afterward, Mitchell, impressed by the performance, shook Rob's hand and promised to call him. Handing the brothers front-row tickets for that night's game, the Crushers' manager headed to the dugout.

Rob and Raymond stayed for the game. But as the contest unfolded, it was clear to Rob that Sonoma, in the process of being shut-out, 7–0, lacked offense. So he volunteered his services. "Hey, Kevin!" he yelled into the Crushers' dugout. "Your team sucks! Put me in. I'll show them how to hit!" Embarrassed, Raymond grabbed his brother by the arm and told him to keep his mouth shut. It was futile. Rob kept up his taunting and was removed from the ballpark by security guards. Needless to say, Mitchell never called.[35]

Denise became desperate. She begged her son to keep his promise to stop using now that his behavior had become so delusional and frightening. She also initiated a three-hour-long family intervention in which Rob was told that he needed to "get help for his drug problem or he could no longer live with them." But Rob insisted that he did not have a problem. "I'm a ballplayer, not a drug addict!" he screamed. "You wouldn't say ballplayers are addicts!" Clearly, Rob refused to make the connection between recreational drugs, which he believed were harmful, and anabolic steroids, which he genuinely believed were a healthy means of enhancing his performance on the baseball diamond. Taking a different approach, and having done some research on the effects of anabolic steroids, Denise told her son about the long-term dangers to his health, including impotence. "That's not important now," replied Rob. "I'll worry about that later." "He just refused to listen to reason," said Raymond. "It took my uncle, a recovering alcoholic, to convince him to go to rehab."[36]

In July, Rob assaulted his father again. Having stolen his car keys, Rob stormed out of the house, got into his car, and drove recklessly around the neighborhood. Once again, Denise, fearing for her son's life, called the police. "I can't believe I'm doing this!" she thought as she paced the floor waiting for the police. "It must be done. But why am I the one doing it? I'm his mother!" Deep down, Denise knew she was the *only* person who could do anything about the situation. She was the only one who understood how dire it had become. Rob was placed on an involuntary hold at Psychiatric Emergency Services, a locked in-patient treatment facility in Santa Rosa, for two weeks. There, he admitted to doing three nine-week cycles of steroids over a period of two years, but those close to him believe that Rob had been doping much longer than that.[37] Shortly thereafter, he agreed to attend a residential treatment program despite his insistence that he was not an addict and did not belong there. But before his twenty-eight-day stint was scheduled to end, Rob was discharged for assaulting an employee.[38]

When Rob returned home on September 26, there was a period of calm. There were no more rages, no more delusional behavior. Instead, Rob appeared to be at peace and actually began talking about a life outside baseball. He was planning to return to SSU to complete his last six credits for a degree in sociology. Rob talked about working with kids, both as a coach and a counselor. He went out during the daytime and visited old friends and returned home to dine with his parents in the evening.[39] One night, Rob told his father of his plans to get a part-time job while completing his degree. Encouraged by the news as well as by his son's improved behavior, Ray returned the keys to his car so Rob could look for work.[40]

On the morning of Monday, September 30, Rob asked his father to play catch, just like they had hundreds of times before. Ray was hopeful that he was getting his son back. In the afternoon, Rob interviewed for a job at a local car dealership. On his way home, he stopped at an indoor shooting range, went up to the counter, and began asking the teller about various kinds of pistols and how to use them. Placing ammunition and three different weapons on the counter, the teller began to explain the firing capacity of each one. When he turned his back to answer the phone, Rob grabbed one of the pistols—a .357 Magnum—and the ammunition and took off.[41]

That evening, he returned home to have dinner with his parents. Afterward, they all sat down in the family room to watch television. Out of the blue, Rob asked his parents, "If I get well—no steroids, no marijuana—and return to school, can I live at home and try out for an independent team in the spring?" Pleased by the query, Denise and Ray agreed. At 10:00 P.M. Rob excused himself and went to bed. Shortly thereafter, Ray and Denise retired for the night. It had become a routine since Rob had returned home from rehab, and the Garibaldis were comforted by it. In fact, Denise would later recall that she "slept better that night than she had in months."[42] But Rob had a change of plans on this particular night.

At 3:30 A.M. on October 1, Ray heard a noise in the garage and went downstairs to investigate. He found Rob starting up his car.

"Where ya going?" he asked his son.

"Just going to get something to eat at McDonald's," said Rob. "Maybe I'll take a drive, too."

Ray thought it was a little strange, because Rob had not kept late-night hours since he had returned from rehab. But it had not been unusual in the past for his son to get up in the middle of the night and go out for some fast food. Thus, he did not give it a second thought.

"Okay, Rob," he said, unaware that those were the last words he would ever say to his younger son.[43]

No one knows for sure what Rob did for the next three hours. Perhaps he paid a final visit to all his old baseball haunts, from the Little League fields in Foster City to the baseball diamond at SRJC, where he had enjoyed his finest season ever. En route, Rob might have reflected on what was and what might have been as he weighed his options for a life without baseball. Whatever he did, the troubled young man just did not see any possibilities outside a game he was born to play.

Having achieved closure, sometime around 6:15 A.M., Rob pulled his car into a parking space a short distance from home. Staring out at Sonoma Mountain, illuminated by the emerging lightness of dawn, the baseball prodigy, just 24 years old, pulled out the .357 Magnum he had stolen the day before, raised it to his temple, and pulled the trigger. A jogger found him and ran from house to house to call for help.[44]

At about 6:45 A.M., the Petaluma police arrived at the Garibaldi home with the news that Rob had shot himself in the head and had been rushed to Santa Rosa Memorial Hospital. Stunned by the news, Ray stood in the doorway, speechless and immobile. Snapping out of his trance, Ray collected himself and went upstairs to get Denise.

"Something's wrong," he uttered, "Terribly wrong."

Denise had heard the sirens from a distance but paid little attention. She did not know what awaited her. Standing at the top of the staircase, she was stunned to see two police officers, a detective, and a chaplain. Somehow keeping her composure, Denise walked past them and took a seat on the sofa.

"Rob shot himself in the head," the chaplain told her. "He's still alive and on his way to Santa Rosa Memorial Hospital. Is there anyone we can call for you?"

Denise let out a blood-curdling scream and began sobbing uncontrollably. She had never wept like this before. It was as if someone had taken a knife and severed her heart. "I tried to keep this from happening!" she shrieked.

Ray did not hear her, though. The shock of their son's suicide was setting in.

Raymond, awakened by the screaming, came downstairs to find his mother in hysterics. Tears flowing down her face, she looked her older son directly in the eye and cried, "Your brother shot himself in the head! He's still alive, and they've taken him to the hospital."

Struggling with a myriad of emotions, Raymond took his mother in his arms and held her. He still did not grasp the full meaning of the tragedy until Denise admitted the painful truth that he had predicted—that his parents' preoccupation with Rob's baseball career would only set him up for failure.

"You were right!' she cried out. "Everything you said was right!"[45]

"I used to think that I'd get some satisfaction if either of my parents admitted that to me," Raymond admitted, years later. "But at that moment, I was sorry I ever said it."[46]

Rob lived another eighteen hours on life support. It was long enough for his extended family, friends, coaches, and teammates to say their good-byes. When everyone but the extended family left, Rob was taken off life support. Denise broke down again, yielding to a convulsion of screams and guttural sobbing. Ray, his eyes streaming with tears, apologized to his son for being such a "bad father." Shortly thereafter, Rob slipped away.[47] He was finally free of the depression, rage, delusions, and disappointments that had haunted him for almost two years.

On Saturday, October 5, 2002, nearly a thousand people gathered at St. James Catholic Church in Petaluma to honor Rob's memory. Coaches, teammates, and friends attended from Casa Grande, SRJC, and SSU, but not a single person came from the USC "family."[48] Denise offered a "meditation," comparing Rob's last years on Earth to a "sailing ship lying silently, waiting for a wind to fill its sails to set off in majestic motion" as people "standing on a dock . . . wave good-bye and go home." She continued:

> Right now, we are like those people on the dock. We've seen Rob go. Bound with ties of despair and failure, he's disappeared through the horizon of death. We cry with sadness and grief, "There he goes." We know that life will be empty and painful without him. But, we who have faith know that the change is not in what we can see from our dock. Rob is still as large as life and larger than life, because he sees Jesus standing on the other shore. Along with Jesus are Josh and Adam [high school friends], Coach [Bob] Leslie, Uncle Pat, [Grandfather] Ben, and all other deceased relatives and friends.
>
> Together they shout, "There he comes!" And as Rob stumbles forth, Jesus steps out to meet him. They instantly recognize one another. Jesus dries Rob's eyes and turns to the crowd. He says once more, as he has so many times before, "Untie him from his despair and failure and set him free!" And then he turns away and says, "Welcome home, Rob!"[49]

Ray embraced his wife and accompanied her back to their seats. Then, Diane and Dan Harvey, Rob's aunt and uncle, delivered the eulogy. "I have no doubt that angels walk among us," began Diane, "and our angel, Rob, has taken flight." "Expressing our sadness at Rob's death is natural, and God gave tears to us to use. I don't want to be brave today. Today, I want to cry . . . knowing that a young man, whom I loved dearly, was robbed of his life." After acknowledging the "special people" in Rob's life, she turned the podium over to her husband. Dan recalled the highlights of Rob's baseball career, his devotion to family and friends, and the "blessing" they felt for having had him in their lives. Then, he read a letter Rob had written to himself as a freshman in high school after returning home from a church retreat:

> Dear Me,
>   I learned a lot on my first retreat. I met a lot of new people. My favorite person was Jesus. Thanks to Father Tom, I got to meet Christ. I think I am going to start going to church again. Now I realize why I go to church. I am very happy I came. I didn't want to come because I thought it was going to be boring. Well, I gotta go.
>   Later,
>   Rob

It was a very touching gesture meant to give comfort to those gathered, reminding them that Rob was a "very spiritual" person. "Rob," said his uncle, was "all about God," and he would want everyone to know that he is "playing on God's team now." "I have no doubt," Dan concluded, "that Rob has already earned his wings, and they are golden."[50]

The eulogy was followed by brief remarks from childhood and high school friends, who remembered Rob as "a caring, generous, respectful young man who loved his family and friends." Some promised that they would "always see a little of [Rob] in themselves." Another admitted that Rob "must have endured pain while on this Earth that he could only imagine," but that he knew his friend was "in a much better place now."[51]

Two days later, Rob was laid to rest at the Italian Cemetery in Colma, California.[52]

Suicide has a devastating effect on a family. Those left behind tend to experience a range of complex and sometimes conflicting emotions. Often, survivors struggle with guilt, wondering whether they could have

Ray and Denise Garibaldi, shown here with a photo of Rob as a Little Leaguer, struggled personally and professionally after their son's suicide. *(By Frederic Larson, San Francisco Chronicle / Polaris Images.)*

prevented the tragic death or the problems that preceded it. Some feel rejected by the deceased or angry at him or her for committing suicide. Others long for the person they lost, only to find relief in his or her death, especially if it was preceded by months or years of mental and/or physical pain. Denial and scape-goating are also common responses.[53] Some families manage to remain intact, finding the support and love necessary to move on with life. Others break up, unable to come to terms with the loss. The Garibaldis experienced all of these feelings after Rob's death.

Within a year, Ray lost his job, in part because of an inability to move on with his life. He punished himself for Rob's suicide, especially for his son's steroids-induced accusations that he was "overinvolved" and that he "should have stayed out of [Rob's] affairs." "I couldn't stop thinking about what I could've done to save him," he admitted:

> I spent so much time with Rob, taking him to practices, games, tryouts. I lived through everything with him—the drafts, every game he played. I flew across the country to watch him play. There was a lot of "windshield time" there. It wasn't like we didn't com-municate. It wasn't like I'd sit there and dictate to him, either.
>
> We'd have conversations. It was a two-way dialogue. We were together constantly. That's why it shocked me. How come I didn't see this coming? If I was a father who wasn't around for his kid, I'd probably understand it, because I wasn't around for him.
>
> I spent a lot of time reflecting on that. You know, the steroids were probably the only secret Rob kept from me. He kept it from me, because he knew how I felt about drug use.[54]

Ray could not bring himself to accept the fact that Rob was grown and responsible for his own decisions. No matter what he said or did, Ray would not have made much of a difference. It is a generations-old problem: parents try to spare their children pain and suffering from the benefit of their own experience, but they rarely, if ever, succeed.

Denise was also struggling with her own demons. "Rob was mad at me, too," she admitted. "He thought I was overprotective. In fact, I had people tell me as much. They said that Rob should have gone to Sonoma State from the start—not to USC. If I had to help him with his papers, he didn't belong at a place like USC, and by doing that, I participated in his demise. All that was hard to hear, but I worked through it."[55] In part, Denise resolved her guilt by sharing the painful experience of Rob's steroid use with others. Her involvement began in March 2004, when she and Ray happened to be watching *60 Minutes* on CBS and learned of Taylor Hooton's steroids-related suicide. Until that moment, they had been hesitant to discuss Rob's story.[56]

"I became energized by hearing Taylor's story," recalled Denise. "I admired Don and Gwen Hooton for having the courage to share their story with others. I also began to see so much purpose in Rob's life. I knew I had to share his story with other families to prevent something similar from happening to them. I hoped that Rob's story would reinforce Taylor's story about the dangers of steroid abuse."[57] But Ray was hesitant, thinking that Denise would be airing their family's "dirty laundry." Although Ray was uncomfortable with the idea, he eventually agreed to it.[58]

On March 25, 2004, the couple traveled to Sacramento to testify at a California State Senate hearing on the dangers of illegal body-enhancing drugs used by amateur and professional athletes. According to Ralph Leef of the *Santa Rosa Press Democrat*, the legislative investigation, which came in the wake of the BALCO scandal, revealed that in California alone, more than twenty thousand teens were believed to have used anabolic steroids either to enhance their athletic performances or to improve their physical appearances.[59] The Garibaldis' testimony provided state legislators with a rude awakening to the realities of teenage doping. It also placed the couple in the national spotlight when they were asked to testify at the 2005 congressional hearings on steroid use in MLB.

Since those hearings, California has taken the lead in the fight against adolescent steroids use. In May 2005, the state's Interscholastic Federation became the first high school association in the nation to adopt an anti-doping policy. The policy requires every student-athlete to sign a contract promising not to use PEDs and requires all coaches to complete a

State Senator Jackie Speier (D–San Francisco) successfully sponsored legislation that barred California's coaches from selling nutritional supplements to students, banned supplement companies from promoting their products at high school sporting events, and legalized the California Interscholastic Federation's anti-doping policy. Today, she serves in the U.S. House of Representatives. *(Courtesy of Congresswoman Jackie Speier.)*

steroids-education course. Later that year, State Senator Jackie Speier (D-San Francisco) sponsored and tried to push through the state legislature SB 1630, a bill that would bar coaches from selling nutritional supplements to students, ban supplement companies from promoting their products at high school sporting events, and legalize the California Interscholastic Federation's anti-doping policy.[60] It took two years to get the bill passed after Governor Arnold Schwarzenegger vetoed the first measure. When he threatened to do the same the following year to a similar bill (SB 37), the Garibaldis filed a conflict-of-interest claim with the California Fair Political Practices Commission. The claim alleged that the governor's veto of SB 1630, a bill to regulate the dietary-supplements industry, came at a time when he had a multi-million-dollar contract for endorsing supplements. Schwarzenegger yielded to the pressure and signed SB 37 into law.[61]

State Senator Speier's efforts caught the attention of the National Federation of State High School Associations, which began an antisteroids campaign aimed at every adolescent athlete in the country. Titled "Make the Right Choice," the initiative includes videos geared toward coaches, athletes, and parents.[62] By December 2005, other states had also joined the fight. New Jersey requires random steroid testing of all athletes at state championships as well as steroids-education programs beginning in middle school. Connecticut updated its chemical health policy to include penalties for athletes caught using steroids. Several other states, including Illinois, Minnesota, Montana, New York, North Carolina, and Pennsylvania, also created steroids-education programs.[63]

Denise and Ray also went on CNN and *48 Hours* to share their story with a national television audience. In those interviews, the Garibaldis faulted USC for their son's problems with steroids. "We sent USC this thriving young athlete with a lot of personality, hope, and determination, and he came back broken," Denise told Troy Roberts, who did the *48 Hours* interview. Ray was more direct. "Rob told me that a trainer advised him to take steroids," he recounted on the August 4, 2004, program. When Roberts asked whether he thought the use of steroids by Division I athletes was done "with a wink and a nod," Ray replied with an emphatic, "Yes."[64] The couple repeated the claim in a live interview with Harry Smith on the *CBS Early Morning Show* on March 18, 2005, emphasizing their belief that they "lost their son long before he took his own life."[65] When Ralph Leef of the *Santa Rosa Press Democrat* contacted Gillespie, USC's head baseball coach, about the Garibaldis' remarks, he insisted that it was "the first [time] [he'd] heard about steroids." "Nobody on our staff knew," he added. "Not the coaching staff, the training staff or the weight room staff."[66] Similarly, a USC spokesperson insisted that the university had "conducted a complete investigation of the [Garibaldi] case and categorically denies all of the allegations made by the [family]." In addition, USC's athletic director also told Ray that the university was "prepared to file a defamation suit."[67] But the threat did not dissuade the Garibaldis.

Instead, they continued to speak to teachers, coaches, and impressionable high school students about the signs and dangers of steroid abuse.[68] They established a scholarship in Rob's memory at Casa Grande High School. The monetary award goes to "a graduating student-athlete in any sport who is in good standing."[69] Denise also wrote letters to advance the antisteroids cause. One of those letters was to Senator George Mitchell, offering advice for a stronger drug-testing policy in MLB.[70] Another letter was hand-delivered by Rich Walcoff, a San Francisco sports-radio broadcaster, to Giants' slugger Barry Bonds at PacBell Ballpark. The letter suggested that Bonds "dedicate his home-run record-breaking baseball to the memories of her son, Taylor Hooton, and other youth who have died under similar [steroid-related] circumstances and place it in the National Baseball Hall of Fame at Cooperstown, New York."[71] And she testified before a federal grand jury in support of Mark Fainaru-Wada and Lance Williams, authors of *Game of Shadows: Barry Bonds, BALCO, and the Steroids Scandal that Rocked Professional Sports*, who were subpoenaed by the government to reveal their confidential sources.[72] For the Garibaldis—especially Denise—the opportunity to state their case before a national audience, the establishment of a stronger drug policy in MLB, and the many educational efforts that were inspired by their efforts gave meaning to Rob's legacy and some small comfort for their loss. Unfortunately, the solace was short-lived.

Ray remained incapacitated by Rob's death. Although he found part-time consulting work and tried to become involved in the lives of his older son and his family, he could not escape the terrible feelings of guilt he was suffering. Unable to pay the mortgage, the couple was forced to sell their home and scale down their lifestyle. Ray also declined invitations to speak about their ordeal, believing that doing so would only make him feel worse about his son's death. "It just wasn't working between us," said Denise. "It got to the point where both of us were going to crash. I just couldn't live like that anymore. I had to move on with my life."[73]

On January 9, 2009, after asking for and receiving her son Raymond's blessing, Denise left their home. She filed for divorce in 2010.[74] Nevertheless, Denise continued to speak out against anabolic steroids, began writing and publishing essays on the subject, and became more involved in the lives of her grandchildren as well as in the activities of her Catholic church.[75] "My mom really needed to get on with her life," said Raymond, recalling the painful years following his younger brother's death. "Dad couldn't do it. He'd just hang around the house, almost as if he was in a trance. He was fading away after Robbie's death. I can't blame my mom for leaving. I really respect her for having the courage to strike out on her own and to move ahead with her life."[76] Raymond was not the only one who admired Denise's resolve. Speier, now a U.S. Congresswoman, was so impressed by Denise's courage and faith that she profiled her in a self-help book titled, *This Is Not the Life I Ordered: 50 Ways to Keep Your Head above Water When Life Keeps Dragging You Down.* In it, Speier refers to Denise as "A Mom on a Mission" and lauds her courage:

> After Rob's death, Denise began to speak out about the trainers and coaches who she believed contributed to her son's death by issuing their daily mantra of "get bigger or get beaten." Many tried to intimidate her into silence, threatening her with lawsuits. But her courage grew threefold, and she joined forces with other parents who were coming forward to tell their own heartbreaking stories.
>
> In less than a year, Denise garnered a worldwide audience for her important message. She had become a "mom on a mission" . . . who otherwise would never have sought a national spotlight. She derived her courage from her hope that Rob's life and death would not be forgotten. Her goal was to alert parents to the dangers of steroids to save them and their families from the pain and loss she had experienced.

But she also wanted to tell our national heroes, the ones our children look up to, that players who take steroids and other performance-enhancing drugs are not only cheaters, but cowards. She wanted them to show our children a different way to compete at the top levels so we can put an end to this madness.[77]

After his parents' divorce, Raymond looked after his father, which was not easy. Raymond was carrying a lot of resentment over all the time Ray had spent with Rob due to their mutual passion for baseball. "Dad supported me until I was sixteen and stopped playing the game," said Raymond. "After that, it was all Rob and his baseball career. There wasn't room for anything else. I would've liked him to do 'father-son' things with me, too. Things that interested me, not just him. Things like working on cars, building things, or duck hunting." But now that Rob was gone, Raymond found ways to make up for the missed opportunities. He encouraged his father to attend his granddaughter's soccer and baseball games. Soon, Ray was not only attending those competitions but also coaching her teams. Raymond also found his father a job working concessions at the Golden Gate Bridge Authority, where he is employed as a chief mechanic. "It was good for both of us," he said. "Dad got to see me at work and learned how much I was respected by the other employees. I think he's really proud of that."[78]

Everything was going well for about six months. Then, in 2011, Ray slipped and fell off the gangway into the bay, breaking some ribs. He was rushed to a nearby hospital, where the staff did an MRI and discovered a huge tumor, the size of a soccer ball. It proved to be cancer. With mixed emotions, Raymond phoned his mother to tell her of the accident and the tumor. "It was hard to do," he admitted. "Sure, I felt bad for my dad, but I felt even worse for my mom, because she was finally living the life she wanted. She was getting herself back together, and now Dad had cancer, and we were going to have to take care of him."[79] There was a silver lining, though.

In the process of caring for her ex-husband, Denise became closer to him than they had been in years. They began to do things together—they spent more time with their granddaughters and traveled across the country, all of which had ceased after Rob's death. They also became especially fond of a second family home in the Sierra foothills. Denise's parents had purchased the house for their extended family. "It was important for our family to establish new memories without Rob," explained Denise. "To this day, however, I feel close to Rob when we're there in the mountains.

It's as if we're together as family again."[80] Denise also became as protective of Ray as she had once been of her two sons. Although she still believes that her ex-husband was "living vicariously through Rob's baseball career," she admitted that it was difficult to blame him. "Just think how exciting it must be to have your son accomplishing all that Rob did," she said. "But I also believe that Ray was doing what Rob asked him to do in terms of helping him with his baseball career." Gradually, Denise taught her ex-husband that their son's hurtful accusations were strongly influenced by doping and that even if Rob genuinely believed that his parents played a role in his demise, it did not mean that those feelings were accurate.[81]

"The divorce was my fault," Ray conceded. "Rob's death was extremely hard for me. I was carrying so much guilt about what I didn't do to save him. But since Denise and I got back together, I've come to realize that I couldn't have done any more for Rob than what I did."[82] Denise also learned to be kind to herself. She now understands that she did the very best she could by her younger son. In fact, she believes that Rob knew it, too. Just as important, Denise reconciled the years of conflicting emotions over her son's reasons for taking his life. "Cognitively, Rob was extremely impaired, and he knew it," she explained. "He sensed that he would never be the same again, and he didn't want me to take care of him for the rest of his life. His love for me was that strong. Robbie was trying to protect me."[83] Those beliefs provide little compensation for Denise's loss, but they do ease the pain, allowing her to move on with her life. And she does not have to do so alone.

On March 15, 2014, Denise and Ray were remarried. Once again, they are best friends.

Rob would be proud, too.

Author's Note: Ray Garibaldi died on February 22, 2015, at age 68, after a three-and-a-half-year battle with metastatic renal cancer. Denise was at his side.

AFTERWORD

T he suicide squeeze is baseball's most daring play. The runner takes off for home plate from third base just before the pitcher releases the ball. If the play is properly executed, the runner will score. Because the squeeze is most often attempted late in a close game, the run usually determines the winner of the contest. If the base runner scores, he is showered with praise from coaches and teammates alike. It is the ultimate glory. But if the batter fails to make contact with the pitch, the runner is likely to be out at home plate (hence, "suicide"). Thus, the suicide squeeze requires a skilled bunter who can make contact consistently, even on difficult pitches, and a base runner bold enough to believe that he can cheat the odds to score.

Like the daring base runner in a suicide squeeze, Taylor Hooton and Rob Garibaldi were determined to score their respective baseball dreams. Both youngsters had the natural ability to achieve those dreams, but they were told by coaches that they needed more. Like the third-base coach prodding the base runner to "get a bigger lead," their coaches told Taylor and Rob they "needed to get bigger" if they wanted to succeed. Those coaches may not have told them *how* to get that "lead," but they certainly did not bother to find out about their methods. Once the runner breaks for home, there is no turning back. Caution is thrown to the wind. It is a ruthless—if not reckless—pursuit of glory. Either the runner scores or is caught dead at home plate by the catcher's tag.

So it was with Taylor and Rob. Once these young ballplayers began using steroids to achieve their dreams, there was no turning back. And no one could stop them—not parents, friends, or family, most of whom had no idea what was driving their reckless behavior. The few friends who did know of Taylor's and Rob's juicing were afraid to tell, much like the batter who, at the very last moment, must lay down a perfect bunt to protect the runner. That batter realizes that the suicide squeeze play is "on" and tries to "cover" for the runner with a diversionary tactic, bunting the ball safely out of the catcher's reach. In the end, the "batters" failed to protect Taylor and Rob from themselves, with each youngster committing suicide at or near home.

More than a decade has passed since the steroid-induced suicides of Taylor Hooton and Rob Garibaldi. Aside from pressuring MLB to rid the sport of doping and to restore a sense of integrity to the game, Congress has done little to further the cause. In fact, former Commissioner Bud Selig was the driving force behind the campaign to prevent the use of steroids and PEDs among our youth. Still, APED use remains a serious problem that currently affects more than one million youngsters and counting.

Recent research indicates that doping among students at the middle and high school levels has ballooned from 500,000 in 2005 to 1.5 million today and that girls are the most rapidly increasing group of users. In other words, approximately 6 to 8 percent of male teens and 2 to 3 percent of female adolescents have used or are using anabolic steroids.[1] The statistics do *not* include homosexual and bisexual male teens, who are at a higher risk of using APEDs due to increased depressive symptoms, suicidal tendencies, and victimization.[2] Nor do the statistics include those kids who are unknowingly taking performance-enhancing dietary supplements laced with anabolic steroids or those using HGH. Several studies indicate that as many as 25 percent of the body-building supplements sold over the counter in health food stores contain anabolic steroids and other substances banned by the WADA.[3] And a recent study released by the Partnership for Drug-Free Kids revealed the doubling of HGH usage to 11 percent between 2013 and 2014. In the average high school with an enrollment of 980 kids, this 11 percent figure translates to more than 100 kids using HGH and 70 using steroids.[4] When these additional groups are added, the total number of adolescents using APEDs is considerably higher than the 1.5 million who have reported their use. What's more, a Zogby poll taken in 2013 by the Digital Citizens Alliance revealed that almost 28 percent of males ages 18 to 25 reported knowing someone who has used APEDs and that one in five males reported believing that doping was the only way to achieve a career in professional sports. Not surprisingly, more than 77 percent of parents of males between the ages of 14 and 25 said the use of PEDs in pro sports places pressure on youths to do the same.[5]

To put these numbers in perspective, consider this: if every single MLB and NFL player using anabolic steroids were gathered together, they would not be able to fill the bleachers in a typical high school football stadium. But the 1.5 million kids using APEDs would fill nearly every MLB ballpark in the nation. If something is not done to address the problem soon, those numbers could possibly double in the near future. Doping is an open secret among adolescents, and one the rest of our society refuses to address in any meaningful way. This point was made clear when I began doing my research for this book.

Many of the individuals intimately tied to the Hooton and Garibaldi tragedies refused to be interviewed, in spite of the fact that the families urged them to speak with me. Some even requested that they not be identified by name in the book, although the statements they made to the press in the immediate aftermath of the suicides are part of the public record. One educational institution threatened a lawsuit if any public allegation of negligence was made. Fortunately, others did agree to be interviewed and were extremely helpful. Their remarks enabled me to arrive at several important conclusions about the Hooton and Garibaldi suicides as well as some constructive reforms to prevent similar tragedies.

First, parents must educate themselves on the symptoms and dangers of anabolic steroids and how to identify them in their children's behavior. The Hootons and the Garibaldis were knowledgeable about recreational drug use, but they were not informed about steroids. Instead, they attributed their sons' behaviors to developmental factors, such as variable hormonal changes and teenage moodiness or psychological disorder. The desire to improve one's physical appearance through muscle building is normal for teens, but telltale signs of steroid use include the following:

- Excessive exercise that goes beyond the athletic training required at school
- Engaging in sports for the sole purpose of improving appearance rather than a love of the sport or the camaraderie of teammates
- A preoccupation with physical appearance
- Overuse of dietary supplements (such as creatine or protein powder)

- Rapid fluctuation in weight caused by fasting, extreme diets, laxatives, and diuretics
- Excessive amounts of time and/or money spent on grooming activities and products
- Constant concern over looking good enough or the need for constant reassurance of physical attractiveness
- Embarrassment over having all or part of one's body seen by others on a beach or in the locker room at school

If a parent identifies these patterns in an adolescent son or daughter, he or she should do the following:

- Do not ignore the warning signs. Get help immediately by consulting a family physician, school counselors, and coaches.
- Role model a positive attitude and behaviors, such as exercising moderately, eating healthy foods, and accepting your own body with its strengths and limitations.
- Never criticize or tease teens about their appearance, which only reinforces the unhealthy obsession.
- Educate your child about the dangers of steroids, weight-loss drugs, and other risky ways of changing appearance.
- Foster your child's self-esteem by promoting their inner qualities, talents, skills, and personal strengths rather than his or her physical appearance.

Second, institutions of secondary and higher education must work together with student-athletes and their parents to discourage the use of APEDs. Current testing programs serve only as a deterrent, and they do not provide schools with an accurate barometer of student use. Until a less expensive and more accurate testing program can be established, schools must be willing to address doping in an open and candid manner with teachers, staff, coaches, students, and parents.

After his son's suicide, Don Hooton initiated a series of seminars to educate administrators, teachers, coaches, students, and their parents in PISD on the signs and dangers of APED use. But Don's efforts were received half-heartedly, and, according to students in the district, there was no sustained commitment to the issue afterward. Schools cannot afford to look the other way, and the claim of "ignorance" is no longer an excuse. Thanks to the Taylor Hooton Foundation, today there is not only a growing awareness of the problem among medical researchers and policy makers but also a valuable educational resource to address it.

Seminars on the signs and dangers of adolescent APED abuse must be a routine part of student orientation programs and parent "back-to-school" nights each fall. The head coach of every team fielded by a junior high and high school should also meet with the parents of the student-athletes prior to the beginning of a season to discuss the issue. Attendance by at least one parent should be required for his or her son or daughter to participate in the sport. Many schools already conduct a preseason orientation program for parents and student-athletes. Thus, the addition of a session on APED abuse would be simple.

Third, junior highs, high schools, and colleges must take steps to actively monitor students for APED use. Administrators, teachers, and coaches have a fundamental responsibility to protect the welfare of those young people placed in their charge by learning as much as they can about APEDs and acting on that knowledge, especially when they suspect doping.

Taylor's and Rob's coaches claimed that they did not suspect their steroid use, and the officials at their educational institutions vouched for them, but only the coaches themselves know whether any of the staff permitted doping among the student-athletes by looking the other way or condoned the practice by failing to overtly discourage it. Greater accountability among coaches and administrators is a necessary part of resolving the problem.

It is crucial that coaches who work with 15- to 25-year-olds not only be trained but also certified in the signs and dangers of APED use and that they be required to report any suspicion of use to their athletic directors. An academic monitor who has no vested interest in the school's sports program should be assigned to each team to reinforce the policy, with responsibility for monitoring not only the academic performance but also the telltale signs of steroid use (e.g., dramatic weight gain and excessive acne) of the students-athletes on the team. In turn, the athletic director should be required by law to inform the suspected user's parents and monitor a test for steroids in his or her presence and in the presence of a narcotics officer. In the case of a positive test result, the team should be required to forfeit three of its victories. In the case of a positive test result for multiple students-athletes, the team should be required to forfeit competition for the district championship and state titles. These penalties would not only make the coaches accountable but also create the necessary peer pressure to discourage steroid use.

Fourth, the U.S. Food and Drug Administration (FDA) must be more responsible in reporting any steroid or steroid precursor contained in over-the-counter nutritional supplements. Consumers can assist in this process by reporting any tainted supplements to the FDA at www.fda.gov/safety/MedWatch. Warning signs of tainted supplements include nausea, weakness or fatigue, fever, abdominal pain, chest pain, yellowing of skin or eyes, and/or brown or discolored urine.

Fifth, federal sentencing guidelines for those distributing APEDs without a prescription must be strengthened. The dealers who sold APEDs to Taylor and Rob knew that they could escape detection by law enforcement because of the many loopholes that exist in online and postal distribution as well as the difficulty of effectively enforcing U.S. border regulations. Even if the dealers were to be identified, they were confident that they would avoid lengthy incarceration because of the extremely lenient sentencing guidelines for steroids. Upgrading the sentencing guidelines for steroids would discourage dealers.

Congress should mete out the very same penalties for illegal steroids distribution as those that exist for Schedule I controlled substances. A first-time offender would receive a three-year sentence without the possibility of parole. Multiple offenses would be punishable by a graduated scale of sentences, all of which would be served without the possibility of parole.

Sixth, the FDA, the U.S. Justice Department, and the FBI must organize and conduct more sting operations in the fight against steroids. Currently local law enforcement agencies do not place a high priority on the issue. If they had, Taylor and Rob would not have had such easy access to PEDs. The identification, arrest, and prosecution of distributors is not worth the human or financial resources they require, considering the current sentencing guidelines. Until the guidelines are strengthened, federal agencies must shoulder a greater responsibility. Since 1992, the FBI has launched a series of successful sting operations in the war against steroids. Codenamed Operation Equine (1992), Operation Gear Grinder (2005), and Operation Raw Deal (2007), the raids resulted in the convictions of more than two hundred distributors and the seizure of millions of dollars of steroids. In the process, the raids slowed the flow of raw steroids into the United States from Mexico and China and made it more difficult for domestic distributors to engage in the black market.[6]

These efforts must be increased, because they are the most effective methods for identifying, arresting, and prosecuting distributors. Federal agencies can obtain the wiretaps and search warrants necessary for sting operations. Afterward, federal prosecutors can force witnesses to testify before grand juries, and the threat of prison time is hugely persuasive. Among the most recent examples are the federal investigation that broke open the BALCO case; testimony obtained through a federal investigation that broke cycling's powerful code of silence and gave the U.S. Anti-Doping Agency the evidence it needed go after Lance Armstrong; and the Mitchell Report's identification of major league players who were doping, which was largely accomplished through a plea bargain for Kirk Radamski, a steroids dealer, pertaining to preexisting charges of money laundering and steroid distribution.

Finally, medical researchers must concentrate their efforts on establishing a safe and effective protocol for weaning adolescent users off APEDs. Taylor and Rob might still be alive today if they had been diagnosed earlier and treated more effectively for the combination of steroids and antidepressants and/or other medications in their bloodstreams. The health care professionals who treated the two young men did not enjoy the benefit of the research on teenage steroid abuse that has emerged in the wake of their suicides. Still, more than ten years later, there is no safe and effective protocol for treating a user in withdrawal.

Congress should allocate funding for further research on adolescent steroid use, with a special focus on creating a more sophisticated test for detecting it and for finding a safe and effective protocol to wean users off this life-threatening drug. In addition, those health care professionals who counsel and/or treat preteens and teens must also be licensed to exercise this protocol.

None of these reforms can be implemented without legislative action. Congress needs to act immediately to prevent another APED-related tragedy. Up to this point, the federal government's failure to act on adolescent doping seems to suggest that our nation's youth are not as important as professional sports or the athletes who play them. That is a pathetic commentary on our federal government's priorities.

Inevitably, there will be harsh and swift criticism if these reforms are enacted. Parents and students will charge that their constitutional rights are being violated. But those parents who place civil rights above their own child's life need to reconsider their priorities. The constitution cannot protect a child who commits suicide. In addition, those students who place a greater priority on physical appearance and/or athletic performance over their long-term health and use the violation of constitutional rights as an excuse simply do not have the maturity to make an informed decision on either issue. Besides, drastic measures are necessary in a time of crisis. Make no mistake: adolescent APED use *is* a growing health care crisis in our country.

Only when Congress acts to eliminate the use of anabolic steroids by our children will the legacies of Taylor Hooton and Rob Garibaldi be fulfilled.

ACKNOWLEDGMENTS

T he research and writing of *Suicide Squeeze* have been very personal and, at times, emotionally challenging experiences, but they have made me a better parent, teacher-coach, and human being. Like all books, this one would not have come to fruition without the help of others.

To Don and Gwen Hooton and Denise and Ray Garibaldi, I owe a tremendous debt of gratitude. They shared with me not only their lives but also the lives of their late sons, Taylor and Rob, respectively. I know how much courage it took for them to do this and can only imagine the pain that resurfaced in the process. But they are so deeply committed to raising public awareness about adolescent APED abuse that they gave themselves wholeheartedly to this enterprise. Over the course of five years, they have restored my faith in human nature and in the belief that people working together toward a common cause can, indeed, make a meaningful impact on this world. Words cannot adequately express the appreciation, respect, and affection I have for these remarkable parents.

Unfortunately, many of the individuals who were intimately tied to the Hooton and Garibaldi tragedies declined to be interviewed, in spite of the fact that the families urged them to speak with me. This refusal only serves to reinforce the toxic nature of steroid abuse and the desperate need for people to find the courage to tell their stories in an effort to resolve the problem. Fortunately, those who did agree to be interviewed went out of their way to be helpful. Among them are Blake Boydston, Patrick Burke, Erica Cavanaugh, Janet Eddy, Mark Fainaru-Wada, Lindsay

Forester, Joe Garibaldi, Raymond Garibaldi, John Goelz, Mark Gomez, Jill Griffin, Donald Hooton Jr., Mackenzie Hooton, Neil Jeffrey, Liz Krause, Paul Maytorena, Ron Myers, Damon Neidlinger, Christina Reed, Jason Wade, and Charles Yesalis. Some of these individuals also gave permission to have their photographs reproduced in the book, and Amy Leslie Frydenlund granted permission for me to include a photo of her late husband, Bob Leslie. For all of this support, I am extremely grateful.

I owe special thanks to Attorney Janet Fries of the Washington, D.C., firm of Drinker, Biddle, and Reath for vetting the manuscript and providing excellent legal counsel; Mark Fainaru-Wada of the *San Francisco Chronicle* for reviewing an earlier draft of the manuscript and offering his constructive criticism; Johnny Bench (Hall of Fame catcher for the Cincinnati Reds), Richard Borkowski (a sports and recreation safety consultant), Stephen Keener (the president and CEO of Little League International), Randy Levine (the president of the New York Yankees), Rob Manfred (the commissioner of baseball), George J. Mitchell (a U.S. senator), Bud Selig (a former commissioner of baseball), and Jackie Speier (a U.S. congresswoman) for endorsing the book; and John Horne at the National Baseball Hall of Fame Library, Vanessa Erlichson at Polaris Images in New York, and Chad Surmick of the *Santa Rosa (CA) Press Democrat* for providing assistance with photographs for the book.

I am also truly grateful to many teacher-coaches, who do not always receive the recognition they so richly deserve. At the top of the list is Ken Farshtey, my high school baseball coach, who instilled in me many of the values and lessons I have tried to teach my own student-athletes. Other teacher-coaches I have worked with over the years have served as either mentors or assistants, and all were instrumental in helping me develop a positive approach to teaching and coaching youngsters: Dave Beccaria, Greg Kannerstein, and Ed Molush of Haverford College, Haverford, Pennsylvania; Jim Lester of Earlham College, Richmond, Indiana; John McCarthy of the Riverdale Country School, Bronx, New York; Steve Chadwin of Abington Friends School, Jenkintown, Pennsylvania; Jim Farrell of the Episcopal Academy, Merion, Pennsylvania; Allan Brown of the William Penn Charter School, Philadelphia, Pennsylvania; Harry Hayman and John Lotz of Berwyn-Paoli (Pennsylvania) Little League; Gary Brooks and Joe Catania of Pennsylvania District 27's Senior Challenger program; and Steve Cook, Karl Keck, and Chris Ray at Grand Slam U.S.A., Malvern, Pennsylvania.

Still others worked with my son Peter, and I have admired their teaching and coaching from a distance: Russ Trachtenberg of Friends Central

School, Philadelphia, Pennsylvania; Chris Baumann of the Conestoga, Pennsylvania, American Legion and Valley Forge, Pennsylvania, Patriots; Chris Cowell of the Colorado Rockies and the On Deck Training Center, Newtown Square, Pennsylvania; Justin Hanley of the William Penn Charter School; and Steve Sakosits and Jared Broughton of Earlham College. Their examples demonstrate that a teacher-coach can place the educational and moral development of his or her student-athletes above everything else and still win games, even championships.

Finally, I thank my parents, William and Balbina; my wife, Jacqueline; and our three sons, Tim, Peter, and Ben. Few men admit to having heroes, but I am truly fortunate to have been born to and raised by, to have married, and to have fathered mine. My love for them is eternal.

**TAYLOR HOOTON
FOUNDATION**

The **TAYLOR HOOTON FOUNDATION (THF)** is a 501(c)3 nonprofit organization that is widely recognized as the national leader in educating youth and their adult influencers about the dangers of appearance- and performance-enhancing drugs, including anabolic steroids, human growth hormone, and unregulated dietary supplements.

If you or a loved one is struggling with anabolic steroids, if you know of someone who is, or if you would like an education program delivered to your group, reach out to the THF by phone at 972-403-7300 or e-mail the organization at info@taylorhooton.org.

NOTES

1. One of the reasons law enforcement does not pursue the possession, distribution, and sale of illicit steroids is the fear of incriminating some of their own officers. Across the United States, police investigations of Internet pharmacies, "anti-aging" clinics, and unscrupulous physicians have revealed police involvement in a web of APED use. Anabolic steroids and human growth hormone (HGH) appeal to officers who seek a tactical edge or an intimidating appearance. (See Commander Kim R. Humphrey et al., "Anabolic Steroid Use and Abuse by Police Officers: Policy and Prevention," *Police Chief* 75, no. 6 [2008]: 32–36; Susan Donaldson James, "Police Juice Up on Steroids to Get 'Edge' on Criminals," ABC News Network, October 18, 2007, available at abcnews.go.com/US/story?id=3745740; and David Johnson, *Falling Off the Thin Blue Line: A Badge, a Syringe, and a Struggle with Steroid Addiction* [Bloomington, IN: iUniverse, 2007].)

2. Recreational drugs can be grouped into four categories: stimulants (cocaine, amphetamines), depressants (alcohol, heroin), narcotics (hydrocodone, Vicodin), and hallucinogens (marijuana, LSD). APEDs do not fit into any of these categories.

3. See Marla E. Eisenberg, Melanie Wall, and Dianne Neumark-Sztainer, "Muscle-Enhancing Behaviors among Adolescent Girls and Boys," *Pediatrics* 130, no. 6 (2012): 1019–1020; Digital Citizens Alliance, "Zogby Poll: Better at Any Cost: The Dangerous Intersection of Young People, Steroids, and the Internet" (Washington DC: Digital Citizens Alliance, 2013); and Partnership for Drug-Free Kids, "National Study: Teens Report Higher Use of Performance Enhancing Substances," July 23, 2014, available at www.drugfree.org.

The University of Minnesota study discussed in *Pediatrics* surveyed data from 2,793 diverse adolescents (mean age = 14.4) collected at twenty urban middle and high schools. The display of five muscle-enhancing behaviors was assessed (changing eating habits, exercising, using protein powders, using steroids, and using other muscle-enhancing substances), and a summary score reflecting the display of three or more of these behaviors was created. Logistic regression was used to test for differences in each behavior across age group, race/ethnicity, socioeconomic status, body mass index (BMI) category, and sports team participation. The study concluded that 5 to 6 percent of middle-school-age and high-school-age students use anabolic steroids to enhance their athletic performance or their physical appearance.

Zogby Analytics conducted the two online surveys from July 19 through July 22, 2013. Zogby surveyed 350 males between the ages of 18 and 25 in the United States, with a margin of error of +/- 5.3 percentage points, and *352 adults with male children between* the ages of 14 and 25 in the United States, with a margin of error of +/- 5.3 percentage points.

Finally, the Partnership for Drug-Free Kids released a July 2014 survey that confirmed a significant increase—a doubling—in the reported lifetime use of synthetic HGH among teens. According to the latest Partnership Attitude Tracking Study (PATS), sponsored by the MetLife Foundation, 11 percent of teens in grades 9–12 reported "ever having used" synthetic HGH without a prescription, up dramatically from just 5 percent in 2012. The survey, conducted by GfK Roper Public Affairs and Corporate Communications, is nationally projectable, with a +/- 2.1 percent margin of error. The survey was administered to 3,705 teens in grades 9–12 in private, public, and parochial schools.

4. Harrison G. Pope Jr., MD, quoted in Mark Fainaru-Wada, "Dreams, Steroids, Death—A Ballplayer's Downfall," *San Francisco Chronicle*, December 19, 2004, available at www.sfgate.com/sports/article/Dreams-steroids-death-a-ballplayers-downfall, accessed April 19, 2013. As early as 1990, Pope stated that he was aware of "several accounts of young men who committed suicide while using or withdrawing from anabolic steroids." (See Pope quoted in Donna Alvarado, "Steroids Linked to Violence Cases of 'Roid Rage' Come under Scrutiny," *San Jose Mercury*, October 19, 1990.)

5. For Pope's research on steroids, see Harrison G. Pope Jr. et al., "Adverse Health Consequences of Performance-Enhancing Drugs: An Endocrine Society Scientific Statement," *Endocrine Reviews* 35, no. 3 (2014): 341–375; Harrison G. Pope, Gen Kanayama, and James I. Hudson, "Risk Factors for Illicit Anabolic-Androgenic Steroid Use in Male Weightlifters: A Cross-sectional Cohort Study," *Journal of Biological Psychiatry* 71, no. 3 (2012): 254–261; Gen Kanayama, James I. Hudson, and Harrison G. Pope, "Illicit Anabolic-Androgenic Steroid Use," *Hormones and Behavior* 58, no. 1 (2010): 111–121; Harrison G. Pope and Kirk J. Brower, "Anabolic-Androgenic Steroid Abuse," in *Comprehensive Textbook of Psychiatry*, edited by Benjamin J. Sadock and Virginia A. Sadock, 8th ed. (Philadelphia: Lippincott, Williams, and Wilkins, 2004), 1318–1328; Harrison G. Pope and David L. Katz, "Psychiatric Effects of Exogenous Anabolic-Androgenic Steroids," in *Psychoneuroendocrinology: The Scientific Basis of Clinical Practice*, edited by O. M. Wolkowitz and A. J. Rothschild (Washington, DC: American Psychiatric Press, 2003), 331–358; Gen Kanayama et al., "Past Anabolic-Androgenic Steroid Use among Men Admitted for Substance Abuse Treatment: An Underrecognized Problem?" *Journal of Clinical Psychiatry* 64, no. 2 (2003): 156–160; Harrison G. Pope, Katharine A. Phillips, and Roberto Olivardia, *The Adonis Complex: The Secret Crisis of Male Body Obsession* (New York: Simon and Schuster, 2000); Harrison G. Pope, Elena M. Kouri, and James I. Hudson, "Effects of Supraphysiologic Doses of Testosterone on Mood and Aggression in Normal Men: A Randomized Controlled Trial," *Archives of General Psychiatry* 57 (2000): 133–140; and Harrison G. Pope and David L. Katz, "Affective and Psychotic Symptoms Associated with Anabolic Steroid Use," *American Journal of Psychiatry* 145, no. 4 (1988): 487–490.

On the other hand, Charles E. Yesalis, a Penn State endocrinologist, whose views are supported by other researchers, insists that "suicide—especially adolescent suicide—is never easily explained" and "cannot be reduced to a singular cause like steroids." "There are a confluence of factors that lead to suicide," he said in a recent interview and then continued, "Mixing steroids with other addictive drugs, whether suicide runs in the family, are just two of many other factors. I'm not dismissing steroids in a causal role, but I just don't see it as a single cause" (interview with the author, Lynchburg, VA, June 19, 2014).

6. In a suicide squeeze, the runner takes off from third base just before the pitcher releases the ball. If the suicide squeeze is properly executed, the runner will score. Since the play is most often executed late in a close game, the run usually determines the winner of the contest. As a result, the base runner who succeeds is showered with praise from coaches and teammates alike. But, if the batter fails to make contact with the pitch, the runner is likely to be put out at home plate (hence, the term "suicide"). Thus, the suicide squeeze requires a skilled bunter who can make contact consistently, even on difficult pitches, and a base runner daring enough to believe that he can cheat the odds to score.

CHAPTER 1

1. Duff Wilson, "McGwire Offers No Denials at Steroid Hearings," *New York Times*, March 18, 2005; and "McGwire Mum on Steroids in Hearing," CNN.com, March 17, 2005, available at www.cnn.com/2005/ALLPOLITICS/03/17/steroids.baseball/index .html.

2. Donald Hooton, "Statement to Congress on Illicit Steroid Use in Baseball," quoted in U.S. House of Representatives, "Restoring Faith in America's Pastime: Evaluating Major League Baseball's Efforts to Eradicate Steroid Use," Hearing before the Committee on Government Reform, U.S. House of Representatives, 109th Congress, 1st Session, March 17, 2005 (Washington, DC: U.S. Government Printing Office, 2005), 116–120; and interview with the author, Frisco, TX, January 10, 2013.

3. Denise Garibaldi, "Statement to Congress on Illicit Steroid Use in Baseball," quoted in U.S. House of Representatives, "Restoring Faith in America's Pastime: Evaluating Major League Baseball's Efforts to Eradicate Steroid Use," Hearing before the Committee on Government Reform, U.S. House of Representatives, 109th Congress, 1st Session, March 17, 2005 (Washington, DC: U.S. Government Printing Office, 2005), 113–115; and Mark Fainaru-Wada and Lance Williams, *Game of Shadows: Barry Bonds, BALCO, and the Steroids Scandal that Rocked Professional Sports* (New York: Gotham Books, 2006), 244–245.

4. In a January 2010 phone interview with *USA TODAY* writer Mel Antonen, Mark McGwire admitted to using steroids in 1989 and 1990 and again from 1993 to 1999. See McGwire to Antonen, "*USA TODAY* Interview: McGwire Details Steroid Use," *USA TODAY*, January 12, 2010, available at http://usatoday30.usatoday.com/sports/baseball/2010-01-11-mcgwire-steroids_N.htm, accessed February 19, 2016. See also Howard Bryant, *Juicing the Game: Drugs, Power, and the Fight for the Soul of Major League Baseball* (New York: Viking, 2005), 134.

5. Bryant, *Juicing the Game*, 183–184. Methamphetamine, or HGH and EPO, were also used by athletes for the same purpose as anabolic steroids.

6. "Draft '01: Top 100 College Prospects," *Baseball America*, February 19 to March 4, 2001, 15. The list was compiled by Allan Simpson of *Baseball America* in association

with major league scouting directors. Garibaldi was ranked no. 91. Among those on the list who starred in the majors are Mark Teixera of George Tech (no. 1), Mark Prior of USC (no. 2), and Ryan Howard of SW Missouri State (no. 16).

7. Garibaldi, "Statement to Congress on Illicit Steroid Use in Baseball"; and Fainaru-Wada and Williams, *Game of Shadows*, 244–245.

8. Jose Canseco, *Juiced: Wild Times, Rampant 'Roids, Smash Hits, and How Baseball Got Big* (New York: HarperCollins, 2005), 3.

9. Ibid., 4–6.

10. Ibid., 6–8, 133.

11. Commissioner Fay Vincent's June 7, 1991, memorandum quoted in David Epstein, "The Rules, the Law, the Reality: A Primer on Baseball's Steroid Policy through the Years," *Sports Illustrated*, February 16, 2009. According to Vincent's 1991 memo, the "possession, sale or use of any illegal drug or controlled substance by Major League players is strictly prohibited" and those players involved "are subject to discipline by the Commissioner and risk permanent expulsion from the game." Some general managers at that time do not remember the circulation of such a memo, and no such policy was emphasized or enforced.

12. Ross Bernstein, *The Code: Baseball's Unwritten Rules and Its Ignore-at-Your-Own-Risk Code of Conduct* (Chicago: Triumph Books, 2008), 211–218.

13. Pete Palmer and Gary Gillette, *ESPN Baseball Encyclopedia* (New York: Sterling Publishing, 2005), 21, 50, 68, 255, 265, 444, 574, 633, 669, 689. The eighteen 50-home-run seasons were recorded by Brady Anderson (50/1996), Albert Belle (50/1995), Barry Bonds (73/2001), Luis Gonzalez (57/2001), Ken Griffey Jr. (56/1997, 56/1998), Mark McGwire (52/1996, 58/1997, 70/1998, 65/1999), Alex Rodriguez (52/2001, 57/2002), Sammy Sosa (66/1998, 63/1999, 50/2000, 64/2001), Jim Thome (52/2002), and Greg Vaughn (50/1998). Four players connected to anabolic steroids were responsible for eleven of the eighteen 50-home-run seasons: Bonds (one), McGwire (four), Rodriguez (two), and Sosa (four).

14. Palmer and Gillette, *ESPN Baseball Encyclopedia*, 213, 224, 432. The three 50-home-run seasons between 1962 and 1994 were recorded by Willie Mays, who hit 52 for the San Francisco Giants in 1965; George Foster, who hit 52 for the Cincinnati Reds in 1977; and Cecil Fielder, who hit 51 for the Detroit Tigers in 1990.

15. Associated Press, *Home Run! The Year the Records Fell* (Champaign, IL: Sports Publishing, 1998); and Rick Reilly, "You Had to See It to Believe It," *Sports Illustrated: The Baseball Book*, edited by Rob Fleder (New York: Time-Warner, 2000), 150.

16. Sporting News, *Baseball's Greatest Players: A Celebration of the 20th Century's Best* (St. Louis: Sporting News, 1998), 196–197; and Mark Vancil and Peter Hirdt, eds., *Major League Baseball's All-Century Team* (Chicago: Rare Air Books, 1999), 112–115.

17. Fainaru-Wada and Williams, *Game of Shadows*, 51; and Shaun Assael and Peter Keating, "Who Knew? Part III: Cause and Effect—the Writer," *ESPN The Magazine*, Special Report, November 2005, available at http://sports.espn.go.com/espn/eticket/story?page=steroids&num=8 sports.espn.go.com/espn/eticket/story?page=steroids, accessed April 17, 2014.

18. Paul White, "McGwire Says He Used Steroids for Health Reasons," *USA TODAY Sports Weekly*, January 13–19, 2010. McGwire would later admit to using andro, but when asked whether he had used any illegal substances, such as anabolic steroids, he denied it repeatedly until 2010.

19. Fainaru-Wada and Williams, *Game of Shadows*, 240–241.

20. Ken Caminiti quoted in Tom Verducci, "Steroids in Baseball: Confession of an MVP," *Sports Illustrated*, June 3, 2002. Caminiti died unexpectedly of an apparent heart attack on October 10, 2004, at the age of 41. A recovering alcoholic and former drug user, his death was attributed to the combined effects of cocaine and opiates. But coronary heart disease and an enlarged heart—side effects of doping—were also contributing factors. (See Michelle O'Donnell, "Ken Caminiti, Baseball MVP in '96, Dies," *New York Times*, October 11, 2004.)

21. Tom Verducci, "To Cheat or Not to Cheat: Steroids and baseball, Ten Years After," *Sports Illustrated*, June 4, 2012.

22. Baseball is the only major sport that has an exemption from antitrust laws, which prohibit actions that unreasonably restrain competition. The exemption dates to a 1922 Supreme Court decision that ruled that antitrust law did not apply to baseball because the games were local affairs, not interstate commerce. The Supreme Court upheld the antitrust exemption twice, first in 1953 and again in the famous 1972 case in which Curt Flood sued Bowie Kuhn in his attempt to have the reserve clause declared illegal and be declared a free agent.

The Supreme Court has made it clear that it would not overturn the exemption, insisting that only Congress could do so. As a result, whenever Major League Baseball is involved in a major controversy, Congress threatens to revoke the exemption.

23. Rep. Henry A. Waxman quoted in an interview that appeared on NBC's *Meet the Press*, March 13, 2005.

24. Hooton, "Statement to Congress."

25. Garibaldi, "Statement to Congress."

26. Richard Carmona, MD, quoted in Associated Press, "U.S. Leaders Worry about Impact of Steroids on Youths," *USA TODAY*, December 6, 2004.

27. Dave Shenin, "Baseball Had a Day of Reckoning in Congress," *Washington Post*, March 18, 2005; Wilson, "McGwire Offers No Denials."

28. Jorge Arangure Jr., "Palmeiro Suspended for Steroid Violation," *Washington Post*, August 2, 2005; Murray Chass, "Palmeiro Cites His Own Naivete and Ponders Mystery of It All," *New York Times*, December 28, 2005. (For Palmeiro's career statistics, see www.baseball-reference.com/players/p/palmera01.shtml.) On August 1, 2005, Palmeiro was suspended for ten days after testing positive for the potent anabolic steroid Stanozolol. He released a public statement that read, "I have never intentionally used steroids. Never. Ever. Period. Ultimately, although I never intentionally put a banned substance into my body, the independent arbitrator ruled that I had to be suspended under the terms of the program." In November 2005, the House Government Reform Committee decided not to seek perjury charges against Palmeiro, although it did not clear him. (See "Congress Won't Charge Palmeiro with Perjury," ESPN.com, November 11, 2005, available at http://espn.go.com/mlb/news/story?id=2219460.)

29. Assael and Keating, "Who Knew? Introduction."

30. Fainaru-Wada and Williams, *Game of Shadows*, 245–246. In 2003, a federal jury began an investigation into BALCO after reports surfaced that the company was providing PEDs to track and field athletes. Several prominent baseball stars were also subpoenaed, including Bonds. In February 2004, BALCO's president, Victor Conte Jr., and three of his associates, one of whom was Bonds's personal trainer, were indicted for conspiring to distribute steroids and other drugs to dozens of professional athletes.

31. Fainaru-Wada and Williams, *Game of Shadows*. *Sports Illustrated* writer Jeff Pearlman followed the publication of *Game of Shadows* with a revealing biography of Bonds titled *Love Me, Hate Me: Barry Bonds and the Making of an Anti-hero* (New York: HarperCollins, 2006). The book, based on more than five hundred interviews with teammates and former friends, describes Bonds as a polarizing, insufferable braggart with a legendary ego and staggering physical ability.

32. "Barry Bonds Convicted of Obstruction of Justice in Performance-Enhancing-Drugs Case," *Los Angeles Times*, April 13, 2011. In 2007, Bonds was indicted on charges of perjury and obstruction of justice for allegedly lying to the grand jury during the government's investigation of BALCO by testifying that he never knowingly took any illegal steroids. In a trial that began on March 21, 2011, Bonds was convicted on the obstruction of justice charge.

33. Toni Ginnetti, "Hall of Fame Says 'No' to Bonds, Clemens, Sosa," *Chicago Sun-Times*, January 9, 2013. On January 9, 2013, Bonds was denied entry into the National Baseball Hall of Fame in Cooperstown, New York, during his first year of eligibility on the ballot. Of the 75 percent of the votes needed for entry, Bonds earned just 36.2 percent.

34. Hooton interview, January 10, 2013.

35. Ray Garibaldi quoted in Harry Smith, "Grieving Parents Talk Steroids," *CBS Early Morning Show*, March 18, 2005, available at www.cbsnews.com/videos/grieving-parents-talk-steroids/, accessed June 1, 2014.

36. George J. Mitchell, *Report to the Commissioner of Baseball of an Independent Investigation into the Illegal Use of Steroids and Other Performance Enhancing Substances by Players in Major League Baseball* (New York: Office of the Commissioner of Baseball, 2007). The Mitchell report is available at http://files.mlb.com/mitchrpt.pdf.

37. See MLB, "Joint Drug Prevention and Treatment Program," Adopted 2006 Basic Agreement: Attachment 18, available at http://mlb.mlb.com/pa/pdf/jda.pdf, accessed January 26, 2013. Prior to the Mitchell investigation, MLB conducted one unannounced mandatory test each year for every player and random tests for selective players during the season and the off-season. The tests examined players for steroids, steroid precursors, and designer steroids. Players who were caught were suspended without pay: the first time for ten days, the second for thirty days, the third for sixty days, and the fourth for one year.

Beginning in the spring of 2006, MLB adopted a new program that "prohibited all players from using, possessing, selling, facilitating the sale of, distributing, or facilitating the distribution of any Drug of Abuse and/or Steroid." Players requiring prescription medication could still use it with a "Therapeutic Use Exemption" granted by MLB. Initially, testing was only administered during the season and on the basis of "reasonable cause"—that is, when a Health Policy Advisory Committee uncovered evidence that a player had used, possessed, or sold banned substances in the previous twelve months. On January 10, 2013, however, MLB and the players' union reached a new agreement that dramatically increased testing and punishments. Random, in-season HGH testing and a new test to reveal the use of testosterone were added, with a test considered positive if any steroid was present in the urine. The new agreement also stipulated that all players would take unannounced tests twice a year and that selective players would be subject to random testing. Testing would also be done for seven different kinds of abusive drugs, forty-seven different kinds of steroids, and thirty different kinds of stimulants. One of the forty-seven different kinds of steroids is HGH, a once-popular substance among major leaguers that was never tested for before the Mitchell Report.

Stiffer penalties were also instituted: a fifty-game suspension for the first positive test, a hundred-game suspension for the second, and a lifetime ban for the third. Despite these stiffer penalties, players continued to violate the policy. As a result, in March 2014, MLB and the Players Association enacted even tougher penalties. First-time suspensions were increased from fifty to eighty games and second offenses from one hundred games to a full season, with suspended players ineligible for postseason play. See AP, "MLB Toughens Drug Penalties," *Philadelphia Inquirer*, March 29, 2014.

38. Barry M. Bloom, "MLB Donates to Hooton Foundation," MLB.com, June 10, 2008, available at http://mlb.mlb.com/news/print.jsp?ymd=20080610&content_id=2882630.

CHAPTER 2

1. Interview with Gwen Hooton, McKinney, TX, December 11, 2013.

2. Interview with Don Hooton Sr., Williamsport, PA, August 16, 2013.

3. Don Hooton Sr. interview.

4. Interview with Donald Hooton Jr., Philadelphia, PA, August 22, 2013.

5. Gwen Hooton interview.

6. U.S. Department of Commerce, "2010 Federal Census," U.S. Census Bureau, available at www.quickfacts.census.gov, accessed December 27, 2013.

7. "Best Places to Live," *Money* (Cable News Network), available at http://money.cnn.com/magazines/fsb/bestplaces/2008/top100/, accessed July 11, 2011. *Money* ranked Plano as one of the best cities to live in 2005, 2006, and 2011. See also Francesca Levy, "America's Safest Cities," *Forbes*, 2010, available at Forbes.com, accessed July 11, 2011.

8. AreaVibes.com compared the median household income for all U.S. cities whose populations were greater than 250,000 and found that Plano, with an $81,822 median income, was among the wealthiest. If renters are eliminated, Plano's median owner-occupied household income jumps to $128,066. In addition, the income per capita in Plano is 77.8 percent greater than the Texas average and 57.9 percent greater than the national average. The median household income in Plano is 65.6 percent greater than the Texas average and 56.4 percent greater than the national average. The median household income in Plano for owner-occupied housing is 108.4 percent greater than the median household income for renter-occupied housing in Plano. Conversely, the poverty level in Plano is 75.9 percent less than the Texas average and 65.1 percent less than the national average. The median earnings for males in Plano are 83.1 percent greater than the median earnings for females in Plano. (See "Plano, TX, Employment, Jobs and Median Income," available at www.areavibes.com, accessed December 27, 2013.)

9. "America's Best High Schools," *Newsweek*, May 20, 2012.

10. Dave Campbell, "All-Time Texas State Football Champions, 1920–2011," available at www.texasfootball.com, accessed December 17, 2013.

11. Plano East produced Charlie Peprah of the Dallas Cowboys and Justin Blalock and John Leake of the Atlanta Falcons, and Plano West produced Kyle Bosworth of the Dallas Cowboys.

12. Jere Longman, "Drugs in Sports: An Athlete's Dangerous Experiment," *New York Times*, November 26, 2003.

13. See Christie Tate and Linda Madon, *Comprehensive Annual Financial Report for Year Ending June 30, 2008* (Plano, TX: Plano Independent School District, 2008),

available at www.pisd.edu/about.us/budget/documents/PlanoISD2008CA, accessed December 27, 2008. For an explanation of the "Robin Hood Law," see pp. v–vi; for PISD expenses, revenue, salaries, changes in net assets, and property tax income for the period 2002–2008, see pp. 83–101; and for the number of school and athletic facilities built between 1999 and 2008, see pp. 102–103.

14. E-mail to author from Gerald Brence, Plano Independent School District Athletic Director, Plano, TX, January 24, 2014.

15. Gregg Jones and Gary Jacobson, "A Life Undone by Doping," *Dallas Morning News*, June 14, 2005. For drug-related deaths, see Carol Marie Cropper, "10 Heroin Deaths in Texas Reflect Rising Use by Young," *New York Times*, November 23, 1997; and Pam Easton, "MTV Documentary Examines Heroin Use, Plano Deaths," *Abilene Reporter-News*, March 31, 1998.

16. Don Hooton Sr. interview, August 16, 2013; and Jones and Jacobson, "A Life Undone by Doping."

17. Dr. Jack Graham, "The Prestonwood Story," Prestonwood Baptist Church, Dallas, TX, available at www.prestonwood.org, accessed December 28, 2013.

18. Interview with Mark Gomez, Plano, TX, May 21, 2013.

19. Don Hooton Sr. and Donald Hooton Jr. interviews.

20. Interview with Reverend Neil Jeffrey, Plano, TX, February 12, 2014.

21. Interview with Jill Griffin, Powell, MI, June 4, 2014.

22. "Alex Rodriguez," *Jockbio.com*, August 20, 2010, available at http://jockbio.com/Bios/ARod/ARod_bio.html, accessed April 7, 2014.

23. For Rodriguez's offensive statistics, see Pete Palmer and Gary Gillette, *ESPN Baseball Encyclopedia* (New York: Sterling, 2005), 574.

24. Gwen Hooton interview.

25. "Alex Rodriguez: Charity Work, Events and Causes," *Look to the Stars/The World of Celebrity Giving*, available at www.looktothestars.org/celebrity/alex-rodriguez, accessed April 6, 2013.

26. Stanley H. Teitelbaum, *Sports Heroes, Fallen Heroes: How Star Athletes Pursue Self-Destructive Paths and Jeopardize Their Careers* (Lincoln: University of Nebraska Press, 2005), 1–16.

27. Donald Hooton Jr. interview.

28. E-mail, Taylor Hooton to Gwen Hooton, Plano, TX, October 28, 2001.

29. Gwen Hooton interview.

30. Interview with Ray Garibaldi, Novato, CA, June 11, 2013.

31. Rob Garibaldi, journal entry, 2000–2001, 1.

32. Interview with Denise Garibaldi, Novato, CA, April 16, 2013.

33. Interview with Raymond Garibaldi, Petaluma, CA, February 19, 2014; and Rob Garibaldi, journal entry, 3.

34. Raymond Garibaldi interview.

35. Rob Garibaldi, journal entry, 2–3; and Ray Garibaldi interview, June 11, 2013.

36. Raymond Garibaldi interview.

37. Raymond Garibaldi interview; Ray Garibaldi interview, June 11, 2013; Denise Garibaldi interview, April 16, 2013; interview with Joe Garibaldi, San Mateo, CA, February 15, 2014; and "In Loving Memory: Robert Michael Garibaldi, September 15, 1978—October 1, 2002," unpublished memorial book, October 2002.

38. Denise Garibaldi interview, April 16, 2013.

39. The *Foster City* (CA) *Progress*, July 11, 1990.

40. Joe Garibaldi interview.

41. Ray Garibaldi interview, June 11, 2013.

42. Ibid.

43. Rob Garibaldi, "Speculating on My Future," English essay, Bowditch Middle School, Foster City, CA, March 17, 1993; and e-mail to author from Denise Garibaldi, Novato, CA, February 6, 2014.

44. Interview with Christina Reed, Petaluma, CA, June 11, 2014.

45. Rob Garibaldi, "Depression," psychology class, Santa Rosa Junior College, Spring 1999.

46. Erwin G. Gudde and William Bright, *California Place Names: The Origin and Etymology of Current Geographical Names*, 2nd ed. (Berkeley: University of California Press, 1998), 287.

47. W. S. Harwood, "A City of a Million Hens: How Poultry Raising Conducted as a Business Has Made Petaluma Known over the World," *The World's Work: A History of Our Time*, 20 vols. (New York, n.p., 1908), 16:10207–10124; and Sue Fishkoff, "When Left-Wingers and Chicken Wings Populated Petaluma," May 7, 1999, available at jweekly.com, accessed September 14, 2012.

48. Petaluma City, California—Fact Sheet—American FactFinder, available at Census.gov, accessed March 26, 2014.

49. See U.S. Census, 2000. Of the 54,548 residents of Petaluma, 84.16 percent were Caucasian, 1.16 percent African American, 0.54 percent Native American, 3.91 percent Asian, 0.17 percent Pacific Islander, 6.08 percent from other races, and 3.98 percent from two or more races. 14.64 percent of the population were Hispanic. Of the 19,932 households, 36.6 percent had children under the age of 18 living with them, 55.3 percent were married couples living together, 10.6 percent had a female head of household with no husband present, and 29.7 percent were nonfamilies. The average household size was 2.70, and the average family size was 3.16, with 26.2 percent being under the age of 18. The median income for a household in the city was $61,679, and the median income for a family was $71,158. Males had a median income of $50,232 versus $36,413 for females. About 3.3 percent of families and 6 percent of the population were below the poverty line, including 6.2 percent of those under age 18 and 7.1 percent of those ages 65 and over.

50. City of Petaluma CAFR, available at http://cityofpetaluma.net/finance/budget.html, accessed March 16, 2013.

51. Petaluma City, California—Fact Sheet.

52. Denise Garibaldi interview, April 29, 2013.

53. Palmer and Gillette, *ESPN Baseball Encyclopedia*, 444.

54. Jonathan Hall, *Mark McGwire: A Biography* (New York: Simon Spotlight Entertainment, 1998), 55–96; and Jay McGwire, *Mark and Me: Mark McGwire and the Truth behind Baseball's Worst-Kept Secret* (Chicago: Triumph, 2010), 55–89.

55. Palmer and Gillette, *ESPN Baseball Encyclopedia*, 444.

56. Denise Garibaldi interview, April 29, 2013.

57. Palmer and Gillette, *ESPN Baseball Encyclopedia*, 67.

58. George Vecsey, "Sports of the Times; The Pirates Lost a Series, Not Respect," *New York Times*, October 16, 1992.

59. Murray Chass, "Giants Make Investment: $43 Million in Bonds," *New York Times*, December 16, 1992.

60. Palmer and Gillette, *ESPN Baseball Encyclopedia*, 67.

61. Rob Garibaldi, "Depression."

62. Rob Garibaldi, "My Best Friend," reflective essay, English 811, College of San Mateo, December 12, 1997.

63. Marianne Costantinou, "Petaluma Loses Beloved Coach," *San Francisco Chronicle*, June 17, 1998.

64. Mike Carey, "A Way to Truly Honor Bob Leslie's Legacy," *Santa Rosa Press Democrat*, May 29, 2011.

65. Interview with Paul Maytorena, Petaluma, CA, September 11, 2013.

66. Ray Garibaldi interview, Novato, CA, July 25, 2013.

67. Andrew Jowers, "Player Gives All to Casa Grande; Rob Garibaldi Crucial Part of Baseball Team," *Santa Rosa Press Democrat*, March 19, 1997.

68. Ray Garibaldi interview, July 25, 2013.

69. Jowers, "Player Gives All to Casa Grande."

70. Bob Leslie quoted in ibid.

71. Ibid.

72. Rob Garibaldi quoted in ibid.

73. Rob Garibaldi, "The Death of an Adolescent," psychology essay, Santa Rosa Junior College, Spring 1999.

74. Rob Garibaldi quoted in Jowers, "Player Gives All."

75. Rob Garibaldi, "Letter of Admission to University of Southern California," Summer 1999.

CHAPTER 3

1. Interview with Mark Gomez, Plano, TX, May 21, 2013.

2. See Mark Gola, *The Five-Tool Player* (New York: McGraw Hill, 2007), 13.

3. Gomez interview; Gregg Jones and Gary Jacobson, "A Life Undone by Doping," *Dallas Morning News*, June 14, 2005.

4. Billy Ajello quoted in Jere Longman, "Drugs in Sports: An Athlete's Dangerous Experiment," *New York Times*, November 26, 2003.

5. Interview with Don Hooton Sr., Williamsport, PA, August 16, 2013.

6. Gomez interview.

7. Paul Kix, "All the Rage," *Dallas Observer News*, August 12, 2004.

8. Gregg Jones and Gary Jacobson, "Whispers from the Weight Room," part 1 of a four-part series titled "The Secret Edge—Steroids in High Schools," *Dallas Morning News*, available at www.dallasnews.com/sharedcontent/dws/spe/2005/steroids, accessed December 28, 2013.

9. Lloyd D. Johnston et al., *Monitoring the Future National Results on Drug Use, 1975–2013: Overview, Key Findings on Adolescent Drug Use* (Ann Arbor: Institute for Social Research, University of Michigan, 2014). The *Monitoring the Future* (MTF) study, also known as the *National High School Senior Survey*, began in 1975 and only focused on that year's senior class. Questionnaires are sent out yearly by mail. Beginning in 1976, a proportion of survey participants were also chosen for biennial reevaluations. In 1991, the survey was expanded to include eighth- and tenth-grade students. The questionnaire is anonymous for eighth- and tenth-grade students but confidential for twelfth-grade students—their names and addresses are collected for longitudinal follow-up surveys. Each year, a total of approximately fifty thousand eighth-, tenth-, and twelfth-grade students are surveyed. In addition, annual follow-up questionnaires are mailed to a sample of each graduating class for a number of years after their initial participation.

10. Centers for Disease Control and Prevention, "Youth Risk Behavior Surveillance—United States, 2003," *Morbidity and Mortality Weekly Report* 53, no. SS-2 (May 21, 2004): 1–3, 15, 61–62. The sampling frame for the 2003 national Youth Risk Behavior Survey (YRBS) consisted of all public and private schools with students in at least one of grades 9–12 in the fifty states and the District of Columbia. For the 2003 national YRBS, 15,240 questionnaires were completed in 158 schools. The school response rate was 81 percent, and the student response rate was 83 percent. Survey procedures for the national, state, and local surveys were designed to protect students' privacy by allowing for anonymous and voluntary participation. The core questionnaire contained 87 questions. States and cities could add or delete questions from the core questionnaire.

11. Jones and Jacobson, "A Life Undone by Doping."

12. Don Hooton Sr. interview, August 16, 2013.

13. Merritt Onsa, "I Love You Guys. I'm Sorry about Everything," *Service in the Light of Truth* (Sigma Nu Fraternity blog), November 27, 2013; Gwen Hooton interview; Jones and Jacobson, "A Life Undone by Doping"; and Longman, "An Athlete's Dangerous Experiment."

14. Taylor Hooton, note to "Mom and Pops," Plano, TX, circa August 2002.

15. Taylor Perrine, "I Will Never Forget," English composition class, Plano West Senior High School, September 22, 2003.

16. Matt Koenig, "Inspiration: The Key to Unlocking Any Door," English composition class, Plano West Senior High School, September 22, 2003.

17. Dr. Babette Farkas, Taylor's psychiatrist, confirmed that he was struggling with self-esteem issues when she was interviewed by *60 Minutes* after the teen's death. (See Jim Stewart, "The Kid Next Door," CBS, *60 Minutes*, Season 6, Episode 8, produced by Andrew Wolff, aired March 3, 2004, available at http://www.cbsnews.com/videos/teen-steroid-use/.)

18. Matthew Futterman, "Why Everything Is Bigger in Texas," *Wall Street Journal*, February 20, 2009; and Associated Press, "Numerous Rangers, Including Steroid Users Rafael Palmeiro, Juan Gonzalez, on Hall of Fame Ballot," *Dallas Morning News*, November 29, 2010. Gonzalez, Rocker, and Velarde were connected to PEDs in Senator George J. Mitchell's 2007 *Report to the Commissioner of Baseball of an Independent Investigation into the Illegal Use of Steroids and Other Performance Enhancing Substances by Players in Major League Baseball*, which is available at http://files.mlb.com/mitchrpt.pdf.

19. Gwen Hooton interview.

20. Alex Rodriguez quoted in Selena Roberts and David Epstein, "Confronting A-Rod," *Sports Illustrated*, February 16, 2009. See also Selena Roberts, *A-Rod: The Many Lives of Alex Rodriguez* (New York: HarperCollins, 2009).

21. Ken Davidoff, "A-Rod's Anti-steroid Message under Fire after Latest PED Allegations," *New York Post*, January 31, 2013.

22. Emily Parker quoted in Kix, "All the Rage."

23. Tom Parker, letter to Mr. and Mrs. Hooton, Plano, TX, circa July 2003.

24. Ibid.

25. Christie Parker, letter to Don and Gwen [Hooton], Plano, TX, circa July 2003.

26. Tom Parker letter.

27. Emily Parker quoted in Kix, "All the Rage."

28. Ajello quoted in Stewart, "The Kid Next Door"; Kix, "All the Rage"; and Longman, "An Athlete's Dangerous Experiment."

29. Interview with Patrick Burke, Plano, TX, February 3, 2014.

30. Emily Parker quoted in Kix, "All the Rage."

31. Gomez interview; and Jones and Jacobson, "A Life Undone by Doping."

32. Interview with Denise Garibaldi, Novato, CA, April 16, 2013.

33. Andrew Jowers, "Player Gives All to Casa Grande; Rob Garibaldi Crucial Part of Baseball Team," *Santa Rosa Press Democrat*, March 19, 1997.

34. Baccala quoted in Denise Garibaldi interview, April 16, 2013; Ray Garibaldi interview, September 4, 2013.

35. Mark Fainaru-Wada, "Dreams, Steroids, Death—A Ballplayer's Downfall," *San Francisco Chronicle*, December 19, 2004, available at www.sfgate.com/sports/article/Dreams-steroids-death-a-ballplayers-downfall, accessed April 19, 2013; Denise Garibaldi interview, April 16, 2013; and Ray Garibaldi interview, September 4, 2013.

36. Rob Bruno quoted in Fainaru-Wada, "Dreams, Steroids, Death."

37. Denise Garibaldi interview, April 16, 2013.

38. Fainaru-Wada, "Dreams, Steroids, Death"; Ray Garibaldi interview, September 4, 2013; and interview with Paul Maytorena, Petaluma, CA, September 11, 2013.

39. Maytorena interview.

40. Gerard Thorne, *Anabolic Primer: Ergogenic Enhancement for the Hardcore Bodybuilder* (Mississauga, ON: Robert Kennedy Publishing, 2009), 26–27. Between May 2008 and June 2009, the IOC tested 240 over-the-counter nutritional supplements. Of that number, 45 (18 percent) contained anabolic steroids. (See Anni Heikkinen et al., "Use of Dietary Supplements in Olympic Athletes," *Journal of the International Society of Sports Nutrition* 8, no. 1 [2011]: 2783–2788.) In another 2007 study of supplements sold at U.S. health food stores, Informed-Choice, the screening company, found that 25 percent of the 58 supplements it tested contained steroids or stimulants banned by the World Anti-Doping Agency. (See David Epstein, "What You Don't Know Might Kill You," *Sports Illustrated Vault*, May 18, 2009, available at www.si.com/vault/2009/05/18/105813732/what-you-dont-know-might-kill-you, accessed May 22, 2016.)

41. Mark Fainaru-Wada and Lance Williams, *Game of Shadows: Barry Bonds, BALCO, and the Steroids Scandal that Rocked Professional Sports* (New York: Gotham Books, 2006), 47–58.

42. Ibid., 43–45.

43. Ibid., 55–56.

44. M. Powers, "Performance-Enhancing Drugs," in Leaver-Dunn, Houglum, and Harrelson, *Principles of Pharmacology for Athletic Trainers* (Thorofare, NJ: Slack, 2005), 331–332.

45. Fainaru-Wada and Williams, *Game of Shadows*, 56–58.

46. A. L. Siren et al., "Erythropoietin Prevents Neuronal Apoptosis after Cerebral Ischemia and Metabolic Stress," *Proceedings of the National Academy of Sciences* 98, no. 7 (2001): 4044–4049; and Z. A. Haroon et al., "A Novel Role for Erythropoietin during Fibrin-Induced Wound-Healing Response," *American Journal of Pathology* 163, no. 3 (2003): 993–1000.

47. Wolfgang Jelkmann and Carsten Lundby, "Blood Doping and Its Detection," *Blood* 118, no. 9 (September 2011): 2395–2404.

48. Fainaru-Wada and Williams, *Game of Shadows*, 56–58.

49. Mark Fainaru-Wada and Lance Williams, "Steroids Scandal: The BALCO Legacy," *San Francisco Chronicle*, December 24, 2005.

50. Ibid.

51. U.S. Food and Drug Administration, "Significant Dates in U.S. Food and Drug Law History," available at www.fda.gov/aboutfda/whatwedo/history/milestones/ucm128305.htm, accessed June 10, 2014.

52. On July 28, 2009, Deborah Autor, a product safety expert for the FDA, issued a public health advisory, stating that the "so-called 'dietary supplements' have been linked to liver disease, kidney failure, blockage of arteries and stroke in both adults and children." (See Autor quoted in "FDA Advisory Warns of Supplements with Steroids," news video, available at article.wn.com/view/2009/07/28/FDA_advisory_warns_of_supplements_with_steroids_s, accessed June 10, 2014.) As a result, any dietary supplement is considered an anabolic steroid if the following four criteria are met: (1) the substance is chemically related to testosterone; (2) the substance is pharmacologically related to testosterone; (3) the substance is not an estrogen, progestin, or a corticosteroid; and (4) the substance is not dehydroepiandrosterone (DHEA). Any substance that meets these criteria is considered an anabolic steroid and must be listed as a Schedule III controlled substance. The DEA found that boldione, desoxymethyltestosterone, and 19-nor-4,9(10)-androstadienedione—which had been sold as nutritional supplements prior to 2009—now meet the definition of anabolic steroid and added them to the list of banned substances under the Anabolic Steroid Control Act.

53. Fainaru-Wada and Williams, "Steroids Scandal."

54. Mike Shumann, "Beyond the Headlines," ABC-7/KGO-TV (San Francisco, CA), 2005.

55. Fainaru-Wada, "Dreams, Steroids, Death."

56. Poiani quoted in ibid.

57. Rob Garibaldi quoted in Jowers, "Player Gives All to Casa Grande."

58. Brian Seibel quoted in Fainaru-Wada, "Dreams, Steroids, Death."

59. Fainaru-Wada, "Dreams, Steroids, Death."

60. Poiani quoted in ibid.

61. Rob Garibaldi, "My Best Friend," English 811, College of San Mateo, December 12, 1997.

62. Interview with Denise Garibaldi, Novato, CA, April 29, 2013.

63. Interview with Raymond Garibaldi, Petaluma, CA, February 19, 2014.

64. Interview with Ray Garibaldi, Novato, CA, July 25, 2013; and Fainaru-Wada, "Dreams, Steroids, Death."

65. Interview with Denise Garibaldi, Novato, CA, April 16, 2013.

66. Ibid.; and Ray Garibaldi interview, July 25, 2013.

67. Rob Garibaldi, "My Best Friend."

68. Rob Garibaldi, "Annoying Things," English 811, College of San Mateo, September 28, 1997.

69. Rob Garibaldi, "How to Clean a Messy Bedroom," English 811, College of San Mateo, October 14, 1997.

70. Paul Maytorena interview.

71. Ibid.

72. Mike Carey, "A Way to Truly Honor Bob Leslie's Legacy," *Petaluma Press Democrat*, May 29, 2011; and Bob Young, "Garagiola Happy to See MLB Make a Move against Smokeless Tobacco," *Arizona Republic*, November 22, 2011.

73. Bob Leslie quoted in Rob Garibaldi, "You've Gotta Believe," English essay, Santa Rosa Junior College, December 3, 1999.

74. Ibid.

75. Marianne Costantinou, "Petaluma Loses Beloved Coach, 32," *San Francisco Chronicle*, June 17, 1998; and Young, "Garagiola Happy to See MLB Make a Move against Smokeless Tobacco."

76. Rob Garibaldi, "Depression," psychology class, Santa Rosa Junior College, Spring 1999.

77. Rob Garibaldi, "Baseball Is More than Just a Game," speech delivered before teammates at Santa Rosa Junior College, June 1999.

78. Maytorena interview.

79. Poiani quoted in Fainaru-Wada, "Dreams, Steroids, Death."

CHAPTER 4

1. Interview with Gwen Hooton, McKinney, TX, December 11, 2013; and interview with Don Hooton Sr., Williamsport, PA, August 16, 2013.

2. Gregg Jones and Gary Jacobson, "A Life Undone by Doping," *Dallas Morning News*, June 14, 2005.

3. Interview with Lindsay Forester, Lubbock, TX, June 2, 2014.

4. Interview with Liz Krause, Dallas, TX, June 3, 2014.

5. Don Hooton Sr. interview, August 16, 2013.

6. Harrison G. Pope Jr. et al., "Adverse Health Consequences of Performance-Enhancing Drugs: An Endocrine Society Scientific Statement," *Endocrine Reviews* 35, no. 3 (2014): 341–375.

7. Ibid., 342–343.

8. Sally Jenkins, "Winning, Cheating Have Ancient Roots," *Washington Post*, August 3, 2007. For homosexuality of ancient Greek and Roman athletes, see Erica R. Freeman, David A. Bloom, and Edward J. McGuire, "A Brief History of Testosterone," *Journal of Urology* 165, no. 2 (2001): 371–373; Thomas K. Hubbard, *Homosexuality in Greece and Rome* (Los Angeles: University of California Press, 2003); Victoria Wohl, *Love among the Ruins: The Erotics of Democracy in Classical Athens* (Princeton, NJ: Princeton University Press, 2002); and Craig Williams, *Roman Homosexuality: Ideologies of Masculinity in Classical Antiquity* (New York: Oxford University Press, 1999).

9. Charles-Édouard Brown-Séquard, "The Effects Produced on Man by Subcutaneous Injection of a Liquid Obtained from the Testicles of Animals," *Lancet* 137 (1889): 105–107.

10. Michael J. Aminoff, "Brown-Séquard: Selected Contributions of a Nineteenth-Century Neuroscientist," *Neuroscientist* 6, no. 1 (2000): 60–65.

11. Michael Bamberger and Don Yeagar, "Over the Edge: Special Report," *Sports Illustrated*, April 14, 1997.

12. Justin Peters, "The Man behind the Juice," *Slate.com*, February 2005, available at www.slate.com/articles/sports/sports_nut/2005/02/the_man_behind_the_juice.html, accessed January 4, 2014.

13. Thomas M. Hunt, *Drug Games: The International Olympic Committee and the Politics of Doping, 1960–2008* (Austin: University of Texas Press, 2011).

14. Michael S. Bahrke and Charles E. Yesalis, "Abuse of Anabolic Androgenic Steroids and Related Substances in Sport and Exercise," *Current Opinion in Pharmacology* 4, no. 6 (2004): 614–620.

15. Lyle Alzado as told to Shelley Smith, "'I'm Sick and I'm Scared,'" *Sports Illustrated*, July 8, 1991.

16. Jim Haslett quoted in Sam Farmer, "Steroid Use Rampant in Old NFL," *Los Angeles Times*, March 23, 2005.

17. Gerard Thorne, *Anabolic Primer: Ergogenic Enhancement for the Hardcore Body-builder* (Mississauga, ON: Robert Kennedy Publishing, 2009), 19.

18. Arnold Schwarzenegger quoted in Chris Hawke, "Arnold: No Regrets about Steroids," *CBS News*, February 26, 2005, available at www.cbsnews.com/news/arnold-no-regrets-about-steroids/, accessed January 7, 2014.

19. International Federation of Bodybuilders, "IFBB Anti-doping Rules" (Madrid, Spain: IFBB, 2009), 7, available at www.ifbb. com/pdf/IFBB_Anti-Doping_Rules_2009_Final.pdf, accessed January 7, 2014.

20. U.S. Department of Health and Human Services, "Title 21, USC-812—Schedules of Controlled Substances," Controlled Substances Act (1990), available at http://www.fda.gov/RegulatoryInformation/Legislation/ucm148726.htm, accessed January 7, 2004.

21. For a concise history of drug use in sports, see Charles Yesalis and Michael Bahrke, "History of Doping in Sport," *International Sports Studies* 24, no. 1 (2002): 42–76. For a more comprehensive treatment, see Paul Dimeo, *A History of Drug Use in Sport, 1876–1976: Beyond Good and Evil* (New York: Routledge, 2007). The WADA oversees the implementation of anti-doping policies in all sports worldwide and maintains a list of substances (drugs, supplements, etc.) that are banned from use in all sports at all times, banned from use during competition, or banned in specific sports. (See WADA, *The 2014 List of Prohibited Substances and Methods*, available at www.wada-ama.org/en/World-Anti-Doping-Program/Sports-and-Anti-Doping-Organizations/International-Standards/Prohibited-List/, accessed June 2, 2014.) For WADA's comprehensive guidelines for best practices in international and national anti-doping programs, see *The World Anti-Doping Code 2014*, available at www.wada-ama.org/en/worldanti-doping-program/sports-and-anti-doping-organizations/the-code, accessed June 1, 2014.

22. Hooton Foundation, "Frequently Asked Questions."

23. Prior to 2002, Taylor's e-mails bore the title "StudDrummerTH" after his name.

24. Gwen Hooton interview.

25. Parker quoted in Jones and Jacobson, "A Life Undone by Doping."

26. Interviews with Mark Gomez, Plano, TX, May 21, 2013, and January 24, 2014; and Jones and Jacobson, "A Life Undone by Doping."

27. Callahan Kuhns quoted in Jones and Jacobson, "A Life Undone by Doping."

28. Ajello quoted in Jim Stewart, "Kid Next Door," CBS, *60 Minutes*, Season 6, Episode 8, produced by Andrew Wolff, aired March 3, 2004, available at www.cbsnews.com/videos/teen-steroid-use/.

29. Paul Kix, "All the Rage," *Dallas Observer News*, August 12, 2004.

30. Ajello quoted in Jere Longman, "Drugs in Sports: An Athlete's Dangerous Experiment," *New York Times*, November 26, 2003.

31. Kix, "All the Rage."

32. Interview with Jason Wade, Argyle, TX, June 5, 2014.

33. Ibid.

34. Ibid.

35. Ibid.

36. Michael Scally, MD, "Anabolic Steroids. A Question of Muscle: Human Experimentation in Anabolic Steroid Research," available at http://asih.net/_scally_anabolic steroids - a question of muscle.pdf, accessed April 21, 2013.

37. Parker quoted in Kix, "All the Rage."

38. Parker quoted in Jones and Jacobson, "A Life Undone by Doping."

39. Ibid.

40. Parker quoted in ibid.

41. Kix, "All the Rage."

42. Gwen Hooton quoted in Stewart, "Kid Next Door."

43. Longman, "An Athlete's Dangerous Experiment."

44. Gwen Hooton interview.

45. Ibid.

46. Longman, "An Athlete's Dangerous Experiment."

47. There are three different types of steroids: anabolic, androgenic, and cortico. Anabolic steroids are derived from the hormone testosterone and promote the processing of protein cells in the muscle. Androgenic steroids contain the testosterone component that gives the masculine characteristics when used. Cortico steroids are anti-inflammatory steroids used for the treatment of allergies, asthma, eczema, and kidney diseases. All three types of steroids can be used for medical treatments, but anabolic and androgenic steroids have been used for nonmedical purposes mostly by athletes and body builders.

Anabolic steroids are by far the most abused. Research shows that aside from athletes and body builders, male nonathletes and non–body builders at the median age of 25 are lured to these types of steroids to enhance masculine characteristics and physical appearance as well as to increase virility.

Athletes use more than one hundred types of AAS. Some are injected, others are taken orally, and still others are stacked. The most common AAS are Nandrolone (Durabolin, Deca Durabolin), Oxandrolene (Anavar/Var), Stanazol (Winstrol/Winny), Oxymetandrolone (Anadrol/droll/Abombs), and Methandrostenolone (Dianabol/Dbol). Each one of these drugs has a specific purpose and function, although there is some overlay in properties and effects. (See "Different Types of Steroids on the Market," available at isteroids.com, accessed June 9, 2014; and "Types of Steroids," available at buysteroids.com, accessed June 9, 2014.)

48. Association against Steroid Abuse, "Steroid Testing," available at www.steroidabuse.com, accessed June 9, 2014.

49. Mary Pilon, "Differing Views on Value of High School Tests," *New York Times*, January 5, 2013.

50. D. H. Catlin et al., "Tetrahydrogestrinone: Discovery, Synthesis, and Detection in Urine," *RCM: Rapid Communications in Mass Spectrometry* 18, no. 12 (2004): 1245–1249. In 2003, Don Catlin, a researcher at UCLA, broke the code for the designer steroid THG. The U.S. Anti-Doping Agency (USADA) received a syringe with barely any liquid left in it. USADA Science Director Rich Hilderbrand rinsed the syringe with methanol and sent the rinse to UCLA as a few drops in a test tube. Within three weeks, Catlin and his team had drawn the molecule for THG and then created a new test to detect it. It was an extremely challenging task, because THG typically breaks down in the lab instrument before it reaches the detector. Since then, Catlin has cracked the code for multiple designer steroids. (See Jill Lieber Steeg, "Catlin Has Made a Career out of Busting Juicers," *USA TODAY*, February 28, 2007.)

51. Taylor Hooton Foundation, "Singapore Bodybuilder Taught Others How to Use Illegal Steroids," *Hoot's Corner*, July 20, 2012; Ute Mareck et al., "Factors Influencing the Steroid Profile in Doping Control Analysis," *Journal of Mass Spectrometry* 43 (2008): 877–891; and Christophe Saudan et al., "Testosterone and Doping Control," *British Journal of Sports Medicine* 40, Suppl. 1 (2006), 21–24.

52. Russell Sabin, "HGH: Aging Baby Boomers Turn to Hormone," *San Francisco Chronicle*, November 17, 2003.

53. Taylor Hooton Foundation, "Will Next PED Fad Be Viagra?" *Hoot's Corner*, November 29, 2012.

CHAPTER 5

1. Interview with Denise Garibaldi, Novato, CA, April 29, 2013; interview with Ray Garibaldi, Petaluma, CA, June 11, 2013.

2. Pete Cava, "Baseball in the Olympics," *Citius, Altius, Fortius* (Summer 1992): 7–15.

3. For a complete account of the 1998 home-run race, see Mike Lupica, *Summer of '98: When Homers Flew, Records Fell, and Baseball Reclaimed America* (Chicago: Contemporary Books, 1999).

4. Claire Smith, "McGwire Wears His Heart on 19-Inch Biceps," *New York Times*, December 27, 1997.

5. Pete Palmer and Gary Gillette, *ESPN Baseball Encyclopedia* (New York: Sterling Publishing, 2005), 444.

6. "Sammy Sosa," available at Biography.com, accessed April 25, 2014.

7. Bill Dedman, "Unlikely Season of Dreams for Cubs," *New York Times*, September 29, 1998.

8. Sammy Sosa and Marcos Breton, *Sosa: An Autobiography* (New York: Time Warner, 2000), 23–32; and Palmer and Gillette, *ESPN Baseball Encyclopedia*, 633.

9. Richard Justice, "McGwire Surpasses Maris with 62nd Home Run," *Washington Post*, September 9, 1998.

10. Denise Garibaldi interview, April 29, 2013.

11. Jim Gullo, *Trading Manny: How a Father and Son Learned to Love Baseball Again* (Boston: DaCapo Press, 2012). Gullo, a Seattle sportswriter, found himself struggling to answer questions about steroid use in Major League Baseball for his 7-year-old son, Joe, after the Mitchell Report was released. Joe, arriving at his own conclusion that those players who had used steroids were cheating, "punished" them by removing their baseball cards from his prized collection and created a "cheater's pile." "Even a 7-year-old knew that taking steroids was cheating," writes Gullo. "And I realized that Joe was absolutely right. It was cheating to take drugs to play better, or prolong a career, and it cheated all of us: the fans, the other players, high school and college players who wanted to 'move up a level,' me, Joe, and you" (Gullo, *Trading Manny*, 4).

12. Denise Garibaldi interview, April 29, 2013; and Denise Garibaldi quoted in Mark Fainaru-Wada, "Dreams, Steroids, Death—A Ballplayer's Downfall," *San Francisco Chronicle*, December 19, 2004, available at www.sfgate.com/sports/article/Dreams-steroids-death-a-ballplayers-downfall, accessed April 19, 2013.

13. Santa Rosa Junior College, "History and Highlights," available at www.santarosa.edu, accessed April 28, 2014.

14. Interview with Ron Myers, Santa Rosa, CA, September 30, 2013; and interview with Damon Neidlinger, Santa Rosa, CA, September 25, 2013.

15. Ron Myers interview.

16. Damon Neidlinger interview.

17. Rob Garibaldi, "Sports Psychology," psychology class, Santa Rosa Junior College, Spring 1999.

18. Neidlinger quoted in Rob Garibaldi, "Baseball Is More than Just a Game," speech delivered before teammates at Santa Rosa Junior College, June 1999.

19. Santa Rosa Junior College, "Baseball Alumni," available at www.santarosa.edu, accessed April 28, 2014.

20. Ron Myers interview.

21. Damon Neidlinger interview.

22. Ibid.

23. Ron Myers interview.

24. John Fay, "Gomes Focused on Outfield Job; Former Ray Must Return to Earlier Form," *Cincinnati Enquirer*, February 25, 2009.

25. Ron Myers interview.

26. Interview with Paul Maytorena, Petaluma, CA, September 11, 2013.

27. Santa Rosa Junior College, "Bear Cub Individual Season Records and Player Statistics," *SRJC Baseball Program* (Santa Rosa, CA: Santa Rosa Junior College, 2000), 10–11.

28. Fainaru-Wada, "Dreams, Steroids, Death"; Troy Roberts, "Making It Big: High School Athletes Turning to Drugs to Get into Shape," *48 Hours Investigates*, August 4, 2004; and Mike Shumann, "Beyond the Headlines," ABC-7 / KGO-TV (San Francisco, CA), 2005.

29. Ron Myers interview.

30. Ibid.

31. Damon Neidlinger interview.

32. Rob Garibaldi, "Motivation," psychology class, Santa Rosa Junior College, Spring 1999.

33. Rob Garibaldi, "College application essay to the University of Southern California." Summer 1999.

34. Rob Garibaldi, journal entry, May 12, 1999.

35. Ibid., Spring 1999.

36. Interview with Ray Garibaldi, Novato, CA, September 4, 2013. The Major League Baseball draft, known officially as the "First-Year Player Draft" or the "Rule 4 Draft," is held every June. Players eligible to be drafted are residents of the United States or Canada who are high school graduates and have not yet started college; college players (from four-year colleges) who have either completed their junior or senior years or are at least 21 years old no later than forty-five days after the draft; or junior college players, who are eligible for the draft at any time. (See Office of the Commissioner of Baseball, "First-Year Player Draft Eligibility Rules," Baseball Operations Department, available at http://mlb.mlb.com/mlb/draftday/rules.jsp, accessed April 27, 2014.)

37. Ron Myers interview; Damon Neidlinger interview; and Denise Garibaldi interview, April 29, 2013.

38. Rob Garibaldi, "The Power of Persuasion," psychology class, Santa Rosa Junior College, Spring 1999.

39. Ray Garibaldi interview, September 4, 2013.

40. Shumann, "Beyond the Headlines"; and Denise Garibaldi interview, April 29, 2013.

41. See "John Savage—Biography," UCLA Baseball, available at UCLABRUINS .com, accessed April 27, 2014.

42. Ray Garibaldi interview, September 4, 2013.

43. Ibid.

44. Fainaru-Wada, "Dreams, Steroids, Death"; and Denise Garibaldi interview, April 29, 2013.

45. Denise Garibaldi interview, April 29, 2013.

46. Ray Garibaldi interview, September 4, 2013; and Denise Garibaldi interview, April 29, 2013.

47. Rob Garibaldi, "College Application Essay to USC."

48. Ray Garibaldi interview, September 4, 2013.

49. For more information on Division I baseball scholarships, see National Collegiate Athletic Conference, "College Baseball Scholarships," http://web1.ncaa.org/ECWR2, accessed April 30, 2013.

50. See "1999 Baseball Draft Results," available at www.thebaseballcube.com/draft/research.asp?Y=1999&P=June-Reg, accessed May 24, 2013. The top pick in the 1999 draft was Josh Hamilton, who was signed by the Tampa Bay Rays. Other first-round picks who went on to become major league stars were Barry Zito (Oakland A's); Josh Beckett (Florida Marlins); and Ben Sheets (Milwaukee Brewers). Other stars went lower, including Albert Pujols (St. Louis Cardinals, 13th round, 402 overall pick); Shane Victorino (Los Angeles Dodgers, 6th round, 194 overall pick); and Brandon Phillips (Montreal Expos, 2nd round, 57 overall pick).

The 1999 draft was not very successful for the New York Yankees. Of their fifty picks, only five (10 percent) played in the majors: Alex Graman, a left-handed pitcher from Indiana State University (3rd round, 111 overall); Andy Phillips, a third baseman from the University of Alabama (7th round, 231 overall); Sean Henn, a left-handed pitcher from Aledo (Texas) High School (30th round, 921 overall); Kevin Thompson, a shortstop from Grayson Community College, Denison, Texas (31st round, 951 overall); and Chad Bentz, a left-handed pitcher from Juneau (Alaska) High School (34 round, 1,041 overall). Of these five draftees, only Phillips spent any substantive length of time in the majors, appearing in 259 games. None of the others appeared in more than sixty major league games.

51. Rob Garibaldi quoted in Fainaru-Wada, "Dreams, Steroids, Death."

52. Ron Myers interview.

53. Ray Garibaldi interview, September 4, 2013; Ron Myers interview; and Damon Neidlinger interview.

54. Damon Neidlinger interview.

55. Rob Garibaldi, "Baseball Is More than Just a Game."

56. Denise Garibaldi interview, April 29, 2013.

CHAPTER 6

1. Interview with Mackenzie Hooton, Frisco, TX, January 3, 2014.

2. Interview with Donald Hooton Jr., Philadelphia, PA, August 22, 2013.

3. Mackenzie Hooton interview.

4. Jere Longman, "Drugs in Sports: An Athlete's Dangerous Experiment," New York Times, November 26, 2003; and Paul Kix, "All the Rage," Dallas Observer News, August 12, 2004.

5. Interview with Mark Gomez, Plano, TX, January 17, 2014.

6. Longman, "An Athlete's Dangerous Experiment"; Kix, "All the Rage"; and Gregg Jones and Gary Jacobson, "A Life Undone by Doping," Dallas Morning News, June 14, 2005.

7. Taylor Hooton, e-mail to "Mom," Plano, TX, March 24, 2003.

8. Dr. Babette Farkas quoted in Jim Stewart, "Kid Next Door," CBS, 60 Minutes, Season 6, Episode 8, produced by Andrew Wolff, aired March 3, 2004, available at http://www.cbsnews.com/videos/teen-steroid-use/.

9. Mark Gomez interview, January 17, 2014.

10. Billy Ajello quoted in Longman, "An Athlete's Dangerous Experiment."

11. Longman, "An Athlete's Dangerous Experiment"; Kix, "All the Rage"; and Jones and Jacobson, "A Life Undone by Doping."

12. R. S. Tan and Michael S. Scally, "Anabolic Steroid-Induced Hypogonadism—Towards a Unified Hypothesis of Anabolic Steroid Action," *Medical Hypotheses* 72, no. 6 (2009): 723–728, available at www.elsevier.com/locate/mehy.

13. Donald A. Malone Jr. et al., "Anabolic Steroid Abuse: Psychiatric and Physical Costs," *Cleveland Clinic Journal of Medicine* 74, no. 5 (2007): 341–344; and Malone et al., "The Use of Fluoxetine in Depression Associated with Anabolic Steroid Withdrawal," *Journal of Clinical Psychiatry* 53, no. 4 (1992): 130–132.

14. Harrison G. Pope and D. L. Katz, "Psychiatric and Medical Effects of Anabolic-Androgenic Steroid Use: A Controlled Study of 160 Athletes," *Archives of General Psychiatry* 51, no. 5 (1994): 375–382; and K. J. Brower et al., "Anabolic Androgenic Steroids and Suicide," *American Journal of Psychiatry* 146 (1989): 1075.

15. Charles E. Yesalis and Michael Bahrke, "Doping among Adolescents," *Clinical Endocrinology and Metabolism* 14, no. 1 (2000): 25–35.

16. Gerard Thorne, *Anabolic Primer: Ergogenic Enhancement for the Hardcore Bodybuilder* (Mississauga, ON: Robert Kennedy Publishing, 2009), 50–51, 76–77, 86–87.

17. Emily Parker quoted in Jones and Jacobson, "A Life Undone by Doping."

18. Callahan Kuhns quoted in ibid.

19. Mark Gomez quoted in ibid.

20. Kix, "All the Rage."

21. Interview with Patrick Burke, Plano, TX, February 3, 2014.

22. Emily Parker quoted in Kix, "All the Rage"; and Jones and Jacobson, "A life Undone by Doping."

23. Kix, "All the Rage."

24. Emily Parker quoted in ibid.

25. Kix, "All the Rage."

26. Ibid.

27. Interview with Blake Boydston, Plano, TX, July 31, 2013. See also Boydston quoted in Longman, "An Athlete's Dangerous Experiment."

28. Interview with Don Hooton Sr., Williamsport, PA, August 16, 2013.

29. Interview with Gwen Hooton, McKinney, TX, December 11, 2013.

30. Ibid.

31. Ibid.

32. Ibid.; Don Hooton Sr. interview, August 16, 2013; Donald Hooton Jr. interview; and Mackenzie Hooton interview.

33. Longman, "An Athlete's Dangerous Experiment"; and Jones and Jacobson, "A Life Undone by Doping."

34. Mackenzie Hooton interview.

35. Taylor Hooton, letter to Emily Parker, London, England, July 14, 2003.

36. Taylor Hooton, "Emily," poem, July 14, 2003.

37. Gwen Hooton interview.

38. Donald Hooton Jr. interview.

39. Mackenzie Hooton interview; Gwen Hooton interview; Don Hooton Sr. interview; Longman, "An Athlete's Dangerous Experiment"; and Kix, "All the Rage."

40. Mackenzie Hooton interview.

41. Kix, "All the Rage."

42. Thorne, *Anabolic Primer*, 82–83.

43. Virginia S. Cowart, "National Institute on Drug Abuse May Join in Anabolic Steroid Research," *Journal of the American Medical Association* 261, no. 13 (1989): 1855–1856.

44. See Pascale Franques, Marc Auriacombe, and Jean Tignol, "Sports Use of Performance Enhancing Drugs and Addiction: A Conceptual and Epidemiological Review," *Annales de Médecine Interne* (Paris) 1521, Suppl. 7 (2001): 37–49. The study, completed by the University of Psychiatry at Bordeaux Hospital, France, concluded that the large majority of sports-practicing subjects have no dependence to either PEDs or addictive drugs. However, a subgroup of individuals who practice sports intensely and make use of both addictive and PEDs appear to be at increased risk for developing a substance-dependence syndrome. This subgroup is even more at risk because some PEDs (i.e., anabolic steroids) could increase the risk for occurrence of a substance-dependence syndrome through neurobiological actions.

45. Harrison G. Pope Jr., MD, et al., "The Lifetime Prevalence of Anabolic-Androgenic Steroid Use and Dependence in Americans: Current Best Estimates," *Drug and Alcohol Dependence* 20 (2013): 1–7.

46. Gen Kanayama et al., "Anabolic Steroid Abuse among Teenage Girls: An Illusory Problem?" *Drug and Alcohol Dependence* 88, nos. 2–3 (2007): 156–162.

47. The ten studies are Pope, "The Lifetime Prevalence of Anabolic-Androgenic Steroid Use and Dependence in Americans"; K. J. Brower et al., "Evidence for Physical and Psychological Dependence on Anabolic Androgenic Steroids in Eight Weight Lifters," *American Journal of Psychiatry* 147, no. 4 (1990): 510–512; J. Copeland et al., "Anabolic-Androgenic Steroid Use Disorders among a Sample of Australian Competitive and Recreational Users," *Drug and Alcohol Dependence* 60, no. 1 (2000): 91–96; D. W. Gridley et al., "Anabolic-Androgenic Steroid Use among Male Gymnasium Participants: Knowledge and Motives," *Sports Health* 12 (1994): 11–14; Gen Kanayama et al., "Anabolic-Androgenic Steroid Dependence: An Emerging Disorder," *Addiction (Abingdon, England)* 104 (2009): 1966–1978; Gen Kanayama et al., "Issues for DSM-V: Clarifying the Diagnostic Criteria for Anabolic-Androgenic Steroid Dependence," *American Journal of Psychiatry* 166, no. 6 (2009): 642–645; D. A. Malone Jr., "Psychiatric Effects and Psychoactive Substance Use in Anabolic-Androgenic Steroid Users," *Clinical Journal of Sports Medicine* 5, no. 1 (1995): 25–31; Simon J. Midgley et al., "Dependence-Producing Potential of Anabolic-Androgenic Steroids," *Addiction Research* 7 (1999): 539–550; P. J. Perry et al., "Anabolic Steroid Use in Weightlifters and Bodybuilders: An Internet Survey of Drug Utilization, *Clinical Journal of Sports Medicine* 15, no. 5 (2005): 326–330; H. Barnett et al., "Psychological and Physical Impact of Anabolic-Androgenic Steroid Dependence, *Pharmacotherapy* 32 (2012): 910–919; and Harrison G. Pope Jr. et al., "Psychiatric and Medical Effects of Anabolic-Androgenic Steroid Use: A Controlled Study of 160 Athletes," *Archives of General Psychiatry* 51, no. 5 (1994): 375–382.

48. Pope, "The Lifetime Prevalence of Anabolic-Androgenic Steroid Use and Dependence in Americans," 5.

49. Harrison G. Pope Jr. et al., "Treatment of Anabolic-Androgenic Steroid Dependence: Emerging Evidence and Its Implications," *Drug and Alcohol Dependence* 109 (2010): 10; emphasis original.

50. Ibid.

51. Gwen Hooton interview; Gwen Hooton quoted in Stewart, "Kid Next Door"; Kix, "All the Rage"; and Longman, "An Athlete's Dangerous Experiment."

52. Kix, "All the Rage"; Longman, "An Athlete's Dangerous Experiment."

53. Gwen Hooton interview; and Stewart, "Kid Next Door."
54. Stewart, "Kid Next Door."
55. Mackenzie Hooton interview.
56. Gwen Hooton interview.

CHAPTER 7

1. Interview with Ray Garibaldi, Novato, CA, September 4, 2013; interview with Denise Garibaldi, Novato, CA, April 29, 2013; and Ralph Leef, "Steroids Blamed in Suicide of Ex–Casa Grande Star," *Santa Rosa Press Democrat*, March 25, 2004. The quote by John Savage comes from interviews with both Ray and Denise Garibaldi.

2. USC Baseball, "History," University of Southern California Baseball website, available at www.usctrojans.com, accessed May 3, 2014. The USC Trojans Baseball team captured national titles in 1948, 1958, 1961, 1963, 1968, 1970, 1971, 1972, 1973, 1974, 1978, and 1998. No other Division I school has more than six national championships in baseball.

3. "Head Coach Mike Gillespie," University of California, Irvine Baseball website, available at www.ucirvinesports.com/sports/m-basebl/coaches/index, accessed May 7, 2014. Arizona's Jerry Kindall is the only other individual to both play for and coach an NCAA-championship baseball team.

4. Ibid.

5. See *College Baseball* on Savage's top-ranked recruiting class of 1999–2000.

6. USC Baseball, "Archives—2000 Season Results," USC Baseball website, available at www.usctrojans.com, accessed May 4, 2014.

7. "Garibaldi's Offensive Statistics—Archives—2000 Season Results," USC Baseball website, January 29 to February 8, accessed May 4, 2014.

8. "USC Falls to Texas Tech, 4–3," USC Baseball website, February 11, 2000, accessed May 5, 2014.

9. Gillespie quoted in Rob Garibaldi, journal entry, February 22, 2000.

10. "USC Falls to Texas Tech, 4–3."

11. Rob Garibaldi, journal entry, February 22, 2000.

12. "USC Defeats University of San Diego, 7–3; Garibaldi's Three-Run Homer Caps Four-Run First Inning to Lead Trojans," USC Baseball website, February 22, 2000, accessed May 5, 2014.

13. "Garibaldi's Offensive Statistics—Archives—2000 Season Results," USC Baseball website, February 11 to March 14, accessed May 5, 2014.

14. Rob Garibaldi, journal entry, March 15, 2000.

15. Denise Garibaldi interview, April 29, 2013.

16. Ibid.

17. Ray Garibaldi interview, September 4, 2013; Denise Garibaldi interview, April 29, 2013.

18. Denise Garibaldi interview, April 29, 2013.

19. "Garibaldi's Offensive Statistics—Archives—2000 Season Results.," USC Baseball website, March 14 to April 18, accessed May 5, 2014.

20. "Baseball Beats UCLA, 6–2," USC Baseball website, April 18, 2000, accessed May 6, 2014.

21. "Garibaldi's Offensive Statistics—Archives—2000 Season Results," USC Baseball website, April 20 to May 2, accessed May 5, 2014.

22. Rick Hellend quoted in Leef, "Steroids Blamed in Suicide of Ex–Casa Grande

Star." Despite this author's many efforts to contact several members of the 2000 and 2001 USC Trojans baseball teams, no one returned phone calls or e-mails.

23. Denise and Ray Garibaldi quoted in Mark Fainaru-Wada, "Dreams, Steroids, Death—A Ballplayer's Downfall," *San Francisco Chronicle*, December 19, 2004, available at www.sfgate.com/sports/article/Dreams-steroids-death-a-ballplayers-downfall, accessed April 19, 2013; Ray Garibaldi interview; Denise Garibaldi interview, April 29, 2013; interview with Denise Garibaldi, Novato, CA, May 10, 2014.

24. Rob Garibaldi, journal entry, December 12, 2000.

25. "Baseball Evens Series with No. 3 Arizona State, 12–2," USC Baseball website, April 29, 2000, accessed May 6, 2014.

26. "Baseball Dispatches Oregon State, 16–7," USC Baseball website, May 13, 2000, accessed May 6, 2014.

27. "Baseball One Win away from Advancing to Super Regional," USC Baseball website, May 28, 2000, accessed May 6, 2014.

28. "Trojan Baseball Bound for the College World Series!" USC Baseball website, June 3, 2000, accessed May 6, 2014.

29. "USC Trojans Baseball, 2000—Final Statistics," USC Baseball website, accessed April 15, 2014 and May 6, 2014.

30. "Rob Garibaldi's Career Statistics—2000," USC Baseball website, accessed April 10, 2014.

31. "Draft' 01: Top 100 College Prospects," *Baseball America*, February 19–March 4, 2001, 15.

32. Ray Garibaldi interview.

33. Denise Garibaldi, letter to Coach Mike Gillespie and Mr. James Ross, Petaluma, CA, August 25, 2000.

34. Fainaru-Wada, "Dreams, Steroids, Death."

35. Ibid.

36. Denise Garibaldi quoted in Leef, "Steroids Blamed in Suicide of Ex–Casa Grande Star"; and Denise Garibaldi interview, May 10, 2014.

37. Ray Garibaldi quoted in Troy Roberts, "Making It Big: High School Athletes Turning to Drugs to Get into Shape," *48 Hours Investigates*, August 4, 2004; Denise Garibaldi, "The Challenge and the Tragedy," *New England Law Review* 40, no. 3 (2006): 718; and Ray Garibaldi interview. Rob never identified the trainer by name.

38. Denise Garibaldi interview, April 29, 2013.

39. The author made repeated efforts to contact Savage, now the head baseball coach at UCLA. But he refused to return phone calls, finally dismissing the inquiry with a curt e-mail that read, "This just isn't a subject I'd like to go on the record about." (John Savage quoted by Mike Leary, UCLA Sports Information director, in e-mail to author, Los Angeles, CA, September 19, 2013.)

40. Denise Garibaldi interview, April 29, 2013; and Fainaru-Wada, "Dreams, Steroids, Death."

41. Rob Garibaldi, journal entry, December 12, 2000.

42. Gen Kanayama et al., "Past Anabolic-Androgenic Steroid Use among Men Admitted for Substance Abuse Treatment," *Journal of Clinical Psychiatry* 64, no. 2 (2003): 158; Pope, Elena M. Kouri, and James I. Hudson, "Effects of Supraphysiologic Doses of Testosterone on Mood and Aggression in Normal Men: A Randomized Controlled Trial," *Archives of General Psychiatry* 57 (2000): 137; and Pope and David L. Katz, "Affective and Psychotic Symptoms Associated with Anabolic Steroid Use," *American Journal of Psychiatry* 145, no. 4 (1988): 489.

43. Rob Garibaldi, journal entry, December 12, 2000.

44. Ray Garibaldi interview, September 4, 2013.

45. This author made numerous attempts to contact Gillespie, now the head base-ball coach at UC Irvine, but was informed that he "decided to pass on participating in the book project." (Fumi Kimura, assistant director, Media Relations, University of California, Irvine, e-mail to author, Irvine, CA, September 19, 2013.)

46. Dr. Edward Roth, director, USC Office of Student Disability Services, e-mail to author, Los Angeles, CA, May 27, 2014.

47. John Soldate, now an athletic counselor and instructor at Butte College in Oroville, California, was the tutorial coordinator for USC's SAAS at the time. Soldate, a native of Petaluma who also played baseball at SRJC, was very familiar with Rob's case, but he refused to discuss the matter with this author. (John Soldate, former USC tutorial coordinator and counselor, phone conversation with author, Oroville, California, May 28, 2014.)

48. Gillespie quoted in "Rob Garibaldi #15," USC Trojans roster, 2001. Archives, USC Baseball website, accessed March 3, 2014.

49. "Garibaldi's Offensive Statistics—Archives—2001 Season Results," USC Base-ball website, January 31 to February 17, accessed May 5, 2014.

50. "Morales Provides Game-Winning Hit in Baseball's 5–4 Win at UCLA," USC Baseball website, February 18, 2001, accessed May 11, 2014.

51. Ray Garibaldi interview, September 4, 2013.

52. "Baseball box score: Loyola Marymount 9, USC 1," USC Baseball website, Feb-ruary 20, 2001, accessed May 11, 2014.

53. "Baseball box scores," USC Baseball website, February 20–March 3, 2001, ac-cessed May 11, 2014.

54. Rob Garibaldi quoted in Ray Garibaldi interview, September 4, 2013.

55. Fainaru-Wada, "Dreams, Steroids, Death."

56. Ray Garibaldi interview, September 4, 2013.

57. Interview with Joe Garibaldi, San Mateo, CA, February 15, 2014.

58. "Garibaldi's Offensive Statistics—Archives—2001 Season Results," USC Base-ball website, April 3 to April 13, accessed May 11, 2014.

59. Fainaru-Wada, "Dreams, Steroids, Death"; Leef, "Steroids Blamed in Suicide of Ex–Casa Grande Star"; and Denise Garibaldi interview, May 10, 2014.

60. Rick Hellend quoted in Leef, "Steroids Blamed in Suicide of Ex–Casa Grande Star."

61. Ray Garibaldi interview, September 4, 2013; Denise Garibaldi interview, May 24, 2014; and Leef, "Steroids Blamed in Suicide of Ex–Casa Grande Star." As it turned out, Rob played his last game for USC on Saturday, April 21. It was a 7–0 win against Stanford in which he went 1-for-3 at the plate. (See "Box score, USC 7—Stanford 0," USC Baseball website, April 21, 2001, accessed May 11, 2014.)

62. Rick Hellend quoted in Leef, "Steroids Blamed in Suicide of Ex–Casa Grande Star."

63. Rob Garibaldi, journal entry, April 28, 2001.

64. Rick Hellend quoted in Leef, "Steroids Blamed in Suicide of Ex–Casa Grande Star."

65. Interview with Paul Maytorena, Petaluma, CA, September 11, 2013; Fainaru-Wa-da, "Dreams, Steroids, Death"; Leef, "Steroids Blamed in Suicide of Ex–Casa Grande Star."

66. Rick Hellend quoted in Leef, "Steroids Blamed in Suicide of Ex–Casa Grande Star"; Ray Garibaldi interview, September 4, 2013; and Denise Garibaldi interview, May 24, 2014.

67. Denise Garibaldi interview, May 24, 2014.

68. Ray Garibaldi interview, September 4, 2013; and Denise Garibaldi, "Notes of May 3, 2002, Meeting with Coach Gillespie."

69. "Janet Eddy," Emeriti Center, University of Southern California website, available at http://emeriti.usc.edu/mini-bios/janet-eddy/, accessed May 12, 2014; and interview with Janet Eddy, Glendale, CA, May 29, 2014.

70. Gillespie quoted in Ray Garibaldi interview, September 4, 2013; Denise Garibaldi, "Notes of May 3, 2002, Meeting with Gillespie"; and interview with anonymous source, Office of Student Disabilities Services, USC, January 20, 2014.

71. Ray Garibaldi interview, September 4, 2013; and Ray Garibaldi quoted in Leef, "Steroids Blamed in Suicide of Ex–Casa Grande Star."

72. Janet Eddy interview; anonymous source interview; Ray Garibaldi interview, September 4, 2013; and Denise Garibaldi, "Notes of May 3, 2002, Meeting with Gillespie."

73. Anonymous source interview; Ray Garibaldi interview, September 4, 2013; and Denise Garibaldi, "Notes of May 3, 2002, Meeting with Gillespie."

74. Janet Eddy interview; anonymous source interview; Ray Garibaldi interview, September 4, 2013; and Denise Garibaldi, "Notes of May 3, 2002, Meeting with Gillespie."

75. Several journal essays address the changing definition of *in loco parentis* in higher education. Among the best are Philip M. Hirshberg, "The College's Emerging Duty to Supervise Students: In Loco Parentis," *Washington University Journal of Urban and Contemporary Law* 46 (1994); Brian Jackson, "The Lingering Legacy of in Loco Parentis: An Historical Survey and Proposal for Reform," *Vanderbilt Law Review* 44 (1991); and Peter F. Lake, "The Special Relationship(s): Between a College and a Student: Law and Policy Ramifications for the Post in Loco Parentis College," *Idaho Law Review* 37 (2001): 531–555. Prior to the 1960s, undergraduates were subject to many restrictions in their private lives, including curfews, sex-segregated dormitories, and the inability to exercise free speech. The student movements of the 1960s severely criticized such restrictions; the Free Speech Movement at the University of California at Berkeley not only challenged them but inspired undergrads across the nation to join in the opposition. (See Terry H. Anderson, *The Movement and the Sixties* [New York: Oxford University Press, 1996].) The landmark case *Dixon v. Alabama* (1961) was the first legal challenge to in loco parentis in U.S. higher education. The U.S. Court of Appeals for the Fifth Circuit found that Alabama State College could not summarily expel students without due process. (See *Dixon v. Alabama State Board of Education*, 294 F. 2d 150 [5th Cir. 1961].)

76. Title I, Section 102a, Americans with Disabilities Act, 1990, available at www.ada.gov/pubs/ada.htm, accessed May 28, 2014.

77. Janet Eddy interview.

78. Ibid.

79. Denise Garibaldi interview, May 24, 2014.

80. Title I, Section 104c, ADA.

81. NCAA, "Banned Substances list," available at http://grfx.cstv.com/photos/schools/domi/genrel/auto_pdf/ncaa-banned-substance-list.pdf, accessed May 28, 2014.

82. Gillespie quoted in Ray Garibaldi interview, September 4, 2013; anonymous source interview; and Denise Garibaldi, "Notes of May 3, 2002, Meeting with Gillespie."

83. John Savage quoted in Ray Garibaldi interview, September 4, 2013; and Denise Garibaldi interview, April 29, 2013.

84. Denise Garibaldi interview, May 24, 2014.

85. Anonymous source interview. The source was corroborated by Denise and Ray Garibaldi. (See Ray Garibaldi interview, September 4, 2013; and Denise Garibaldi, "Notes of May 3, 2002, Meeting with Gillespie.")

86. Janet Eddy interview.

87. Ray Garibaldi interview, September 4, 2013; and Denise Garibaldi, "Notes of May 3, 2002, Meeting with Gillespie."

88. Anonymous source interview; Ray Garibaldi interview, September 4, 2013; and Denise Garibaldi, "Notes of May 3, 2002, Meeting with Gillespie."

89. Ray Garibaldi interview, September 4, 2013; and Denise Garibaldi, "Notes of May 3, 2002, Meeting with Gillespie."

90. Denise Garibaldi interview, May 24, 2014.

91. Leef, "Steroids Blamed in Suicide of Ex–Casa Grande Star."

CHAPTER 8

1. Paul Kix, "All the Rage," *Dallas Observer News*, August 12, 2004; and Gregg Jones and Gary Jacobson, "Father Makes Truth His Purpose," *Dallas Morning News*, June 8, 2005.

2. Jones and Jacobson, "Father Makes Truth His Purpose."

3. Interview with Don Hooton Sr., Williamsport, PA, August 16, 2013.

4. Jere Longman, "Drugs in Sports: An Athlete's Dangerous Experiment," *New York Times*, November 26, 2003; and Kix, "All the Rage."

5. Jones and Jacobson, "Father Makes Truth His Purpose."

6. Interview with Reverend Neil Jeffrey, Plano, TX, February 12, 2014.

7. Interview with Gwen Hooton, McKinney, TX, December 11, 2013.

8. Don Hooton quoted in Jones and Jacobson, "Father Makes Truth His Purpose."

9. Interview with Don Hooton Sr., McKinney, TX, May 21, 2013.

10. Interview with Mark Gomez, Plano, TX, January 17, 2014.

11. Ibid.

12. Don Hooton Sr. interview, May 21, 2013; and Jones and Jacobson, "Father Makes Truth His Purpose."

13. Jones and Jacobson, "Father Makes Truth His Purpose."

14. Ibid.

15. Don Hooton Sr. interview, August 16, 2013.

16. Don Hooton Sr., letter to R.W., Plano, TX, September 9, 2004.

17. Don Hooton Sr. interview, August 16, 2013.

18. Jones and Jacobson, "Father Makes Truth His Purpose."

19. Curtis Howard, Senior Police Legal Adviser, Plano Police Department, e-mail to author, Plano, TX, August 29, 2013.

20. Robert J. Cramer, "Anabolic Steroids Are Easily Purchased without a Prescription and Present Significant Challenges to Law Enforcement Officials," GAO-06-243R Anabolic Steroids (Washington, DC: U.S. Government Accountability Office, 2005), 5, available at www.gao.gov/new.items/d06243r.pdf, accessed on January 24, 2013. The report was written in response to a request by U.S. Representative Tom Davis, the chairman of the House Committee on Government Reform. For informa-

tion on the use and abuse of anabolic steroids by police officers, see Kim R. Humphrey, "Anabolic Steroid Use and Abuse by Police Officers: Policy and Prevention," *Police Chief*, August 2014, available at www.policechiefmagazine.org/magazine/index .cfm?fuseaction=display_arch&article_id=1512&issue_id=62008, accessed August 11, 2014; David Johnson, *Falling Off the Thin Blue Line: A Badge, a Syringe, and a Struggle with Steroid Addiction* (Bloomington, IN: iUniverse, 2007); Sabrina Rubin Erdely, "Cops on Steroids: It's the 'Other' Doping Scandal, and We're Breaking It Wide Open," *Men's Health*, September 19, 2005, available at http://www.menshealth.com/health/ scandals-cops-and-steroids, accessed August 12, 2014; and Charles Swanson, Larry Gaines, and Barbara Gore, "Abuse of Anabolic Steroids," *FBI Law Enforcement Bulletin* 60, no. 8 (1991): 19.

21. George Dohrmann and Luis Llosa, "The Mexican Connection," *Sports Illustrated*, April 24, 2006, 66–69.

22. U.S. Drug Enforcement Administration (DEA), "DEA Announces Largest Steroids Enforcement Action in U.S. History," News Release, September 24, 2007, available at www.justice.gov/dea/divisions/hq/2007/pr092407p.html, accessed May 20, 2014; Robert Miller, "Steroids: Made in China," *Stamford (CT) Advocate*, April 7, 2011; Ted Sherman, "Black Market Steroids Pipeline Leads from NJ to China, Feds Say," *Newark (NJ) Star Ledger*, June 18, 2013; and George Spellwin, "China: Massive Steroids Pipeline to America," available at Elitefitness.com, accessed May 20, 2014. In September 2007, another DEA probe, "Operation Raw Deal," shut down twenty-six underground steroid labs and instigated more than fifty arrests across the United States in what was the largest PED crackdown in U.S. history. The DEA also identified thirty-seven Chinese factories that purportedly supplied the raw materials for the labs. The raids capped an eighteen-month probe netting 124 arrests in twenty-seven states and closing fifty-six labs. The agency also seized $6.5 million and 532 pounds of raw steroid powder. Most of the raids took place in quiet suburban neighborhoods. The investigation also focused on message boards where advice is traded about obtaining raw materials as well as on the websites that help the labs sell finished products to the public. (See Shaun Assael, "'Raw Deal' Busts Labs across U.S., Many Supplied by China," *ESPN the Magazine*, September 24, 2007.)

23. Cramer, "Anabolic Steroids Present Significant Challenges to Law Enforcement," 5–6.

24. Ibid., 6–7.

25. According to the DEA, Schedule III drugs are substances that are accepted for medical use in the United States but have the potential for abuse and addiction. In addition to anabolic steroids, Schedule III controlled substances include LSD, ketamine, and certain codeine combinations. (See U.S. Drug Enforcement Administration, "Drug Schedules" [Washington, DC: U.S. Department of Justice, 2014], available at http:// www.justice.gov/dea/druginfo/ds.shtml, accessed January 25, 2014.)

26. *2010 U.S. Sentencing Guidelines Manual*, § 2D1.1, Notes to Drug Quantity Table (G).

27. *2004 U.S. Sentencing Guidelines Manual*, § 2D1.1, Notes to Drug Quantity Table (G).

28. Cicero A. Estrella, "Federal Sentencing Rules for Steroids Offenses Toughened," *San Francisco Chronicle*, March 28, 2006.

29. Interview with Charles Yusalis, State College, PA, June 10, 2014.

30. Humphrey, "Anabolic Steroid Use and Abuse by Police Officers."

31. Swanson, Gaines, and Gore, "Abuse of Anabolic Steroids."

32. Humphrey, "Anabolic Steroid Use and Abuse by Police Officers."

33. Matt Goodman, "Feds: Arlington Cop Offered Confidential Info to Steroid Dealer," WFAA.com, June 12, 2013, available at www.wfaa.com/news/local/tarrant/Feds-allege-Arlington-officer-provided-confidential-information-to-steroid-dealer-211235291.html, accessed August 12, 2014.

34. Harrison Pope, MD, quoted in Erdely, "Cops on Steroids."

35. Erdely, "Cops on Steroids."

36. Carol Marie Cropper, "10 Heroin Deaths in Texas Reflect Rising Use by Young," *New York Times*, November 23, 1997; and Pam Easton, "MTV Documentary Examines Heroin Use, Plano Deaths," *Abilene Reporter-News*, March 31, 1998.

37. Don Hooton Sr. interview, August 16, 2013.

38. Jones and Jacobson, "Father Makes Truth His Purpose"; and Kix, "All the Rage."

39. Jones and Jacobson, "Father Makes Truth His Purpose."

40. Don Hooton Sr. interview, August 16, 2013; and Jones and Jacobson, "Father Makes Truth His Purpose."

41. For Billy Ajello, Blake Boydston, Mike Hughes, and school official quotes, see Longman, "An Athlete's Dangerous Experiment."

42. Cliff Odenwald quoted in ibid.

43. Larry Gwyn quoted in Jim Stewart, "Kid Next Door," CBS, *60 Minutes*, Season 6, Episode 8, produced by Andrew Wolff, aired March 3, 2004, available at http://www.cbsnews.com/videos/teen-steroid-use/.

44. Don Hooton Sr. interview, August 16, 2013; and Don Hooton quoted in Stewart, "Kid Next Door."

45. Don Hooton Sr. interview, August 16, 2013.

46. Douglas Otto, superintendent of schools, "Statement on Steroid Use in the Plano Independent School District," delivered at Plano East Senior High School in March 2004; and Kix, "All the Rage."

47. Ajello quoted in Kix, "All the Rage." There were also several problems with the Texas A&M survey. First, the data had been collected in 2001, so they were obsolete. Second, there were no follow-up questions, such as "What type of steroids have you taken?" The response to such a question would confirm use. If the student were unable to identify the steroid, chances would be good that he had not used steroids at all. Finally, the poll did not address Plano West in much detail, even though that was the school where students said the steroids problem was greatest. (See Public Policy Research Institute, "Survey of Steroid Use among Dallas-Area High School Students" [College Station, TX, Texas A&M University, 2001].)

48. Emily Parker quoted in Kix, "All the Rage."

49. Gomez quoted in ibid.

50. Patrick Burke quoted in ibid.

51. Kix, "All the Rage."

52. Merritt Onsa, "I Love You Guys. I'm Sorry about Everything," *Service in the Light of Truth* (Sigma Nu Fraternity blog), November 27, 2013; and Selena Roberts, "Congress' Waning Roid Rage," available at *Sportsonearth.com*, October 16, 2013.

53. Don Hooton quoted in Stewart, "Kid Next Door."

54. Don Hooton Sr. interview, August 16, 2013.

55. Barry M. Bloom, "MLB Donates $1.5 million to Hooton Foundation," MLB.com, June 10, 2008, available at http://mlb.mlb.com/news/print.jsp?ymd=20080610&content_id=2882630.

56. "Taylor Hooton Foundation Launches All Me League," July 30, 2014, Archives, Taylor Hooton Foundation website.

57. For more information about the Taylor Hooton Foundation, access the organization's website at http://taylorhooton.org/about-us/. Shortly after the congressional hearings on steroids in MLB had concluded, Commissioner Selig, deeply moved by the testimonies of Don Hooton and Denise Garibaldi, made a significant financial commitment on behalf of MLB to further the mission of the Taylor Hooton Foundation. MLB remains the chief sponsor of the nonprofit organization.

58. Interview with Donald Hooton Jr., June 3, 2014.

59. Interview with Donald Hooton Jr., Philadelphia, PA, August 22, 2013.

60. See Christopher Lawlor, "Texas High Schools Get Tough on Steroid Abuse," *USA TODAY*, July 6, 2007; and Gary Scharrer, "UIL Posts Rules on High School Steroid Tests," *Houston Chronicle*, November 29, 2007.

61. See Jeff Miller, "Steroid Testing Program for High School Athletes Shrinks as State Cuts Funds," *Dallas Morning News*, January 2, 2011.

62. Don Hooton Sr. interview, August 16, 2013.

63. "Charged Doc Says He Wrote A-Rod Script," Associated Press, March 8, 2010; and Michael S. Schmidt, "Taking Balco Approach, Authorities Interview Athletes Linked to Galea," *New York Times*, February 28, 2010.

64. Selena Roberts and David Epstein, "Confronting A-Rod," *Sports Illustrated*, February 16, 2009, 28–31. The revelation that A-Rod had used steroids had been part of a government-sealed report detailing 104 major leaguers who tested positive during a 2000 drug survey of 1,200 players. Approved by the players themselves with the promise of anonymity, the survey was conducted by MLB to determine whether a mandatory drug-testing program was necessary. At the time, baseball's collective-bargaining agreement did not assign a penalty or punishment for a positive test. But because more than 5 percent of the samples taken from players in 2003 came back positive, mandatory testing of MLB players began in 2004, with penalties for violations. The 2003 test results were supposed to remain anonymous, with the samples destroyed. However, a coded master list of 104 players was seized during the BALCO investigation, turning up in a 2004 federal raid on Comprehensive Drug Testing's facility in Long Beach, California. Shortly afterward, the list was released to the Players Association, which leaked the news of A-Rod's positive test results. Meanwhile, the physical samples of the positive tests were subpoenaed by federal authorities in November 2003. (See Peter Gammons, "A-Rod Admits, Regrets Use of PEDS," *ESPN The Magazine*, February 11, 2009; and Michael S. Schmidt, "Alex Rodriguez Said to Test Positive in 2003," *New York Times*, February 7, 2009.)

65. Michael S. Schmidt, "Rodriguez Admits to Using Performance-Enhancing Drugs," *New York Times*, February 9, 2009; and "Selig Considering Options on A-Rod," *ESPN The Magazine*, February 11, 2009.

66. Rodriguez quoted in Tyler Kepner, "As Team Looks on, Rodriguez Details His Use of Steroids," *New York Times*, February 17, 2009.

67. Don Hooton Sr. interview, August 16, 2013.

68. Tim Elfrink and Gus Garcia-Roberts, *Blood Sport: Alex Rodriguez, Biogenesis, and the Quest to End Baseball's Steroid Era* (New York: Dutton, 2014), 118.

69. "Transcript of Alex Rodriguez's Press Conference," *New York Times*, February 18, 2009; Kepner, "As Team Looks on, Rodriguez Details His Use of Steroids"; and Alan Schwarz, "As It Happened: The A-Rod News Conference," *New York Times*, February 17, 2009.

70. Don Hooton Sr. interview, August 16, 2013.

71. Tim Elfrink, "A Miami Clinic Supplies Drugs to Sports' Biggest Names," *New York Times*, January 31, 2013; and Elfrink and Garcia-Roberts, *Blood Sport*, 251–253.

The other stars identified by the newspaper were Melky Cabrera, Bartolo Colon, Tasmani Grandal, Ryan Braun, and Nelson Cruz.

72. Tim Brown, "Alex Rodriguez, 12 Other Players Suspended by MLB for Biogenesis Ties," *Yahoo! Sports*, August 5, 2013, accessed August 13, 2013. Rodriguez was allowed to play the remaining forty-nine games of the 2013 season, pending his appeal of that decision. An arbitrator later upheld the suspension in January 2014, technically reducing the suspension to 162 games, representing the entire 2014 regular season and postseason. (See Ronald Blum and Larry Neumeister, "A-Rod Drug Saga Goes to Extra Innings," *Philadelphia Inquirer*, January 14, 2014.)

73. "A-Rod Suspended through 2014 Season," available at MLB.com, August 5, 2013, accessed August 15, 2013.

74. Ibid.

75. Ibid.

76. Don Hooton Sr., "Statement on the Suspension of Alex Rodriguez," press release, August 5, 2013, Taylor Hooton Foundation website, available at http://taylorhooton.org/thf-supports-mlbs-efforts-to-rid-the-sport-of-steroids/, accessed June 3, 2014.

77. Gwen Hooton interview.

CHAPTER 9

1. Dr. Brent Cox quoted in Mark Fainaru-Wada, "Dreams, Steroids, Death—A Ballplayer's Downfall," *San Francisco Chronicle*, December 19, 2004, available at www.sfgate.com/sports/article/Dreams-steroids-death-a-ballplayers-downfall, accessed April 19, 2013.

2. Dr. Brent Cox, letter "To Whom It May Concern," Petaluma, CA, August 27, 2001.

3. Interview with Denise Garibaldi, Novato, CA, May 10, 2014.

4. John Daly quoted in Ralph Leef, "Steroids Blamed in Suicide of Ex–Casa Grande Star," *Santa Rosa Press Democrat*, March 25, 2004.

5. Dr. Brent Cox quoted in ibid.

6. Denise Garibaldi interview, May 10, 2014.

7. Interview with Ray Garibaldi, Novato, CA, September 20, 2013.

8. See P. Y. Choi, A. C. Parrott, and D. Cowan, "High-Dose Anabolic Steroids in Strength Athletes: Effects upon Hostility and Aggression," Human Psychopharmacology 5 (1990): 349–356; Paul J. Fudala et al., "An Evaluation of Anabolic-Androgenic Steroid Abusers over a Period of 1 Year: Seven Case Studies," *Annals of Clinical Psychiatry* 15, no. 2 (2003): 121–130; Thomas A. Pagonis et al., "Psychiatric Side Effects Induced by Supraphysiological Doses of Combinations of Anabolic Steroids Correlate to the Severity of Abuse," *European Psychiatry* 21, no. 8 (2006): 551–562; Thomas A. Pagonis et al., "Psychiatric and Hostility Factors Related to Use of Anabolic Steroids in Monozygotic Twins," *European Psychiatry* 21, no. 8 (2006): 563–569; and C. Wilson-Fearon and Andrew C. Parrott, "Multiple Drug Use and Dietary Restraint in a Mr. Universe Competitor: Psychobiological Effects," *Perceptual and Motor Skills* 88, no. 2 (1999): 579–580.

9. Pope et al. "Adverse Health Consequences of Performance-Enhancing Drugs: An Endocrine Society Scientific Statement," *Endocrine Reviews*, December 2013, 13, ePub ahead of print. For the specific studies, see Manuel Estrada, Anurag Varshney, and Barbara E. Ehrlich, "Elevated Testosterone Induces Apoptosis in Neuronal Cells,"

Journal of Biological Chemistry 281, no. 35 (2006): 25492–25501; Filippo Caraci et al., "Neurotoxic Properties of the Anabolic Androgenic Steroids Nandrolone and Methandrostenolone in Primary Neuronal Cultures," *Journal of Neuroscience Research* 89, no. 4 (2011): 592–600; Rebecca L. Cunningham, Andrea Giuffrida, and James L. Roberts, "Androgens Induce Dopaminergic Neurotoxicity via Caspase-3-Dependent Activation of Protein Kinase Cdelta," *Endocrinology* 150, no. 12 (2009): 5539–5548; and Stefano Pieretti et al., "Brain Nerve Growth Factor Unbalance Induced by Anabolic Androgenic Steroids in Rats," *Medicine and Science in Sports and Exercise*, August 14, 2012, ePub ahead of print. It is important to note that these studies are not definitive but raise the possibility of AAS-induced neurotoxicity. Research in this area demands further study.

10. Ray Garibaldi interview, September 20, 2013.

11. Interview with Denise Garibaldi, Novato, CA, April 29, 2013.

12. Interview with Joe Garibaldi, San Mateo, CA, February 15, 2014.

13. Rob Garibaldi quoted in interview with Ray Garibaldi, September 4, 2013.

14. Leef, "Steroids Blamed in Suicide of Ex–Casa Grande Star."

15. Interview with Paul Maytorena, Petaluma, CA, September 11, 2013.

16. Interview with John Goelz, Rohnert Park, CA, October 3, 2013.

17. Ibid.

18. Leef, "Steroids Blamed in Suicide of Ex–Casa Grande Star."

19. John Goelz interview.

20. Denise Garibaldi interview, May 10, 2014.

21. Interview with Raymond Garibaldi, Petaluma, CA, February 19, 2014.

22. John Goelz interview.

23. Paul Maytorena interview.

24. John Goelz interview.

25. Ibid.

26. Paul Maytorena interview; and Paul Maytorena quoted in Fainaru-Wada, "Dreams, Steroids, Death."

27. Denise Garibaldi interview, May 10, 2014.

28. Gerard Thorne, *Anabolic Primer: Ergogenic Enhancement for the Hardcore Bodybuilder* (Mississauga, ON: Robert Kennedy Publishing, 2009), 82–83; and Harrison G. Pope et al., "Treatment of Anabolic-Androgenic Steroid Dependence: Emerging Evidence and Its Implications," *Drug and Alcohol Dependence* 109 (2010): 10.

29. Denise Garibaldi interview, May 10, 2014; and Raymond Garibaldi interview.

30. John Goelz interview.

31. Denise Garibaldi interview, May 10, 2014; Ray Garibaldi interview, September 20, 2013; Fainaru-Wada, "Dreams, Steroids, Death"; Leef, "Steroids Blamed in Suicide of Ex–Casa Grande Star"; Troy Roberts, "Making It Big: High School Athletes Turning to Drugs to Get into Shape," *48 Hours Investigates*, August 4, 2004; and Mike Shumann, "Beyond the Headlines," ABC-7 / KGO-TV (San Francisco, CA), 2005.

32. Raymond Garibaldi interview.

33. Ray Garibaldi interview, September 20, 2013.

34. Denise Garibaldi interview, May 10, 2014; Ray Garibaldi interview, September 20, 2013; and Raymond Garibaldi interview.

35. Raymond Garibaldi interview.

36. Interview with Denise Garibaldi, Novato, CA, May 24, 2014; Ray Garibaldi interview, September 20, 2013; Raymond Garibaldi interview; and Denise Garibaldi quoted in Shumann, "Beyond the Headlines."

37. Denise Garibaldi, "Statement to Congress on Illicit Steroid Use in Baseball," quoted in U.S. House of Representatives, "Restoring Faith in America's Pastime: Evaluating Major League Baseball's Efforts to Eradicate Steroid Use," Hearing before the Committee on Government Reform, U.S. House of Representatives, 109th Congress, 1st Session, March 17, 2005 (Washington, DC: U.S. Government Printing Office, 2005).

38. Fainaru-Wada, "Dreams, Steroids, Death."

39. Ray Garibaldi interview, September 20, 2013; Denise Garibaldi interview, May 10, 2014; Raymond Garibaldi interview; and Paul Maytorena interview.

40. Ray Garibaldi interview, September 20, 2013.

41. Ibid.; and Fainaru-Wada, "Dreams, Steroids, Death."

42. Ray Garibaldi interview, September 20, 2013; and Denise Garibaldi interview, May 10, 2014.

43. Ray Garibaldi interview, September 20, 2013.

44. Will Wallman, Chief Deputy Coroner, Sheriff's Department, Sonoma County, letter to Mr. and Mrs. Raymond Garibaldi, Santa Rosa, CA, October 2, 2002; Fainaru-Wada, "Dreams, Steroids, Death"; and Leef, "Steroids Blamed in Suicide of Ex–Casa Grande Star."

45. Denise Garibaldi interview, May 24, 2014.

46. Raymond Garibaldi interview; Fainaru-Wada, "Dreams, Steroids, Death"; and Leef, "Steroids Blamed in Suicide of Ex–Casa Grande Star."

47. Denise Garibaldi interview, May 24, 2014; Ray Garibaldi interview, September 20, 2013; and Raymond Garibaldi interview.

48. Fainaru-Wada, "Dreams, Steroids, Death"; and Leef, "Steroids Blamed in Suicide of Ex–Casa Grande Star."

49. Denise Garibaldi, "A Meditation," Mass of Christian burial for Robert Michael Garibaldi, St. James Catholic Church, Petaluma, CA, October 5, 2002.

50. Diane and Dan Harvey, "Eulogy of Rob Garibaldi," St. James Catholic Church, Petaluma, CA, October 5, 2002, Garibaldi Family Papers.

51. Christopher Parker, "Robbie Garibaldi"; P.J. Poiani et al., "Dear Baldi"; and Derek Pasisz, "Rob," Garibaldi Family Papers.

52. Obituary, "Robert Michael Garibaldi," Santa Rosa Press Democrat, October 4, 2002.

53. For studies on the impact of suicide on survivors, see Julie Cerel, John R. Jordan, and Paul R. Duberstein, "The Impact of Suicide on the Family," Crisis: The Journal of Crisis Intervention and Suicide Prevention 29, no. 1 (2008): 38–44; Jie Zhang, Hui Qi Tong, and Li Zhou, "The Effect of Bereavement Due to Suicide on Survivors' Depression: A Study of Chinese Samples," Omega (Westport) 51, no. 3 (2005): 217–227; and Pierre Baume, "Suicide: A Crisis for the Whole Family," in Preventing Youth Suicide, edited by Sandra McKillop (Canberra: Australian Institute of Criminology, 1992), 279–287.

54. Ray Garibaldi interview, September 20, 2013.

55. Denise Garibaldi interview, May 24, 2014.

56. Ibid.

57. Ibid.

58. Ray Garibaldi interview, September 20, 2013.

59. Leef, "Steroids Blamed in Suicide of Ex–Casa Grande Star."

60. "Lawmakers Approve High School Steroid Bill," News 10 ABC San Francisco, September 8, 2005; and Soraya Sarhaddi Nelson, "Governor Signs Bill Limiting Supplement Use," Orange County (CA) Register, October 8, 2005.

61. Robert S. Arns et al., attorneys, "Schwarzenegger Conflict of Interest Claim Filed with Fair Political Practices Commission," press release, July 18, 2005; and Denise Garibaldi to Governor Arnold Schwarzenegger, letter, Petaluma, CA, July 14, 2005.

62. Mark Fainaru-Wada and Lance Williams, "Steroids Scandal: The BALCO Legacy: From Children to Pros, the Heat Is on to Stop Use of Performance Enhancers," *San Francisco Chronicle*, December 24, 2006.

63. Ibid.

64. Denise and Ray Garibaldi quoted in Roberts, "Making It Big."

65. Denise and Ray Garibaldi quoted in Harry Smith, "Grieving Parents Talk Steroids," *CBS Early Morning Show*, March 18, 2005, available at http://www.cbsnews.com/videos/grieving-parents-talk-steroids/, accessed June 1, 2014.

66. Mike Gillespie quoted in Leef, "Steroids Blamed in Suicide of Ex–Casa Grande Star."

67. For USC's response to the Garibaldis' allegations, see Roberts, "Making It Big"; and Fainaru-Wada, "Dreams, Steroids, Death."

68. For an example of presentations, see Denise Garibaldi, "Rob Garibaldi: Baseball Was His Life," delivered at El Molino High School, Sebastopol, CA, November 12, 2005.

69. Denise Garibaldi interview, May 24, 2014.

70. Denise Garibaldi, letter to Senator George Mitchell, Petaluma, CA, November 27, 2006.

71. Denise Garibaldi, letter to Barry Bonds, Petaluma, CA, June 22, 2006; and U.S. District Court, Northern District of California, "Affidavit of Denise Garibaldi in Support of the Motion to Quash and/or for a Protective Order by Mark Fainaru-Wada and Lance Williams," San Francisco, CA, May 2006.

72. U.S. District Court, "Affidavit of Denise Garibaldi."

73. Denise Garibaldi interview, May 24, 2014.

74. Ibid.; and Raymond Garibaldi interview.

75. One of the best-received papers was Denise Garibaldi, "The Challenge and the Tragedy," *New England Law Review* 40, no. 3 (2006): 717–730.

76. Raymond Garibaldi interview.

77. Jackie Speier, Deborah Collins Stephens, and Michaeline Cristini Risley, *This Is Not the Life I Ordered: 50 Ways to Keep Your Head above Water When Life Keeps Dragging You Down* (San Francisco: Conari Press, 2009), 96–98.

78. Raymond Garibaldi interview.

79. Ibid.

80. Denise Garibaldi interview, May 24, 2014.

81. Ibid.

82. Ray Garibaldi interview, September 20, 2013.

83. Denise Garibaldi interview, May 24, 2014.

AFTERWORD

1. Marla E. Eisenberg, Melanie Wall, and Dianne Neumark-Sztainer, "Muscle-Enhancing Behaviors among Adolescents," *Pediatrics* 130, no. 6 (2012): 1019–1020; and Digital Citizens Alliance, "Zogby Poll: "Better at Any Cost: The Dangerous Intersection of Young People, Steroids, and the Internet" (Washington DC: Digital Citizens Alliance, 2013). Charles E. Yesalis, a Penn State endocrinologist, identified significant female adolescent steroid use as early as 2000. (See Charles Yesalis and Michael

Bahrke, "Doping among Adolescents," *Clinical Endocrinology and Metabolism* 14, no. 1 [2000]: 25–35.)

2. In 2014, Harvard University researchers completed the first known study examining the prevalence rates of AAS misuse as a function of sexual orientation. Participants were 17,250 adolescent boys taken from a pooled data set of the fourteen jurisdictions from the 2005 and 2007 Youth Risk Behavior Surveys that had assessed sexual orientation. The study revealed that adolescent boys who are a sexual minority (e.g., those who are homosexual or bisexual) reported a higher incidence of using (21 percent versus 4 percent) compared with their heterosexual counterparts. (See Aaron J. Blashill and Steven A. Safren, "Sexual Orientation and Anabolic-Androgenic Steroids in U.S. Adolescent Boys," *Pediatrics* 133, no. 3 [2014]: 1–7.)

3. Gustavo de Albuquerque Cavalcanti et al., "Detection of Designer Steroid Methylstenbolone in 'Nutritional Supplement' Using Gas Chromatography and Tandem Mass Spectrometry," *Journal of Steroids* 78, no. 2 (2013): 228–233; Anni Heikkinen et al., "Use of Dietary Supplements in Olympic Athletes," *Journal of the International Society of Sports Nutrition* 8, no. 1 (2011): 2783–2788; David Epstein and George Dohrmann, "What You Don't Know Might Kill You," *Sports Illustrated Vault*, May 18, 2009; H. Geyer et al., "Analysis of Non-hormonal Nutritional Supplements for Anabolic-Androgenic Steroids—Results of an International Study," *International Journal of Sports Medicine* 25, no. 2 (2004): 124–129; and Norbert Baume et al., "Research of Stimulants and Anabolic Steroids in Nutritional Supplements," University of Lausanne/Swiss Olympic Association, 2003, available at www.doping.chuv.ch/files/nutritionalsupplements_04.pdf, accessed June 10, 2014.

4. Partnership for Drug-Free Kids, "National Study: Teens Report Higher Use of Performance Enhancing Substances," July 23, 2014, available at www.drugfree.org.

5. Digital Citizens Alliance, "Zogby Poll."

6. Sarah Pullen, "DEA Announces Largest Steroid Enforcement Action in U.S. History," press release, September 24, 2007, available at www.justice.gov/dea/divisions/la/2007/la092407p.html, accessed June 10, 2014; "DEA Leads Largest Steroid Bust in History—Operation Gear Grinder," press release, December 15, 2005, available at www.justice.gov/dea/pubs/pressrel/pr121505.html, accessed June 10, 2014; and T. J. Quinn, Christian Red, and Michael O'Keefe, "Muscling inside Ring of Steroids: How FBI Sting Operation Exposed Dealers and Users," *New York Daily News*, March 14, 2005.

SELECTED BIBLIOGRAPHY

Assael, Shaun, and Peter Keating. "Who Knew? Part III: Cause and Effect—the Writer." *ESPN The Magazine*, Special Report, November 2005.

Bahrke, Michael, and Charles E. Yesalis, eds. *Performance-Enhancing Drugs in Sport and Exercise*. Champaign, IL: Human Kinetics, 2002.

Bamberger, Michael, and Don Yeagar. "Over the Edge: Special Report." *Sports Illustrated*, April 14, 1997, 64–68.

Bryant, Howard. *Juicing the Game: Drugs, Power and the Fight for the Soul of Major League Baseball*. New York: Viking, 2005.

Canseco, Jose. *Juiced: Wild Times, Rampant 'Roids, Smash Hits, and How Baseball Got Big*. New York: Harper Collins, 2005.

Centers for Disease Control and Prevention. "Youth Risk Behavior Surveillance—United States, 2003." *Morbidity and Mortality Weekly Report* 53, no. SS-2 (2004): 1–62.

Dimeo, Paul. *A History of Drug Use in Sport, 1876–1976: Beyond Good and Evil*. New York: Routledge, 2007.

Elfrink, Tim, and Gus Garcia-Roberts. *Blood Sport: Alex Rodriguez, Biogenesis, and the Quest to End Baseball's Steroid Era*. New York: Dutton, 2014.

Fainaru-Wada, Mark. "Dreams, Steroids, Death—A Ballplayer's Downfall." *San Francisco Chronicle*, December 19, 2004. Available at www.sfgate.com/sports/article/ Dreams-steroids-death-a-ballplayers-downfall, accessed April 19, 2013.

Fainaru-Wada, Mark, and Lance Williams. *Game of Shadows: Barry Bonds, BALCO, and the Steroids Scandal that Rocked Professional Sports*. New York: Gotham Books, 2006.

———. "Steroids Scandal: The BALCO Legacy." *San Francisco Chronicle*, December 24, 2005.

Garibaldi, Denise. "The Challenge and the Tragedy." *New England Law Review* 40, no. 3 (2006): 717–730.

Gullo, Jim. *Trading Manny: How a Father and Son Learned to Love Baseball Again*. Boston: DaCapo Press, 2012.

Jenkins, Sally. "Winning, Cheating Have Ancient Roots." *Washington Post*, August 3, 2007.

Johnston, L. D., P. M. O'Malley, R. A. Miech, J. G. Bachman, and J. E. Schulenberg. *Monitoring the Future National Results on Drug Use, 1975–2013: Overview, Key Findings on Adolescent Drug Use.* Ann Arbor: Institute for Social Research, 2014.

Jones, Gregg, and Gary Jacobson. "Father Makes Truth His Purpose." *Dallas Morning News*, June 8, 2005.

———. "A Life Undone by Doping." *Dallas Morning News*, June 14, 2005.

———. "The Secret Edge—Steroids in High Schools." Four-part series. *Dallas Morning News.* Available at www.dallasnews.com/sharedcontent/dws/spe/2005/steroids.

Kix, Paul. "All the Rage." *Dallas Observer News*, August 12, 2004.

Leef, Ralph. "Steroids Blamed in Suicide of Ex–Casa Grande Star." *Santa Rosa Press Democrat*, March 25, 2004.

Longman, Jere. "Drugs in Sports: An Athlete's Dangerous Experiment." *New York Times*, November 26, 2003.

Lupica, Mike. *Summer of '98: When Homers Flew, Records Fell, and Baseball Reclaimed America.* Chicago: Contemporary Books, 1999.

McGwire, Jay. *Mark and Me: Mark McGwire and the Truth behind Baseball's Worst-Kept Secret.* Chicago: Triumph, 2010.

Mitchell, George J. *Report to the Commissioner of Baseball of an Independent Investigation into the Illegal Use of Steroids and Other Performance Enhancing Substances by Players in Major League Baseball.* New York: Office of the Commissioner of Baseball, 2007.

Pearlman, Jeff. *Love Me, Hate Me: Barry Bonds and the Making of an Anti-hero.* New York: HarperCollins, 2006.

Pope, Harrison, Katharine A. Phillips, and Roberto Olivardia. *The Adonis Complex: The Secret Crisis of Male Body Obsession.* New York: Simon and Schuster, 2000.

Roberts, Selena. *A-Rod: The Many Lives of Alex Rodriguez.* New York: HarperCollins, 2009.

Roberts, Selena, and David Epstein. "Confronting A-Rod." *Sports Illustrated*, February 16, 2009, 28–31.

Roberts, Troy. "Making It Big: High School Athletes Turning to Drugs to Get into Shape." *48 Hours Investigates*, August 4, 2004.

Shumann, Mike. "Beyond the Headlines." ABC-7 / KGO-TV (San Francisco, CA), 2005.

Smith, Harry. "Grieving Parents Talk Steroids." *CBS Early Morning Show*, March 18, 2005.

Speier, Jackie, Deborah Collins Stephens, and Michaeline Cristini Risley. *This Is Not the Life I Ordered: 50 Ways to Keep Your Head above Water When Life Keeps Dragging You Down.* San Francisco: Conari Press, 2009.

Stewart, Jim. "The Kid Next Door." CBS, *60 Minutes*, Season 6, Episode 8. Produced by Andrew Wolff. Aired March 3, 2004.

Thorne, Gerard. *Anabolic Primer: Ergogenic Enhancement for the Hardcore Bodybuilder.* Mississauga, ON: Robert Kennedy Publishing, 2009.

U.S. House of Representatives. "Restoring Faith in America's Pastime: Evaluating Major League Baseball's Efforts to Eradicate Steroid Use." Hearing, Committee on Government Reform, U.S. House of Representatives, 109th Congress, 1st Session, March 17, 2005. Washington, DC: U.S. Government Printing Office, 2005.

Verducci, Tom. "To Cheat or Not to Cheat: Steroids and Baseball, Ten Years After." *Sports Illustrated*, June 4, 2012, 40.

INDEX

William C. Kashatus is a historian, a longtime educator, and an amateur baseball coach. A regular contributor to the *Philadelphia Inquirer,* he is also the author of several books on baseball, including *Jackie and Campy: The Untold Story of Their Rocky Relationship and the Breaking of Baseball's Color Line.*